Designing for Humans

Nature aside, the world in which we live should be designed for us, from everyday products like scissors and chairs to complex systems in avionics, medicine and nuclear power applications. Now more than ever, technological advances continue to increase the range and complexity of tasks that people have to perform. As a discipline, human factors psychology (ergonomics) therefore has an increasingly important role to play in ensuring that the human user's physical characteristics, cognitive abilities and social needs are taken into account in the development, implementation and operation of products and systems.

In this book, *Jan Noyes* provides a comprehensive and up-to-date overview of human–machine interaction and the design of environments at work. Focusing on topics relevant to user-centred design, she includes coverage of the capabilities and limitations of humans, human–machine interactions, work environments, and organisational issues. Health and safety issues underpin a large amount of work on the human factors of design, and these are addressed fully in this book. Each chapter includes case studies that demonstrate the real-world relevance of the points being made and concludes with a list of key points.

Although aimed primarily at advanced undergraduates, postgraduates and researchers in organisational and occupational psychology, this book will also be of relevance to students on engineering, computing and applied psychology/human factors programmes.

Jan Noyes is currently Graduate Dean of Science at the University of Bristol. Her research and teaching interests are in the area of human factors psychology, and more specifically, the design of interfaces for advanced and emerging technologies such as automatic speech recognition, pen-based products and high level warning systems. In 1999 she was awarded the prestigious Otto Edholm medal for her contributions to applied research in ergonomics. She is the co-editor (with Chris Baber) of *Interactive speech technology: Human factors issues in the application of speech input/output to computers*, published by Taylor & Francis in 1993.

Psychology at Work
Series Editor: Peter Robinson
Professor of Social Psychology, University of Bristol

The *Psychology at Work* series provides comprehensive coverage of the central issues and debates in work and occupational psychology today. Its aim is to take specific areas or problems within the world of commerce, industry and public service, and establish a dialogue between their practical concerns and the academic theory and research of work and organisational psychologists. It is hoped that the series will provide a resource that generates debate and facilitates the process by which policy and practice become informed by (and inform) critically evaluated evidence-based research.

The comprehensive text by Christine Doyle; *Psychology in Organisations: An Introduction*, covers the central areas of the subject. Further texts cover options found on advanced courses in work and organisational psychology or examine contemporary and controversial topics within the field. The series will be of use to undergraduate and postgraduate students on work and occupational psychology courses, and will be particularly suitable for the British Psychological Society specification syllabus of accredited MSc courses in occupational psychology. It will also be of interest to those professionals in business and management eager to find out more about how work and organisational psychology can inform and improve the working environment.

Other forthcoming titles in this series:

Psychology in Organisations: An Introduction
Christine Doyle

The Psychological Contract at Work
Jackie Dyer and Nicky Hayes

The Psychology of Health and Safety at Work
Robert Parkinson, Paul Lyons and Andrew Tattersall

Personal Development and Employment
David Williams and Judi Irving

Designing for Humans

Jan Noyes

First published 2001 by Psychology Press Ltd
27 Church Road, Hove, East Sussex, BN3 2FA

Simultaneously published in the USA and Canada
by Taylor & Francis Inc,
29 West 35th Street, New York, NY 10001

Psychology Press is part of the Taylor & Francis Group

http://www.psypress.co.uk

British Library Cataloguing in Publication Data
A catalogue record for this book is available from the British Library

Library of Congress Cataloging-in-Publication Data

Noyes, Janet M.
    Designing for humans / Jan Noyes.
      p. cm. – (Psychology at work)
    Includes bibliographical references and index.
    ISBN: 0-415-22721-6 – ISBN: 0-415-22722-4 (pbk)
    1. Human engineering. 2. Human-computer interaction.
  3. Work environment. I. Title. II. Series.

  TA166 .N63 2001
  620.8'2–dc21
                                                        2001019886

ISBN: 0-415-22721-6 (hbk)
ISBN: 0-415-22722-4 (pbk)

Cover design by Jim Wilkie
Typeset in the UK by Mayhew Typesetting, Rhayader, Powys
Printed and bound in the UK by Biddles Ltd, Guildford and
King's Lynn

For Emily Ceri

The reasonable man adapts himself to the world: the unreasonable one persists in trying to adapt the world to himself. Therefore, all progress depends upon the unreasonable man.

George Bernard Shaw, 1903, Man and Superman 'Maxims for Revolutionists: Moderation'

Ergonomists must be 'unreasonable' in the sense that they will strive vigorously and increasingly to support a meaningful and productive relationship between technology and mankind, that technology and its products might be used for the ennoblement and fulfilment of mankind and not for its disenfranchisement and, finally, that instead of attempting to be the master of nature with its animals and flowers, man must learn to live harmoniously with them and with each other.

J.M. Christensen, 1976

Contents

Tables

Figures

Preface

A chair should be judged by one's pants, a jewel by the light in a lady's eyes, a typewriter by the hovering fingers.

Time Magazine, On good design, 12 January 1959

When this quote was written, the study of human–machine interaction from a psychological perspective was in its infancy. Today, over 40 years later, we have a greater understanding of the design issues associated with human–machine interactions and work environments. This is in part due to the growing discipline of Ergonomics/Human Factors psychology. In 1996, for example, the International Ergonomics Association (IEA) had thirty-five federated and affiliated member societies. Today, this has grown to thirty-nine member societies. In 1996 there were about 17,000 ergonomists representing forty-five countries involved in professional activities under the umbrella of the IEA. The true number is likely to be higher given that the IEA does not include student members, associates or retired members. Further, some ergonomists do not belong to a professional organisation – some estimates place this at around 40 per cent. Finally, these figures are from 1996 and the overall trend has been towards an annual increase in numbers.

Although the IEA includes countries from around the world, there is greater representation from some areas. Geographical areas that are well-represented include Australasia, Japan, Northern Europe, North America and Scandinavia. Although several new societies are currently being formed, there is comparably little ergonomic representation (and therefore, activity) in Africa, Latin America and the Middle East. This is important from the perspective of where the research is primarily being carried out and from where the material has been gathered in order to write this book. It has to be stated from the outset that this book has been written from a developed-world perspective. No attempt has been made to consider human–machine interactions and working conditions in communities and cultures where the emphasis is on manual labour rather than technologically driven systems. Writing such a book would indeed pose a considerable challenge. However, when considering the distribution of the world's population, relatively few live in the developed world. Whittaker (1994) estimated that in the year 2000, approximately 20 per cent of the population of the world would live in Europe (including Russia and surrounding countries) and North America. This is in comparison to the 62 per cent that he estimated would live in Asia. Hence, the vast majority of people do not live in the world that provided the inspiration and material for this book. This places a further twist on the developed world perspective when one considers that so relatively few people in the population are 'practising' ergonomics.

Ergonomics is a discipline that seeks to maximise safety, efficiency and comfort by shaping the design and operation of the technology to the physical and psychological capabilities and social needs of the user. It extends to encompass the context in which the product or system is being used and this can include the workplace, the physical environment as well as the organisation. Stated very simply, we live in a world where all the objects and artefacts that humans create should be designed for our use. Admittedly, the natural world does not meet this requirement and, indeed, we would not expect it to. But, for whatever reason, neither does the human-made world. One has only to look around a home to find videos that are difficult to programme, light switches where you never remember to flick the right switch for the light you want, microwave ovens where nothing is ever cooked that is more complicated than 2 minutes on 'high' because no one knows how to and the instructions were lost long ago. The list is endless. One is tempted to say that if interfaces were designed to be intuitive, these problems would be resolved. The problem being, of course, that 'intuitive' means something different to each person. Further, some of the best designs are counterintuitive. For example, you could argue that the brake pedal on a car is operated in a counterintuitive manner. In terms of movement compatibility, it does not make sense that pushing forward on one foot pedal makes the vehicle go faster while the same action on the adjacent pedal results in deceleration. We have a counterintuitive design that works extremely well. One of the reasons for this is that humans adapt. This is partly the reason why we are so successful in our natural environment – because we have the ability and intelligence to adapt to situations. It does mean, however, that we eventually adapt to poor designs, perhaps to the point where we do not even notice the inappropriate design. Having invested the time in acquiring the skills to operate the poorly designed object, we are then unwilling to change to a better design. The ubiquitous QWERTY keyboard is one example where this has happened. The application of ergonomics is therefore a complicated business when one considers all the other factors at work.

Having said that, interest in ergonomics around the world is gathering momentum, and it could be concluded that the very fact this book has been written specifically to address part of the British Psychological Society's syllabus for the Postgraduate Certificate in Occupational Psychology is further evidence. The postgraduate syllabus covers eight areas, of which two are 'human–machine interaction' and 'design of environments and work: health and safety'. Details are given in the Annex. This book has been written to cover the topics covered by the syllabus with respect to these two areas; topics that I have taught to MSc students for the last 10 years. It should be noted that some topics, e.g. stress and training, are covered more extensively elsewhere in the syllabus for the other six areas, and may be treated fairly superficially here. A further comment concerns the approach taken in this book, which is primarily a systems one that considers issues relating to the individual. There are many approaches that can be taken to design, e.g. a social or environmental perspective, but the stance taken here has been to approach the subject from a system's viewpoint with the human system being one part of the overall system. The 'individual' approach mirrors the psychological literature that has focused more on the activities and functioning of the individual than that of the group. Admittedly, there are areas where research is active, e.g. computer-supported co-operative work, but these are not covered in any detail here. It might also be noted that frequently the examples given are from avionics – the only explanation (excuse!) offered for this is that it reflects the research background of the author. A final note concerns the case studies. These are derived from a diverse set of topics but it is the intention that it is the application of the various points being made that is of interest and relevance rather than the specific topic being discussed.

Finally, to return to the quote. Ergonomics is all about design. And we know as psychologists that there is little benefit to be gained from knowing about design if we cannot assess and evaluate human reactions to it. There is nothing exceptional about this – psychology courses throughout the UK teach statistics, experimental design and computing in order to help their students 'measure' the human traits and behaviour that they are studying. (It is perhaps worth noting that this is often to the chagrin of under-graduates who came to study the interesting clinical cases and not 'push' numbers around in complex statistics packages!) However, this book is not a text on methods – the reader is referred to other books that do this extremely well. But, having said that, ergonomics is all about design, assessment and evaluation, and it would be remiss of me if I did not draw attention to this. It is also about placing the human at the centre of the design process; one of the ways of facilitating this is to work closely with the users and find out about their opinions and feelings with regard to the design of a product or system. The concept of 'user-centred design' taking into account users' requirements, preferences and performance will undoubtedly lead to better designs. Hence it could be concluded that, more than forty years later, nothing has changed – the answer is still to be found via the seat of one's pants (or the eyes or the fingers)!

Jan Noyes
Bristol, 2000

Acknowledgements

With special thanks to Dad for his proof-reading, Lara Heard for drawing the figures, and Professor W. Peter Robinson for his support and guidance.

1   Human Factors

Life was simple before World War II. After that, we had systems.
Grace Hopper, Developer of the COBOL computer language, 1987

'Human Factors' is one of those nebulous expressions that is frequently used in everyday life, and in this sense defining it is not easy. Human factors are omnipresent in that we are all aware of the influence of humans in whatever we do or attempt to do and, when taken literally, the term conveys little precise meaning to the reader or listener. However, for one group of psychologists, this term has a very specific definition and meaning. It refers to the area of work concerned with the interaction of humans with machines, and the many implications arising from this. To differentiate the more general meaning of human factors, i.e. 'aspects relating to the nature of people' (Edwards and Edwards, 1990: 7), the term will be given capital letters when referring to the discipline.

Origins

The origins of Human Factors are often quoted as residing in a study of shovel design carried out in the late 1890s. The study was conducted by the Quaker engineer Frederick W. Taylor, who is primarily remembered for his principles of scientific management (see biographies by Kakar, 1970; Nelson, 1980; Zalesnik, 1966). In 1878 Taylor began work as a foreman at Bethlehem Steel Works in the US eventually becoming promoted to chief engineer. During this time, he had begun to take a keen interest in the best way to do a job in order to ensure the workers' productivity (see Taylor, 1911). Taylor studied the actions of the workers, their use of equipment and their rest periods, and related this to levels of productivity. He began by collecting baseline data, i.e. information about the workers, their tools and the materials (iron ore and steel) to be moved. Anywhere between 400 and 600 full-time workers brought their own shovels to work and used them to shift different types of material. Shovel loads varied from 3.5 pounds for coal to 38 pounds for iron ore – pounds being the imperial measure in use at this time – equivalent to 1.6 kilograms for coal to 17.2 kilograms for iron ore. Taylor's optimal shovel load was 9 kilograms; this is in the middle of the range of 5–11 kilograms specified by Frievalds (1986) in a review of the ergonomics of spade design and shovelling. Once Taylor had collected his baseline information, he began the second phase of his study. This was an experimental investigation in which two men moved materials with an array of shovels that decreased in size. Taylor concluded that the best shovel load was one weighing around 21 pounds (9.5 kilograms), and that different sized shovels would be needed to shift the various materials. He used this information to persuade the management at the steel works to purchase a range of shovels for different people and various shovelling tasks. More-over, he kept records of individual worker productivity and provided training for those who were not meeting targets. Over a 3-year period, the costs of shovelling fell by a half. However, this was probably in part due to the fact that the number of shovellers fell to 140. Taylor's now well-known shovelling study comprised one of the first 'time and motion' studies (Taylor, 1903). He found that through these time and motion studies he could break jobs down into smaller, well-defined tasks and then devise a better, more efficient way to perform the same jobs, i.e. increase the worker's productivity. Taylor also generalised from one situation to another. For example, he carried out about 40,000 experiments to find the best ways of cutting metal (Taylor, 1907). Although Taylor's early work at the Midvale Steel Company focused on how workers managed their jobs, i.e. the time and motion studies, his later interest concerned managing workers. He was particularly interested in the piecework method of pro-duction and payment. The principles of scientific management for which Taylor is probably best remembered emanated primarily from this later work. Taylor's primary interest was in increasing productivity and, because of this, it has been argued that Taylor's motives were not entirely for the benefit of the workers, i.e. human-centred (Ryan and Smith, 1954). Hence, many workers considered 'Taylorism' to be a form of exploitation and, in 1912, Taylor's system of shop management was investigated by the US House of Representatives (Taylor, 1947). In his defence, Taylor did denounce the exploitation of workers at a public forum in 1916 (Berry and Houston, 1993).

The principled approach of Taylor's early work, i.e. systematic and empirical observation of workers in time and motion studies, was continued by Frank and Lillian Gilbreth – a husband and wife team – who replicated some of Taylor's early work (although they had no direct contact with Taylor) by conducting time and motion studies of bricklayers. Frank Gilbreth began his working career as a bricklayer's apprentice in 1885. He was promoted rapidly and subsequently became interested in work methods. Soon, he was studying how workers carried out building tasks in the construction industry. One particular study considered the actions of bricklayers, and experimented with modifying the scaffolding for the picking up of bricks, techniques for sorting and stacking the bricks before laying, and methods of bricklaying (Gilbreth and Gilbreth, 1921). The Gilbreths found that the development of a new method of laying bricks could decrease the number of actions required to lay one brick from eighteen to less than five. Consequently, they found that they could improve the workers' productivity by increasing the number of bricks laid from 120 per hour to 350 per hour. The Gilbreths also refined the techniques for observing human behaviour with the development of a motion picture camera that time-marked the film. By 1917, they had developed a technique for recording the time, speed and acceleration of movements (Barnes, 1940). This and other work comprised a significant step forward in the study of human performance. For example, their research with hospital surgical teams has had long-lasting effects in the procedures associated with instrument selection. The Gilbreths observed that surgeons were spending a lot of their operating time looking for the required instrument and so introduced the procedure whereby the accompanying nurse selected and orientated the tools for the surgeons. Apart from having a large family – Lillian Gilbreth gained some notoriety as the key figure in *Cheaper by the Dozen*, a story of a woman with a PhD in psychology who combined research with a houseful of children – their other 'claim to fame' was generating the term 'therblig' for a (very small) unit of work (Konz, 1990). This was an anagram of their surname and it hardly needs to be stated that it has not become common usage. Like the reasons for Taylor's work, the motives behind some of the Gilbreth's studies must be questioned because their primary interest was not the welfare of the workers, but how to increase productivity. However, this perspective needs to be viewed within the context of the times in which they lived. Towards the end of the nineteenth century and the industrial revolution, the heavy industries (iron, coal, steel) were flourishing and there was no shortage of work or people to carry out what was predominantly manual work (Flinn, 1966). In many ways, the human was the expendable part of the system – if anyone dropped out for whatever reason (illness, injury, even death), there was usually another person waiting to take their place. This situation was exacerbated in the early part of the 1900s when recession hit the economies of the western world and work was in short supply for manual labourers. Hence, it is reasonable to conclude that consideration of the human (and their needs and requirements for satisfaction) took a low priority in the workplace.

In the 1920s, Elton Mayo and F.J. Roethlisberger conducted the Hawthorne studies (Roethlisberger and Dickson, 1939). They were named this because the work was carried out at the Hawthorne Works of the Bell System's Western Electric Company in the US. Between 1924 and 1933, Mayo and Roethlisberger looked at a number of issues relating to human behaviour in the workplace. The so-called Hawthorne effect emanated from the now famous illumination experiments and the bank wiring observation room study. Briefly, the illumination experiments considered workers' productivity under different levels of lighting. It was hypothesised that higher levels of illumination would result in greater output, and indeed they found that this was the case. However, lowering the levels of illuminations also had the same effect, i.e. productivity improved. The researchers had come across a phenomenon that was unrelated to illumination levels; namely, attention and interest from the researchers had apparently motivated the workers to greater output. The bank wiring assembly room study demonstrated a similar effect. Mayo and Roethlisberger noticed that when a new worker joined the bank wiring assembly room their output was high, but after a few weeks it dropped. As the workers were paid according to the amount of equipment they assembled, this observation appeared puzzling. It was subsequently noticed that the more experienced workers were putting pressure on the new individual to conform to group norms of productivity – the established group was concerned that higher productivity would result in management shifting the base rates. This would result in them having to work harder to achieve the equivalent payment. Like the illumination experiments, this finding underlined the importance of interpersonal relationships in the workplace and reinforced the complexity of workplace management in that workers did not work solely for financial reward (see Parsons, 1974; 1990). The Hawthorne studies also indicated the complexity of relating productivity to efficiency in that there was no simple linear relationship (Blum and Naylor, 1968), although some have argued that the research methods were flawed (Bramel and Friend, 1981). For a detailed account of the Hawthorne studies, see Gillespie (1991).

In the UK, a major milestone was the formation of the Health of Munitions Workers' Committee in 1915. This development was in response to the number of problems relating to people that had been experienced in the munitions factories at the start of World War I when it was important to the war effort that work was carried out efficiently and productivity was high. At the end of the war, the Committee was reconstituted as the Industrial Fatigue Research Board (IFRB). As the name suggests, its primary interest was to consider issues associated with fatigue as well as determinants of productivity in the workplace such as job rotation. In 1929, the IFRB became the Industrial Health Research Board and, correspondingly, its scope was broadened to consider the health of workers *per se* within the context of industrial efficiency. The Board comprised psychologists, engineers and medics who worked on a wide range of problems relating to job design, the working environment, selection and training. A further significant development was the formation of the National Institute of Industrial Psychology that focused on selection, recruitment and training issues. In fact, testing, selection and training issues had already become established as the primary area of interest for the applied psychologists. As Berry and Houston (1993) pointed out, the 1935 issues of *Psychological Abstracts* provide evidence of a continuing emphasis on vocational topics.

It can be seen that formal interest in the worker was gradually gathering momentum both in the UK and US with the formation of a number of committees and the execution of some large-scale research studies. This situation was about to be accelerated by the outbreak of World War II and the rapid development and implementation of new ideas, activities and technologies. It was quickly realised that no amount of training of carefully selected personnel could ensure good human–machine interactions. The approach of 'FMJ – fitting the man to the job', i.e. selecting workers for the job, was soon to be replaced by the approach of 'FJM – fitting the job to the man' (Rodger and Cavanagh, 1962).

World War II

One of the significant differences between World War I and World War II was that the former was fought mainly on the land and at sea, rather than in the air. For World War II to involve air battles, a number of rapid technological developments had taken place both prior to and during the war. This was certainly the case in cockpit design, where developments could be traced back to the success of getting the first aeroplanes airborne by the Wright brothers in 1909. One of the outcomes of the war was that equipment had to be designed and implemented urgently without ample opportunity for testing. This was especially the case with the human element, which was often the neglected component in system design. Subsequently, a number of mistakes were made. For example, radar operators were placed on 8-hour shifts until it was noticed that they were missing a large number of targets after a fairly short time (Mackworth, 1948, 1950). We now know from work on vigilance that in some monitoring situations detection performance declines after the first 20–30 minutes, and it is generally hard for people to maintain good monitoring skills, especially if searching for a low frequency target. Humans are not good 'monitors' and tasks need to be designed, whenever possible, to take this into account. This is especially the case when we are doing nothing but monitoring (Warm *et al.*, 1996).

Another example of hasty design concerns the Douglas escape hatch that allowed parachutists to exit the aircraft when airborne. It was not realised until the aircraft was actually flying and the parachutist was attempting to exit via the hatch that the designers had not allowed enough clearance room. The size of the aircraft hatch had been designed to accommodate basic human dimensions and had not taken into account the extra width needed because of the parachute. Hence, the person could leave on his or her own but not with the parachute!

A third example concerns the seat design for anti-aircraft gunners onboard ships. These personnel were given standard car-like seats that were fine when sighting aircraft in the distance close to the horizon, but not when trying to locate aircraft directly overhead. The problem was that it was not possible to adjust the seats and tilt them backwards as and when appropriate.

A final example of poorly designed aircraft systems could be found on the B-52 bombers. On some aircraft, similar-looking controls operating the landing gear and steering flaps were placed next to each other. As a result, several B-52s landed on their 'bellies' because the pilots had believed that they had operated the landing gear control when they were actually operating the steering flaps.

Although these design errors may seem obvious, even amusing now, it did mean that people began to question the need for better designs and research into human–machine interaction. Psychologists were brought into direct contact with Human Factors issues, and one individual who made a significant contribution to this work was Sir Frederic Bartlett. He was responsible for building a simulator of the Spitfire aircraft cockpit in order to investigate the effects of stress and fatigue on pilot behaviour. The shift of attention from machine to human had occurred and the area of Human Factors was born.

Birth of Human Factors

It is never easy to date the exact moment that an organisation is formed. But, shortly after World War II, several groups of individuals around the world began to discuss the need to set up professional bodies on Human Factors. In the UK, an interdisciplinary group (the 'Human Performance Group') was formed at a meeting held at the British Admiralty in July 1949. It should be noted that there is a discrepancy here in terms of the date of the actual meeting in Room 1101 of the Admiralty building at Queen Anne's Mansions. Some sources date it as 8 July and others as 12 July – there may of course have been two meetings of the working group! The following year, this group formed the Ergonomics Research Society, which is now the UK Ergonomics Society (Edholm and Murrell, 1973). At about the same time, a group in the US was laying the foundations of the Human Factors Society. At the end of the war in 1945 a number of engineering psychology laboratories had been established in the US by the armed forces. These led to the formation of the Human Factors Society in 1957. In the same year, the organisation of Division 21 (Society of Engineering Psychology) of the American Psychological Association (APA) took place; the APA itself had been founded in 1892. 1957 was also the year in which the UK journal *Ergonomics* was launched. Two other significant publication milestones were the first article on human engineering in the *Journal of Applied Psychology* and the publishing of one of the first books on Human Factors in 1949 by Chapanis, Garner and Morgan. Ten years later, in 1959, the International Ergonomics Association (IEA) was formed with the intention of linking the various Human Factors and ergonomics societies and groups around the world (Chapanis, 1990). In 1964, the Ergonomics

Society of Australia and New Zealand (ESANZ) was formed (see Welford, 1976a). As evidence of the growth of ergonomics, the IEA professional body now has thirty-six member societies around the world (Shackel, 1997).

It should be noted that the UK and Australasian communities favour the term 'ergonomics' – derived from the Greek '*ergon*' meaning work and '*nomos*' meaning natural laws. The word, or variations of it, is now used in many parts of the world, e.g. 'ergonomie' in France and Holland, and 'ergonomia' in Hungary and Brazil. Taken literally, the word ergonomics means 'the customs, habits or laws of work'. It was 'coined to denote an approach to the problems of human work and control operations which came into prominence during the second world war in relation to equipment for the fighting services' (Editorial, 1957: 1). The word is not new, having been used by the Polish scholar, Wojciech Jastrzebowski in his now classic 1857 treatise *An Outline of Ergonomics, Or the Science of Work* (Karwowski, 1991). Jastrzebowski's work was republished as a Special Commemorative Edition by the Central Institute for Labour Protection (Koradecka, 2000). Post-war, initial reaction to the word was not positive and there was some resistance to it. To quote Welford (1976a: 277), people thought it was 'ugly, incomprehensible, and easily confused with economics, and it took considerable persuasion to obtain the agreement of the publishers for its use as the title of a journal'.

The difference between ergonomics and Human Factors is not obvious, and indeed it could be argued that the terms are synonymous, i.e. one side of the Atlantic favoured ergonomics and the other, Human Factors. In the past, the term ergonomics has often been used in the context of 'knobs and dials' ergonomics, suggesting a narrower definition than Human Factors, which could be thought to encompass any aspect involving humans in their work (Hawkins, 1993). Another view is that ergonomics is more concerned with the physical aspects of human work (Grandjean, 1988). Indeed, it is generally thought that ergonomics was grounded in the biological sciences whereas Human Factors is grounded in psychology. A perusal of the first volume of *Ergonomics* would probably support this, with papers on fatigue, stress, physiological aspects of human–machine interaction, training, effects of environment (noise, light, flicker, heat, vibration). Interestingly, the situation has become less clear. On the 1 January 1993 the Human Factors Society adopted the word ergonomics in its title, i.e. the Human Factors and Ergonomics Society (Editorial, 1993). This followed many months of discussion that indicated a reluctance to abandon the term 'Human Factors' while there was some support for the more technical sounding term 'Ergonomics'. Some discussants considered that the latter was a subclass of Human Factors while others held the reverse opinion. However, there was considerable support for the view that the terms were synonymous. Sanders and McCormick (1987) supported the viewpoint that the terms were synonymous by stating that any distinctions were arbitrary and have not been maintained. To some extent, the Canadian Society 'solved' the problem

Table 1.1   Topics from the First International Conference on Cognitive
Ergonomics and Engineering Psychology (1996)

Discipline	Topic
Cognitive ergonomics	Design of control and display systems
	Human error and human reliability
	Human–computer interaction
	Artificial intelligence and decision support
	Automation
	Training for skill acquisition and retention
	Techniques for the evaluation of human machine systems
Engineering psychology	Applications of theories of human perception
	Human information processing
	Human performance modelling
	Mental workload and stress
	Situation awareness
	Human skilled performance
	Physiological correlates of performance

by using 'Human Factors' in their English name and 'ergonomie' in its
French version. Other phrases used to describe this area are 'industrial
psychology', 'human psychology', 'I/O (input/output) psychology' and
'engineering psychology'. The term 'human engineering' has also been
employed, but there is a concern here of confusion with exercises in genetic
intervention (Edwards and Edwards, 1990). It can be seen that many of these
phrases include the word 'psychology' and, hence, could be thought of as
disciplines within psychology. In the UK, the last term has gained some
prominence with the formation of a Special Interest Group on engineering
psychology by the British Psychological Society and the launch of a new
biennial conference on Engineering Psychology and Cognitive Ergonomics.
Table 1.1 lists the topics covered in the first conference in 1996. In the US, a
new journal – *The International Journal of Cognitive Ergonomics* – was
launched in 1997. Wickens (1992) argued that the goal of engineering
psychology was understanding human performance within the context of
designing systems whereas Human Factors was more concerned with
applying the findings on understanding human performance to the design of
systems. Some recent developments have included the word 'cognitive' –
cognitive ergonomics, cognitive engineering and cognitive technology (the
name of an International Conference convened in Hong Kong in 1994, an
Indiana State conference in 1997 and a journal launched in 1996). As the
word 'cognitive' relates to the high-level information-processing activities of
the human, e.g. decision making and problem solving, as opposed to the
physical/physiological aspects, it could be concluded that the shift of interest
has been towards this area. Wright (1997) stated that cognitive technology
has its roots in research and applications related to memory; hence it is of no
surprise to find that the journal *Cognitive Technology* is the official journal of
the Practical Memory Institute. In contrast, Gorayska and Mey (1996) in

their book *Cognitive Technology* focused on the human–computer interface. Rasmussen *et al.* (1995) stated that cognitive engineering was closely related to Human Factors. Its recent prominence is probably due to the increasing interest in cognitive activities and the continuing complexity of technological developments, e.g. expert systems, and the modelling of machine operations on human activities, e.g. the use of software agents (gophers, alter-egos, knowbots).

Given the background to the formation of the professional bodies, it is not surprising that much of the work and research in this field has been carried out either by or for the aerospace and defence industries (see Kraft, 1958). Prior to the 1960s there had been a tremendous need for Human Factors input in the space programme in the race to place a human on the moon. One Human Factors anecdote that exemplifies the rush has been told by Muchinsky (1997) and concerns the operation of switches in the space capsule – astronauts were given instructions relating to switch position that were subsequently found to be meaningless when they were weightless and free-floating. This was the position in the 1940s and 1950s, and to a certain extent it still exists today. It serves to illustrate the influence of these industries on the development of this area.

Case study: moral tales – Three Mile Island

A notable event in the development of the field of Human Factors was the Three Mile Island incident that has subsequently entered the annals of literature as a so-called moral tale (USNRC, 1980). Three Mile Island was a nuclear power station located near the East Coast of the US in Pennsylvania. In March 1979, the plant experienced a major incident (see Rubinstein and Mason, 1979 for a detailed account). One of the pilot-operated relief valves which should have opened automatically to allow coolant (i.e. water) to flow around the reactor to reduce the temperature and pressure, did not open and the flow of water was interrupted. This could have resulted in a melt-down, i.e. an uncontrolled nuclear reaction. However, although there was a small release of radioactive material into the atmosphere, an accident was averted. The workers in the control room battled for 2 hours 18 minutes to resume normal operating conditions with the emergency continuing for over 16 hours. There was no loss of life but the cost to the operating companies and insurers was estimated at the time to be in the region of one billion dollars. From a Human Factors perspective, there are several interesting aspects to this incident. More importantly this 'near miss' encouraged the nuclear power industry and others to learn a lot to prevent something similar happening in the future. The subsequent Nuclear Regulatory Commission (NRC) report (Malone *et al.*, 1980) highlighted the following points:

1. Operators did commit a number of errors, which certainly had a contributory if not causal influence in the events of the accident
2. These errors resulted from grossly inadequate control room design, procedures and training rather than from deficiencies on the part of the operators.

A number of problems emanated from the design of the control room. For example, at the start of the incident, more than 100 alarms (including forty auditory ones) were activated, and operators had to scan 1,600 windows and gauges to try to make sense of the situation. Around 200 of these had warning lights that were flashing when the incident began (Smither, 1994). In these early stages, the operators were subject to a cacophony of sound and visual activity. This undoubtedly overloaded them with information; a situation exacerbated by the fact that many of the instruments went off-scale, making them impossible to read (Kemeny, 1979). Diagnosis was also hindered by the fact that critical information was missing from the control panels, e.g. there was no display indicating that the secondary cooling system had failed to halt the reaction or a display of relevant valves to help locate the one that had not acted automatically. Further, relevant gauges relating to the amount of coolant escaping (that would have provided information on how hot the core was becoming) had been placed away from the centre of activity and were located behind the main controls some 12 metres away. Tags left by the maintenance personnel to identify controls that needed attention covered some of the lights relating to valve position making them difficult to see. For example, operators could not see a gauge showing the level of coolant water in the reactor, as a large tag covered it. This tag stated that another (unrelated) gauge needed repair. A maintenance tag also covered another relevant gauge and the workers failed to realise that the generator was overheating. And, finally, the situation was also subject to a printer failure. Messages were arriving at the rate of ten to fifteen every second and the printer became overloaded and jammed (Perrow, 1981). As a result, relevant information was not recovered for over 2 hours, as well as the fact that one operator's time was totally taken up with sorting out the printer. A further shortcoming highlighted was training. It is interesting to note that as part of their training, operators had been required to learn fifty different procedures for use in an emergency (Feuer, 1985). However, when the emergency occurred in 1979, none of these procedures were applicable. One of the outcomes of the Three Mile Island incident was the installation of a control room simulator that was an exact replica of the actual workplace. This was subsequently used for training and rehearsal of critical situations.

In conclusion, it can be seen that the Three Mile Island incident illustrated a number of shortcomings relating to design of the control room, operating procedures and training and, as Perrow (1984) pointed out, it is the concatenation of these supposedly trivial events that came together to form the accident. It also indicated the deficiency in designing an industrial environment in isolation, i.e. the individuals involved in the physical design of the control centre were not those writing the procedures. As a result, several groups of individuals were present but they did not communicate with each other despite their common goal – the smooth running of the nuclear power plant (Moray, 1999a). Many would regard it as unfortunate that it took a disaster such as Three Mile Island to raise the profile of Human Factors, but this is in fact what happened. Before this incident, there were virtually no Human Factors psychologists on the staff of the NRC or in the firms hired to design, build, and operate nuclear power plants. Subsequently, and as a direct result of Three Mile Island, the NRC now includes dozens of Human Factors psychologists on its staff.

Influence of computers

Modern-day computing and information technology could be seen as developing from the 'analytical engine' devised by Charles Babbage in the nineteenth century. Between the two world wars the potential of the computer was gradually being realised, with the development of analogue machines and digital systems, e.g. the Massachusetts Institute of Technology (MIT) differential analyser, Harvard Mark 1, developed by Howard H. Aiken, and Konrad Zuse's computers Z1 to Z4 in Germany. These early machines were large and cumbersome. Evans (1983: 37–8) described the Harvard Mark 1 as 'a monster, fifty-five feet long, eight feet high and containing not much less than a million individual components'. The first digital computer using electronic valves (tubes) has been cited as the Colosseus (Shackel, 1997). This computer was built in the UK during World War II for code breaking, although its existence remained a secret from the general public for more than 30 years. The Colosseus computer was responsible for breaking the codes that the Germans produced on their Enigma Machine. As soon as Colosseus had demonstrated its capabilities, a further ten were built – these were undoubtedly the first electronic digital computers (Evans, 1983). However, due to the secrecy surrounding Colosseus, the ENIAC (Electronic Numerical Integrator And Calculator) developed at Pennsylvania University in the US in 1946 is publicly recognised as the world's first electronic digital computer. Like all these early computers, ENIAC was also enormous filling a huge room. It 'covered 3000 cubic feet, weighed 30 tons, and consumed 140 kilowatts of power' (Large, 1980: 35). Compared to Colosseus, it was faster, had a larger capacity and was capable of more than one job. This last point was important. Colosseus could carry out only one task – cracking codes – whereas ENIAC was programmable, in the sense that it could switch from one job to another. This 'programmability' was an important step forward.

The next major step, engineered by Von Neumann, was the development of the stored-program computer. This embodied the concept of storing a set of instructions in the computer to guide operations. Von Neumann, who had been working on ENIAC, began work on EDVAC (Electronic Discrete Variable Automatic Computer) but a number of engineering difficulties proved difficult to resolve. Consequently, the earliest stored-program computer to operate was probably a small, experimental machine – the Manchester Mark I in1948. However, the limited storage capacity of this machine often means that it is not recognised as being the world's first and the EDSAC (Electronic Delay Storage Automatic Calculator) developed at Cambridge is often cited as being the first stored-program computer, executing its first program in 1949. EDVAC managed to do this in 1951.

These machines represented the first generation of computers. A further major development was that of the transistor in 1948, opening the way for high speed processing and the second generation of computers. Again, the space race provided a motivating force. In 1957, the Russians successfully launched a series of satellites, one containing a dog. In comparison, the US had suffered a number of setbacks, with rockets either blowing up on the launch pad or rising only a few hundred feet. One of the outcomes was that the Americans began to take the space race more seriously and began pouring huge amounts of money into the venture. The next significant development was the integrated circuit (IC), comprising the third generation of computers (1964–71). As techniques for manufacturing ICs improved, large-scale integration became possible, and this led the way for the fourth generation of computers. Work on the fifth generation of computers is still ongoing. The aim of the fith generation is 'to solve complex problems which demand expertise and powers of reasoning when tackled by humans' (Hunt and Shelley, 1988: 164). The quest for smaller and smaller silicon chips is also underway, with predictions that, by 2010, chip components will have been reduced in size to one ten-millionth of a metre (McKie, 1999). As a comparison, this is roughly one hundred times thinner than an average human hair. The end result could be a machine that processes data a billion times faster than today's computers, but is small enough to be hidden by a speck of dust.

Throughout the 1960s and 1970s, technological advances resulted in computers with greater processing power (faster operating speeds and larger memory capacities), smaller units and accompanying decreasing costs. Many analogies abound concerning these advances. A rather dramatic one is that if cars had developed at the same rate as computers in terms of price and performance 'a Rolls Royce car would cost £1.35 and do over a million miles to the gallon' (Sherman, 1985: 70). (Note that Large, 1980, had previously stated that the Rolls Royce would do three million miles to the gallon!) The outcome was that computing began to move from the province of the specialist to the general population, i.e. within the reach of the so-called Joe Public. A milestone in this was the launch of the first personal computer (PC) in February 1978. The primary task carried out by the early PCs was word processing. Computers began to replace the electrical typewriters of the 1960s, which in turn had replaced the mechanical typewriters first devised in the nineteenth century. The 1980s witnessed a major upheaval in the workplace as computers were brought to the masses. Typed work was no longer exclusively produced by highly trained individuals who could attain various typing speeds with minimum errors. This was particularly evident in the academic environment. Within a relatively short period of time, untrained individuals were word processing without a typing qualification between them. The PC started to become a standard piece of office furniture. It is therefore not surprising that the topic of human–computer interaction (HCI) began to attract interest. This was exemplified in the launch of a number of HCI events. For example, in 1984 the first International Conference on HCI (INTERACT '84) was held, and the British Computer Society (BCS) initiated their own HCI conference. A year later, the ACM (Association of Computing Machinery) CHI (Computer Human Interaction) held its first conference; BCS HCI conferences have become established as annual events. The 1980s also witnessed the launch of a number of new journals: *Behaviour and Information Technology* in 1982, *Human–Computer Interaction* in 1985, *Interacting With Computers*, and the renaming of the *International Journal of Man–Machine Studies* as the *International Journal of Human–Computer Studies* in 1989. Recent additions to the market place include the launch of new journals entitled *Theoretical Issues in Ergonomics Science* (Editorial, 2000), *Cognition, Technology and Work*, and *Cognitive Systems Research*.

It would be remiss when considering the influence of computers to omit the development of networking and in particular, the World Wide Web (WWW). In 1990, the WWW was developed for the sharing of knowledge amongst a few remote sites (see Berners-Lee *et al.*, 1994). Since its inception, the WWW has become increasingly popular by users connected to the Internet (Lightner *et al.*, 1996). Although the terms 'Internet' and 'WWW' are used interchangeably, strictly speaking, the former is the underlying communications framework. Computer networks that did not exist a few decades ago now cover the world. Yet it is only 30 years since the first experimental network was implemented by the Advanced Research Projects Agency of the US Department of Defense (Nickerson, 1997). Figures from January 1999 indicate that the Internet network is fast approaching 45 million host sites (Network Wizards, 1999), with no evidence that rates of increase are reducing. Again, the move has been from the specialist user to the general population and, in 1993 only about one-third of Internet usage was attributed to scientists and engineers, i.e. people who were computer-literate and using the Internet for their own professional needs (Anderson,

1993). Today, the Internet is viewed primarily as an information source, as people have access to a range of material (and other people) on a scale at the limits of our imaginations. However, it is generally thought that the full potential of working with electronic presentation and exchange of information has yet to be realised. This is partly because the Internet was not designed as an electronic library and does not have the features or tools to perform this function properly (Lynch, 1997). Furthermore, the potential richness of the interaction (e.g. animations, simulations, voice and other sounds) and the learning possibilities have yet to be defined. We are still some way from the concept of the 'global village' whereby electronic communication alone allows us to create, edit, exchange and broadcast information amongst selected groups of individuals. Hence, there are many Human Factors problems relating to information organisation, access, security, management and communication, as well as issues relating to the interface design of computer-based systems.

Today

It is tempting to think that Human Factors/ergonomics has come of age (Table 1.2). Societies in both the UK and US continue to thrive, as do other ergonomics groups in Australasia, India, Japan and Europe. In 1999, the UK Ergonomics Society celebrated its fiftieth anniversary. A number of shared events with other professional bodies took place, thus demonstrating the extent to which this area continues to be multidisciplinary and collaborate with other groups. There is a growing awareness of the importance of considering the human factor in system and product development and operation. Some of this interest stems from the need in safety-critical systems to ensure that accidents are avoided. Some of the emphasis on Human Factors must relate to the altruistic need to make the lives of humans easier – the technology continues to advance and become more sophisticated but the human operator remains fairly fixed in terms of ability to evolve and keep up with this expanding complexity. The end result for the human can be information overload – an increasing problem as we enter the twenty-first century (Noyes and Thomas, 1995). Various design issues relating to the wealth of electronically stored information also pose a significant Human Factors problem. Looking to the future, there is discussion about requiring all products for human use to have passed certain tests and be certified by Human Factors specialists before release into the marketplace.

Perspectives

It has already been stated that Human Factors is the study of the interaction between humans and machines. However, a more precise definition would

Table 1.2   Summary of milestones

Year	Milestone
1903	Taylor's study on shovelling and spade design
1915	Formation of the Health of Munitions Workers' Committee
1918	Health of Munitions Workers' Committee reconstituted as the Industrial Fatigue Research Board
1920s	Hawthorne studies
1921	Gilbreth's bricklaying study
1929	Industrial Fatigue Research Board became the Industrial Health Research Board
1946	First electronic digital computer developed
1949	Formation of the UK Ergonomics (Research) Society
1949	First stored-program computer developed
1957	Formation of the US Human Factors Society
1959	Formation of the International Ergonomics Association
1978	Launch of the first PC (personal computer)
1979	Three Mile Island incident
1982	Launch of journal – *Behaviour and Information Technology*
1984	First international conference on human–computer interaction
1985	Launch of journals – *Human–Computer Interaction* and *Interacting With Computers*
1989	Renaming of the journal *International Journal of Man–Machine Studies* as the *International Journal of Human–Computer Studies*
1990	Formation of the World Wide Web
1994	The Human Factors Society adopts 'Ergonomics' in its title
1996	Launch of journal – *Cognitive Technology*
1997	Launch of journal – *International Journal of Cognitive Ergonomics*
1999	Fiftieth anniversary of the Ergonomics Society
2000	Launch of journal – *Theoretical Issues in Ergonomics Science*

extend this to encompass other temporal and spatial aspects of the workplace and environment. The main reason for this is that it is not feasible to consider human–machine interaction without reference to other influencing factors. For example, an interface might be well designed to facilitate good interactions for a variety of users. However, this design is of little use if the workplace is poorly designed or the working environment is inappropriate. Consequently, a more complete definition of Human Factors/ergonomics would encompass these other aspects, as shown in the following definitions by Chapanis (1999: 214):

Human Factors (Ergonomics) is a body of knowledge about human abilities, human limitations, and other human characteristics that are relevant to design.

Human Factors Engineering (the practice of Ergonomics) is the application of human factors (ergonomic) information to the design of tools, machines, systems, tasks, jobs, and environments for safe, comfortable and effective human use.

- Psychology (cognitive psychology, social psychology, and occupational psychology)

- Anatomy (anthropometry and biomechanics)

- Physiology (exercise and work physiology)

Figure 1.1   Principal components of Human Factors

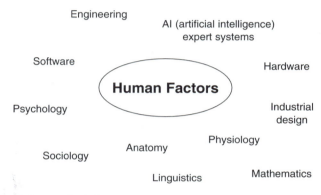

Figure 1.2   Relevant disciplines to Human Factors

It should be noted that there are several definitions in the literature; for example, Wogalter *et al.* (1998) provided a set of definitions from seventy-eight sources. A useful mnemonic for remembering what ergonomics is:

> Ergonomics is concerned with Ease of learning and Ease of use, Efficiency, Errors and Enjoyment (EEEEEE).

From the definitions, it can be seen that Human Factors/ergonomics covers a number of design issues relating to the workplace, the working environment and the organisation within which the interactions between human and machine take place. It also comprises a number of basic components and encompasses a number of other disciplines (Figures 1.1 and 1.2). In addition to the human–machine interface, there are also interfaces between the human and the working environment, and the human in the organisation. These various interfaces will be considered in the following chapters. The existence of the interfaces also provides evidence as to why some prefer to refer to task design rather than interface design, because the former delimits the extent of the subject under study.

There are a number of different ways of considering the application of Human Factors and these range from the conceptual to the more concrete. Descriptions of four typical perspectives are given below.

A promotional tool

Many consider Human Factors/ergonomics as 'a way of looking at the world, of thinking about people and how they interact with all aspects of their environment, their "equipment" and their working situation' (Oborne, 1995: 1). Hence, Human Factors/ergonomics has a philosophical perspective. The premise being that people invented machines in order to make their lives easier, and hence, they needed them to be as well-designed as possible in order to make their interactions as successful as possible. When humans and machines are in harmony, the outcome is good, i.e. tasks will be completed successfully and, in an industrial setting, productivity will increase. As a result, Human Factors/ergonomics is often used as a promotional tool. An example of this type of approach is the number of adverts that have appeared in recent times stating that objects are ergonomically designed. These claims are unlikely to be true, i.e. no formal (or even informal) attempts will have been made to consider ergonomics in the development of the product. But advertisers view the addition of the term 'ergonomics' positively and include it despite lack of evidence. Pheasant (1997) cited the example of an account of 'ergonomically designed pasta' in a Sunday newspaper; the pasta had been designed to facilitate straining and sauce retention. Other examples include vacuum cleaners, cutlery and, more recently, an advertisement describing ergonomically designed nylon tights.

A craft

A different approach is to consider Human Factors/ergonomics as a craft. It is a specialist activity that a few take great pride in doing and, like most crafts, it requires a lot of training, skill, time and perseverance to attain acceptable results – in this case, good designs by comparison with previous designs. As a result, ergonomics is only applied in a small number of 'special' products and systems. Most are mass-produced without any regard to applying ergonomics. Although this may imply that ergonomics is being viewed as an unnecessary addition to the design process, this may not be a deliberate ploy if ergonomics is being considered within the context of being a craft. An example of this might be some of the computer keyboards such as the Maltron (Hobday, 1996). This keyboard was carefully designed according to ergonomic principles and has targeted those members of the user population who have musculoskeletal problems when they use a standard computer keyboard. The designers individually crafted early versions of the Maltron keyboard.

An engineering discipline

As already mentioned, the term 'engineering psychology' has been applied to this area. The use of the word 'engineering' suggests that another approach might be that of the engineering disciplines and in fact 'Human Factors engineers' is a commonly used term to refer to ergonomists. In the engineering approach, the primary focus is on attaining solutions, i.e. the goal is to produce a working product or system according to design specifications. The Human Factors input is therefore to enable this end product to be reached. In this context, it is very practical in nature in that it provides the 'answers' for the main engineering disciplines involved in the design of the product. As an example, aeronautical, electronic and mechanical engineers are among those who might design the hardware of a human–machine system, computer scientists design the software and Human Factors engineers focus on the humans who have roles in the system. This emphasises the view that Human Factors works best in a multidisciplinary context where a team of individuals come together to design a system (or product). Each person has his or her own skills to contribute, with the Human Factors specialist bringing knowledge and understanding about the human component.

An applied psychology

Psychology is concerned with the study of human behaviour and it endorses the scientific method, i.e. it attempts to understand humans through the systematic application of basic principles and theories that have been rigorously derived. As an applied psychology, Human Factors draws on research from a number of areas of human performance and seeks to apply the natural laws of human behaviour (and resultant human performance) to the design of equipment, workplaces, environments and organisations. In this sense, one could argue that Human Factors is frequently a parasite living off the findings from experimental psychology. However, this suggests that the primary function of an applied psychologist is 'to apply the results of fundamental research to practical problems' (Nickerson, 1997: 9). The situation is, of course, more complex. Much of the work of the founders of experimental psychology was motivated by practical concerns – Bartlett has already been mentioned in this context earlier in this chapter – and in psychology there are many examples of the symbiotic relationship of basic and applied research where they inform and benefit each other (Leibowitz, 1996). It is also interesting to note that human factors is now recognised as 'one of the best known areas of applied psychology' (Gavin, 1998: 16).

Key points

- Taylor's work on shovel design was one of the first documented studies of human performance in the workplace.

- In the early part of the twentieth century, psychologists became particularly interested in vocational issues, and the concept of 'fitting the man to the job'.
- Events emanating from World War II established the need for well-designed human–machine interactions – training and selection of personnel could no longer 'fix' the equipment-associated problems.
- The terms 'Human Factors' and 'ergonomics' can be taken to be synonymous for most purposes – the primary difference stems from their origins in the psychological and biological sciences, respectively.
- Since World War II, organisations have begun to employ specialists to investigate Human Factors issues and to design tasks. Previously, tasks have been viewed as being fixed by the machine and/or the workplace (and even by tradition), whereas increasing technological developments allowed them to be viewed as something that could be designed to meet the requirements of the situation.
- Human Factors/ergonomics is first and foremost about design, and 'fit' between the human and their activities.
- The current shift is towards the cognitive aspects of human–machine interactions, as can be seen from the number of recent developments in this area, e.g. journals, articles and conferences.

2 Humans: capabilities and limitations

Man is still the most extraordinary computer of all.

John F. Kennedy, 21 May 1963

The Human Factors approach is to position the human at the centre of all activities and to consider the human system and interactions from this perspective. An example of a simple model that portrays this is the SHEL concept (Edwards, 1972; Hawkins, 1984). The SHEL concept was named after its components: software, hardware, environment and liveware. The latter, liveware, represented the human. There have been a number of pictorial representations of the SHEL concept as ideas concerning the system resources have been refined. An example of one diagrammatic representation of the model is to place L (for liveware) in the centre of a square surrounded by four other squares (S, H, E, and L) in a symmetrical cross shape. This is shown in Figure 2.1.

A feature of the model was that all five squares were given undulating edges to demonstrate the need to 'match' each of the components to the human, i.e. the edges were not deliberately simple or straight. The model also indicates the need to consider human to human communications in system design because liveware appears twice – at the centre and at the edge. This and other similar models (such as the user-centred design model illustrated by Noyes and Baber, 1999: xi) indicate how essential it is to have a sound and thorough understanding of human beings, their capabilities and limitations, both physical and psychological.

Physical aspects

The physical aspects relating to the human can be considered in relation to the anatomy and physiology of the human body/system, because these are two key components of Human Factors (see Figure 1.1). Anatomy relates to describing and measuring various dimensions of the body, and includes anthropometry (studying the human when at rest, i.e. static – also referred to as 'structural') and biomechanics (studying the human when moving, i.e.

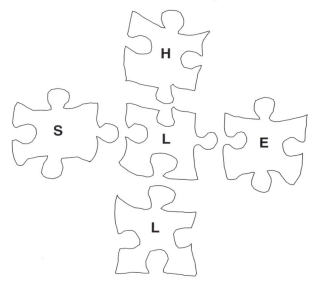

Figure 2.1   The SHEL concept

dynamic – also referred to as 'functional'). Application of the principles of anthropometry and biomechanics helps ensure attainment of the basic Human Factors aims. The Human Factors professional uses anthropometric and biomechanical data to ensure that the human operator has a good 'fit' with his or her environment. However, a full description of the anatomy of the human body is inappropriate here and the reader is referred to Bridger (1995: Chapter 2 'Anatomy, posture and body mechanics'), Oborne (1995: section on 'Body size: anthropometry' in Chapter 2), Kroemer *et al.* (1994: Chapter 1 'The anatomical and mechanical structure of the human body') and Pheasant (1997: Chapter 2 'Principles and practices of anthropometrics'). For physiology, the reader is referred to Bridger (1995: Chapter 7 'Physiology, workload and work capacity' and Chapter 8 'Industrial applications of physiology').

For anthropometry, there is a wealth of well-established information relating to different populations (Kemsley, 1950; Kroemer, 1989; Pheasant, 1997: Chapter 10 'Anthropometric data'). As an example, Oborne (1995) listed fourteen surveys of civilian populations carried out between 1950 and 1992, and ranging from twenty-three people to 33,562 individuals. One of the more global (and ambitious) anthropometric datasets was devised by Juergens *et al.* (1990), who divided the world's population into twenty groups and attempted to compile data on nineteen anthropometric measurements for each group. Anthropometric data is available in the form of tables containing one-dimensional measurements, two-dimensional models in the form of drawing templates, and three-dimensional models simulating puppets and human participants (Molenbroek, 1994). Historically, it is worth noting that much of this data has been compiled from the personnel in the armed forces, and 'cookbooks' with tables of anthropometric data exist in both hardcopy and electronic form. Oborne (1995) put forward two reasons for the prevailing use of this special population, which can obviously prove misleading for civilian applications. First, anthropometric surveys need to include data collected from a large number of people, and in this sense, military personnel provide an easily accessible population. Second, space is at a premium in combat vehicles; hence, appropriate anthropometric data is needed in order to ensure optimal designs. A massive database is currently being compiled that should become available to the scientific community within the next few years. This work emanates from the CAESAR (Civilian American and European Surface Anthropometry Resource) project (see Rioux and Bruckart, 1995). More than 10,000 civilian participants from the US, Netherlands and Italy have contributed by providing data on three-dimensional whole body surface scans. This work comprises a significant step forward from the classical anthropometric dataset, which is traditionally one-dimensional (Hoekstra, 1999).

The compilation of anthropometric data is a time-consuming and expensive activity. The extensive databases that exist are more likely to emanate from populations living in developed countries, and would be scarce in developing regions in the world (Singh *et al.*, 1995). Further, they do not account for secular trends, as Lovesey (1998) pointed out in his paper questioning the extent to which we may be getting larger. As an example, Kroemer *et al.* (1994) stated that body weight has increased in North America and Europe by about 2 kilograms per decade. Greiner and Gordon (1990) supported this in their anthropometic survey of the American Army. However, it is generally accepted that we are growing taller – Pheasant (1986) stated that an increase of 1 centimetre every 10 years had been observed in the US and UK, while Holland witnessed 15 centimetres over the twentieth century (Henneberg, 1992). Given that much of the data emanates from the military population in the developed world, the anthropometric data that exists may not fit the application under consideration (Dutra, 1997). Moreover, information may be out of date due to the unavoidable time taken to compile anthropometric survey data. One solution, suggested by May *et al.* (1999) was to ask users (or potential users) to generate the anthropometric measurements themselves.

Case study: anthropometry – go-kart design (from Jackson and Monnington, 1999)

There have been several serious accidents involving go-karting. This has led the Health and Safety Executive in the UK to consider the ergonomic design principles of go-karts with particular reference to the anthropometric dimensions. Go-karts are relatively simple vehicles with a steering wheel, an accelerator and a brake pedal – some have an adjustable harness for the driver. The aim of Jackson and Monnington's study was to generate a template for go-kart designers of the factors that need to be taken into account in order to provide a safer environment for go-kart users. Consequently, they identified four main safety critical dimensions relating to the driver's posture whilst operating the go-kart:

1. the upper seat-belt mount
2. the horizontal measurement from the seat back to the steering wheel
3. the horizontal measurement from the seat back to the undepressed pedal
4. the vertical measurement between the knee and the steering wheel.

Various positions for the seat-belt mount were considered in conjunction with the horizontal measurements taking into account that the optimum posture for operating foot controls is achieved with a knee angle of 150° (Woodson, 1981). It was concluded that the position of the seat-belt mount should be based on anthropometric (body size) information, some adjustability on the seat/pedal position will be needed to accommodate the various heights of a driver and a smaller diameter steering wheel may give the knees greater clearance. An alternative to providing adjustable equipment is to focus on designing go-karts for specific size ranges, e.g. anthropometric data relating to British teenagers. The authors acknowledged that it is difficult to be prescriptive about go-kart design given that not all machines will have the components described and, more importantly, the dimensions of the go-kart are interdependent so that varying one will have an impact on another. However, they did conclude that anthropometry had an important role to play in informing go-kart design and leading to a safer operational environment.

For biomechanics, information tends to be more specific and the large databases that there are for anthropometry understandably do not exist for biomechanics data. However, comprehensive data is slowly becoming available relating to locomotion (e.g. walking, running, slipping, falling, tripping), handling materials (e.g. lifting, repetitive movements) and various working and resting postures. One of the authoritative sources is still Dempster's (1955) study of joint ranges. In terms of anatomy, 206 bones make up the human skeleton, all of which perform either a protection or a working function or, in some cases, both. As pointed out by Bridger (1995: 31) 'the human body is a mechanical system that obeys physical laws'. In this sense, it will become unstable when subject to stresses and strains outside tolerable limits. These may be generated internally, i.e. by the individual, or imposed externally, i.e. by factors in the environment. Likewise, these effects may be fleeting or long lasting. Like anthropometry, detailed descriptions of the mechanics of the bony skeleton, joints and associated muscles are outside the scope of this book and the reader is referred to Bridger (1995), Oborne (1995: Chapter 3 'The structure of the body II: body size and movement') and Kumar (1999).

Case study: biomechanics – design of shovels: a study of digging (from Bridger et al., 1995)

A great deal of research has been carried out on manual handling and, in particular, on digging and shovelling. It has been suggested that the design of a shovel can be improved by fitting a second handle to its neck, thus reducing the need for the user to stoop (Degani *et al.*, 1993; Sen, 1984). Consequently, it is predicted that the second handle would reduce both the musculoskeletal and physiological load of digging. A study of digging from a biomechanics perspective was conducted to see if this was indeed the case.

Ten participants were videotaped while performing the same task of shovelling sand using a conventional spade and two spades with slightly differently fitted second handles. The modified shovels allowed the person digging to have their wrists either pronated or supinated, depending on how the second handle was fixed. Forces and feet movements were measured in three axes using a force platform while lower back movements were recorded with a lumbar motion monitor (for more information on the specific apparatus and methodology employed, see Marras *et al.*, 1992). Actual body posture in two dimensions was ascertained from the video recording. Biomechanics data was generated from three sources: the joint markers on the participants, the force platform and the lumbar motion monitor.

Results indicated that the times taken to shift the same weight of sand were similar across all three conditions.

- Joint markers – automatic analysis of the joint markers on the participants indicated that the mean trunk–thigh angles with the conventional shovel were significantly lower throughout the digging cycle than with the modified tools. Hence, it was found that use of the latter resulted in 30° less bending of the trunk.

- Force platform – the force platform data was analysed in terms of peak forces and moments in the three dimensions (x-, y- and z-axes). Significant differences were reported for moments in the x-axis that were lower with the modified handle, and the peak forces in the y-axis that were greater when this shovel was used. This was in contrast to the peak forces in the z-axis, which were found to be greater with the conventional shovel. Finally, the peak moment in the z-axis was shown to be greater when the modified handle was used. Interpretation of these results was in keeping with the joint marker analysis that indicated that although more bending was required with the conventional shovel, there was less twisting of the body. The modified handle was slightly heavier than the conventional one and this may in part explain these findings.
- Lumbar motion monitor – the lumbar motion data was analysed according to the model of Marras *et al.* (1995). This model suggests that a combination of five factors (lifting frequency, load moment, trunk lateral velocity, trunk twisting velocity and trunk sagittal angle) can be used to predict the probability of low back disorder. When applied to the three shovels under consideration here, it was found that the conventional shovel had a slightly greater overall probability of low back problems.

It was concluded from the results of the three sets of biomechanical data that the conventional shovel had a higher risk of back disorder, especially when it is considered that the study took place in the laboratory, i.e. under ideal environmental conditions with soft sand.

Psychological aspects

System processes are generally thought to be orderly and discrete, and consisting of three phases – input, conversion, output. In comparison, human behaviour is not so discrete and linear: humans receive information, process it and make decisions from it, which can culminate in various actions. Therefore, a common approach to considering the psychological aspects of human–machine interaction is to view them within the context of information-processing models. A number of these models exist (Broadbent, 1958; Welford, 1976b; Wickens, 1992) and an amalgam of these is presented in Figure 2.2. As models, they are inevitably abstractions of what actually happens when we process information. They are often simplistic and leave out numerous feedback loops and filters, and do not allow for individual and task differences. They suggest a linear approach, i.e. that physical stimuli are changed into a form that the human can utilise in a

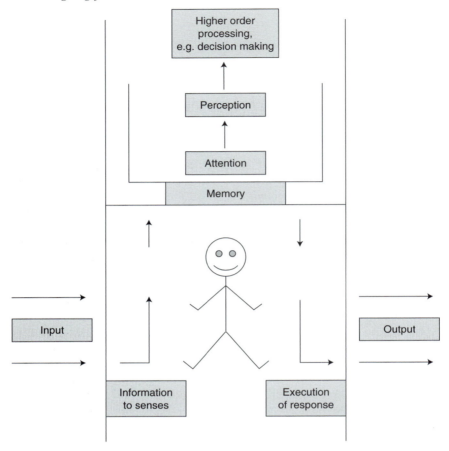

Figure 2.2   Human information-processing model

sequential manner. Movement through the model is sequential and assumes that each stage results in transforming information from one stage to the next. In reality, it is likely that one process of transduction does not begin after the previous one has finished, but that some cascade (McClelland, 1981). This behaviouristic approach is thought to be invalid by individuals who support a more ecological model (Flach, 1989; Vicente and Harwood, 1990). Instead of viewing the components of information processing as separate entities, they propose that they should be studied simultaneously rather than as sequential interactions. However, there has been much support for these information-processing models (Hendy *et al.*, 1997) and they do provide a useful starting point from which to consider how we process information within the context of human–machine interaction.

Attention

In order to process information about the world, it has initially to be gathered. The first point of contact between the human and the external world is through our sensory system. The five primary Aristotelian senses (vision, audition, smell, touch and taste) are widely recognised as providing this initial interface between the human and the physical stimulus. Vision is the dominant sense in human–machine interaction; Anshel (1998) stated that it accounted for over 80 per cent of our learning as well as being the sense that we most feared losing. In contrast, the touch sense has been little researched (Kroemer *et al.*, 1994). There are other senses, e.g. the kinaesthetic and proprioceptive; these inform us about our body's orientation and limb position in space. As a large amount of sensory information falls continually on our senses, a filtering mechanism is needed. Wickens (1992) put forward the view that, for each of the senses, there is a central mechanism that preserves a representation of the physical stimulus for a short period of time. This pre-attentive store does not require conscious attention and decays rapidly.

The searchlight metaphor has been applied to attention, i.e. we are selective in the information sources to which we attend and everything within the beam of the light is processed (Wachtel, 1967). This includes those aspects that we want to process (the 'penumbra') and those that we must process but do not want (the 'umbra'). A further refinement of the searchlight metaphor is to consider the breadth of the beam, i.e. the penumbra in terms of divided attention, and the umbra as focused attention, while the direction of the beam describes the properties of selective attention (see Wickens, 1992). Each of these three types of attention is briefly considered here.

Divided attention

This type of attention occurs when we are forced to attend to two or more tasks simultaneously, i.e. our attention has to be divided. For example, when driving, we may have to watch out for when and where to change direction at the same time as controlling the car. In other words, we have to time-share our resources. An indication that our attention resources have finite capacity can be demonstrated by the fact that whilst driving and talking, we will shut down one channel, usually driving, when increasing demands are made on the other. For example, most experienced drivers can effortlessly control the car whilst talking to a passenger or listening to music. However, on overtaking a bus, most drivers will cease talking as they focus more of their attention on driving. Failure to divide attention successfully can result in total degradation of both the primary and secondary tasks.

Focused attention

This type of attention occurs when we have to attend to a specific activity and make a conscious effort to ignore competing activities in the immediate environment. For example, trying to find a piece of information on a full display screen or holding a telephone conversation in a busy room. Failure of focused attention results in suboptimal processing of the activity.

Selective attention

This type of attention occurs on occasions when we need to attend to an activity and become distracted, i.e. our attention is inappropriately turned to some other aspect of the environment. A classic example of selective attention was given by Wiener (1977) when describing the behaviour of the flight deck crew onboard the fated Eastern Airlines L-1011 flight that crashed into the Everglades swamps in Florida in 1972. In summary, the crew became fixated with the problem of replacing a light bulb to the point that no one was flying the aircraft, and it rapidly lost height, eventually flying into the ground. Although it seems unbelievable, in retrospect, the crew selectively placed their attention on an inconsequential secondary task, ignoring the primary task needed in that particular environment.

Attention usually leads to the processes of perception and interpretation of the sensory information, and an interactive loop involving memory contributes to perception and decision processes. Consequently, the human system does not function in a serial fashion, e.g. decisions can be made as information is being processed. In terms of designing systems, the attention demands of the task are an important consideration. If undivided attention is required then the design of the interface must prevent distraction from other parts of the immediate environment. In some applications, the only way to avoid this may be to change the operator's job. For example, displays that require continuous monitoring (with undivided attention) can be problematic if the operator is scanning other displays simultaneously. This then leads to consideration of the overall cognitive workload of the operator, and when designing the system, workload needs to be taken into account. The topic of workload is considered further in Chapter 5.

Perception

Once information has passed through the pre-attentive and attention stages, it is then ready for higher order processing. The process of perception is two-fold, in that we have to make sense and understand sensory information and we have to integrate this with stored information. It is only after this stage that some higher-order processing can begin to occur. This is demonstrated in the following: when a human observes a scene, the image of this scene falls on the retina of the eye. At this stage, the information is purely visual. To make sense of it, the person has to interpret the situation, i.e. draw on both the sensory and stored information, resulting in perception of the situation. Gibson (1979) argued from his work with pilots landing aircraft that sensory information was more important in the perceptual process. It has been known for some time that pilots can experience a visual illusion upon landing where the point to which the aircraft is moving appears stationary, but the rest of the visual environment appears to move away from that point. A similar type of illusion can occur while flying at night, when fixed lights on the ground appear to move. Gibson's view was that pilots would only use sensory information that in this particular case is rich and detailed. One flaw in this argument concerns errors, i.e. what happens in the situation when we respond incorrectly to perceptual information that is predominantly sensory. In opposition to Gibson's theory of direct perception, Gregory (1972) and Neisser (1976) put forward a constructivist theory, i.e. perceptions are constructions from both types of information. A further alternative theory has been suggested by Marr (1982), who proposed that visual perception involves a series of steps of increasing complexity: these steps are processes that abstract information from the external and internal worlds, and add it to the previous step. Marr has attempted to generate a computer model of his ideas on visual perception. However, he has met with limited success, suggesting that there is greater complexity in visual perception than was once thought. In conclusion, it is generally accepted that 'this complexity is probably due to *all* the theories being partially correct' (Gavin, 1998: 28).

When considering human–machine interaction, one type of perception of particular interest is pattern matching. In pattern matching, the pattern is uniquely identified by a number of features along several physical dimensions (Wickens, 1992). Humans are excellent pattern matchers and can see at a glance when a pattern has been broken. For example, when viewing a number of dials, recognition of a malfunction on one display can be very easily and quickly spotted, i.e. unique combinations (patterns) of indicators (features) on displays (dimensions) can be quickly identified. Likewise, external door handles on trains make a horizontal bar when viewed by the guard, thus making it easy to see at a glance that all doors are securely closed. This aspect of perception is particularly important when considering the design of objects in our environment when we need to respond quickly to an abnormal situation.

Higher-order processing

After a person has perceptually categorised a situation, they then have to decide whether to act and what to do. The higher-order processing that takes place is collectively known as cognition, and covers the various diverse types of thinking (from imaging and fantasising, to problem solving and remembering). Of course, it could be argued that there are other parts of the information-processing model that include higher-order processing, e.g. visual perception, so this term is not exclusive to the aforementioned activities. From a psychological perspective, much of the research emphasis has gone into decision making and there have been three main approaches to this over the decades:

- normative models
- descriptive models
- prescriptive models.

Normative models

The early decision-making models of the 1950s were normative in that they defined a standard way in which decisions should be made in order to optimise outcomes (Edwards, 1954). They have subsequently become known as 'classical decision theory' (Sternberg, 1999). An example of a normative model is some form of Utility Theory or Bayesian decision theory where we seek pleasure and avoid pain; hence, in decision making, we will maximise pleasure (the positive utility) and minimise pain (the negative utility). The expected utility of a particular outcome is defined as the probability multiplied by the cost or benefit. The normative model suggests that the rational decision strategy is to select the option with the maximum expected utility. For example, if you had to decide whether to go out for the evening or visit a friend, you would weigh up the positive utilities (the pleasure to be attained from having a good time) against the negative utilities (the pain associated with the fact that you have not been getting on well with the friend recently).

Descriptive models

These models describe how people actually make decisions, i.e. they take into account human irrationality and biases. They were popular in the 1970s and replaced the normative models when it was realised that people do not always act rationally when making decisions. As a result, the aim of research became not so much to demonstrate that humans are suboptimal decision makers but rather to describe the information-processing strategies that result in non-optimal decision making. An example of a descriptive model is Expected Utility Theory (Yates, 1990) where the utility of the outcomes is determined by the particular characteristics of the individual. Utility theorists assumed they could predict what people would do because decision makers always seek the highest possible utility. However, in practice it is difficult to assign objective utilities to decision making. In the example given above about whether to go out for the evening or visit a friend, there may be other factors, such as guilt because you have not seen the friend recently, or lack of finance, that govern the decision making. The work of Tversky and Kahneman (1974) was particularly influential in the move from normative to descriptive models. They demonstrated that people reduce the cognitive demands imposed by decision making by relying on a limited number of heuristic principles. This work was subsequently confirmed and extended by a large body of research on judgements under uncertainty (see reviews by Kahneman *et al.*, 1982; Scholz, 1983).

Prescriptive models

The more recent approach has been the development of prescriptive models that describe how people should make decisions to conform to the normative model. These models study decision making in natural and operational settings and hence address the criticisms that the early theories often used unrealistic problems and scenarios (Klein, 1993; Rasmussen, 1993). For example, decisions on the civil flight deck can sometimes be made under time pressure, with incomplete information and in a changing environment where the stakes are high in terms of making the 'right' decision. Hence, the term 'naturalistic decision making' defined by Zsambok (1997) as the way in which people use their experience to make decisions in the field.

Research has tended to focus on decision making by an individual but, in many workplace settings, team decisions will need to be made. On these occasions, groups must perceive, encode, store and retrieve information at the same time. Cannon-Bowers *et al.* (1993) hypothesised that teams will only be effective at making decisions when they have a shared understanding of the task, the context and each other, i.e. when they have common mental models. Further, we know that the status of group members also influences group processes and hence, the outcome of any decision making.

Memory

The storage and retrieval of information are fundamental to the information-processing activities. Multistore theories of memory suggest that there are many separate and distinct types of memory but there is much contention amongst memory researchers about the detail of the actual categorisation (see Baddeley, 1992). It is not the intention here to discuss the research evidence for different memory structures, characteristics and operation, other than to draw attention to the fact that memory limitations can be a major bottleneck in many human–machine systems. Individuals may fail to carry out a correct action because of a failure of working memory. In 1987, Northwest Airlines flight 255 crashed because it was alleged the crew had forgotten to lower the flaps during take-off (National Transportation Safety Board, 1988).

In conclusion, it can be seen that we process information through a variety of cognitive operations, which include decision-making and action-planning processes, as well as perception, memory and aspects of attention. People differ in their natural abilities to perform these cognitive operations and these are also occasions when external stimuli will inhibit or disrupt information-processing activities. It is worth noting that some cognitive operations can be improved with training. When considering the design of products, understanding human information-processing is vital. However, it is not that straightforward. In theory, if the information-processing capacities of the human can be understood and taken into account by a designer, an interface should be produced that will be as 'usable' as possible. However, there has been a considerable amount of research relating to motor control, perception and lower level cognitive activities, but relatively less on the role of models relating to higher level cognitive processing.

Execution of action

The output from the human information-processing model is usually some form of motor action. The actual length of neural pathways in our nervous system, and hence the time taken for nerve impulses to travel, limits our response times. Consequently, it will not in the foreseeable future be possible to execute a response in less than a second. This has implications with respect to some military applications and the time needed for the human to respond to attacking missiles from the enemy. Manual control has been studied from two very different perspectives: skilled behaviour and dynamic systems (Wickens, 1992). Skilled behaviour in this context relates to the execution of complex movements in a highly controlled, i.e. predictable, environment. For example, the worker on a production line makes a number of repetitive actions over and over again. In contrast, dynamic systems often lack the element of certainty, e.g. crew flying an aircraft are engaging in a more open-loop task. In the laboratory setting, the latter is often investigated through the use of the tracking paradigm where participants control a system whose dynamics are being determined by another (computer) system. Execution is a vital component of human information processing, since it is sometimes the only way that the higher order cognitive processes can be studied.

Case study: higher order processing – development of an integrated decision-making model for avionics application (from Donnelly et al., 1998)

The flight deck on civil aircraft provides a unique environment for human decision making. Although most of the crew's time is spent in relative calm, with monitoring being the primary activity, there are occasions when decisions relating to complex and dynamic situations will have to be made quickly and with too much information coming in too fast. Hence, there is a need for us to understand the dynamics of information processing in this type of environment (Abbott *et al.*, 1996). With reference to the decision-making theories, the naturalistic ones are the most appropriate to the flight deck environment, although there are certain aspects of this setting that are not covered by existing models and theories. In response to this, Donnelly *et al.* generated an Integrated Decision Model (IDM; Figure 2.3), which enhances existing work by producing a more descriptive model of crew behaviour. A further feature of the IDM is that it highlights areas of weakness in decision making, thus enabling the intervention of decision support strategies.

The model indicates that there are three paths for crew decision making:

- Path 1 – if information is complete, the crew might form intentions to act (they may also consider the consequences of their actions and perhaps perform a mental simulation, as described by Klein, 1993).
- Path 2 – if information is incomplete, the crew might seek to find out more, i.e. to enhance their mental representation.
- Path 3 – in some instances, completeness of information is not an issue and the crew will bypass the stage of forming intentions and considering alternatives. This automaticity might occur when a situation is routine or there is little time available; one of the frequent consequences of this is error.

The two issues of time pressure and automaticity were considered in an experimental study. It was hypothesised that decision makers would make more errors under conditions of time pressure and when procedures had resulted in automatic responses. A process control task was designed that was analogous to a flight deck in that it contained some of the key characteristics of naturalistic decision making. The process control task was interspersed with a secondary task where participants had to respond to a simple message; this event was controlled, thus ensuring that responses became automatic. An 'independents' subject' design was employed with fifteen participants in the experimental condition (time pressure and automaticity) and fourteen in the control condition. The number of correct responses and response times were measured. It was found that time pressure greatly affected the way in which participants made decisions, whereas increasing routineness (i.e. automaticity) had little effect.

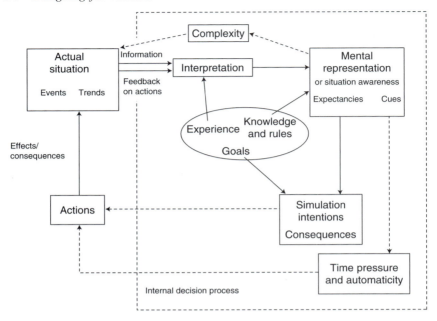

Figure 2.3   The proposed integrated decision model

Obviously, the IDM needs further validation but it does seem that two of the main areas of weakness in the human decision-making process are the formation and maintenance of an accurate mental representation and the consideration of the outcome of actions, including inaction. These two aspects lie within the internal decision-making process, as shown by the dashed line in Figure 2.3, and intervention at this point is naturally difficult. Moreover, the IDM does indicate the points at which decision support could aid the crew. For example, an effective intervention would be to provide a predictive facility for crew to find out about the consequences of their actions – an aspect of flight deck design highlighted in research carried out by Noyes and Starr (2000). In this respect, it seems a useful model.

Users

Having considered the physiological and psychological aspects of humans, it is necessary within the context of the topic of human–machine interaction to consider how we view humans as a group. In this sense, the humans who have direct contact with the machines are often collectively referred to as users. Note that these people can be defined as primary users because they use interfaces and accompanying information to achieve their goals. In contrast, there is a group of secondary users who will be affected by the performance abilities of the primary users (Hackos and Redish, 1998). If an example relating to computer databases is considered, the primary users would be the individuals managing and having direct access to a computer database, whereas the secondary users would be the people who needed to use the information provided by the database. For whatever reason, these people would not have direct access to the database and hence would be reliant on the primary users. Inevitably, users exhibit a number of individual differences relating to age, sex, background, experience, level of motivation, etc. Despite this, there will be occasions when it is necessary to define and classify them according to a single category, e.g. when carrying out user evaluations. One commonly used classification is to consider users according to their level of experience, i.e. experienced, intermediate and novice. This broad-brush classification is easier to apply than others that divide the first category into 'expert' and 'skilled', and the third category into 'beginner' and 'naïve' users. These four groups were distinguished by Sutcliffe (1988) in his book on human–computer interaction, who defined them as follows:

- Naïve – these individuals have no experience of using the machines/technology. In reality, they are often quite difficult to locate because it is quite common for individuals to have used similar machines and technologies. Hence, the truly naïve individual is a rarity.
- Novices – these are the users who are beginners at using the machines/technology; however, this does not preclude them from being skilled or even expert at other applications.
- Skilled – these individuals are competent users, but lack the 'extra' knowledge and understanding or motivation to be classed as experts. It could be hypothesised that the majority of users would fall into this category.
- Experts – these are the individuals who have extensive knowledge and understanding about how the machines/technology works to the point where they could take it apart and rebuild, if necessary. There are relatively few expert users.

To allow for the skilled users transferring from one application to another (and thus becoming 'temporary' novice users), Hackos (1994) suggested that the category of 'transfer users' would be a useful addition. This highlights the fact that the situation being described here is a dynamic one and is continually changing. Hackos also recommended that the classification should take into account the type of use. For example, rote users are individuals who may use the system competently but do this primarily by following instructions and procedures. Hence, in one sense, they are skilled users, but their lack of understanding may exclude them from this group. The classification favoured by Hackos and Redish (1998) was: novice users,

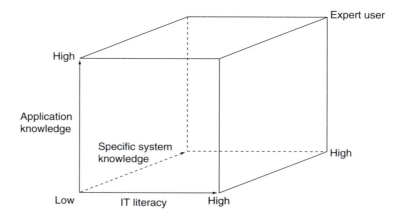

Figure 2.4 Smith's (1997) three-dimensional classification of user types (reproduced with permission of the McGraw-Hill Publishing Company)

advanced beginners, competent users, and expert users. These four user types represented a continuum based upon their stages of use. The Hackos and Redish model was based on one developed by Dreyfus and Dreyfus (1986). At any one time, users will be somewhere on the continuum. However, one of the problems of this model is that it does not take into account that users may be skilled at one component of a task but a novice at another. Carey (1982) suggested that computer users can be better classified according to a two-dimensional model that takes into account their knowledge of and skills relating to both the general application and the specific software system. She described four categories of users: naïve (someone with little knowledge of either the application or the system); novice (having little application knowledge but considerable system knowledge); casual (having considerable application knowledge but limited system knowledge); experienced (having considerable knowledge of both dimensions). Smith (1997: 38) added a third dimension of general information technology (IT) literacy in order to generate the 'skill level user cube'. By classifying knowledge of the application, the system and IT literacy as either high or low, Smith generated eight different user types: novice, parrot, literate, trained, casual, specific, transferring, expert (Figure 2.4). In one corner of the cube can be found the novice (scoring 'low' on all three dimensions) while in the opposite corner resides the expert (scoring 'high' on all three dimensions). In between can be found the other user types emanating from the various combinations of high and low knowledge of the application, system and IT literacy.

It soon becomes apparent that any classification of users quickly becomes problematic. This may beg the question as to why we need to classify users at all. Although frequency of use may seem an obvious starting point for this, it comprises a narrow description and does not take into account the other skills that individuals may have in the workplace. For example, being an expert at collating data on Excel spreadsheets is of little use if you cannot complete the work by the required deadline. In conclusion, it would seem that the rather crude, three-part classification will probably suffice as a general rule to defining users, and anything more precise needs to take into account the specific characteristics of the application.

Key points

- The physical characteristics of the human are often considered in terms of anatomy (anthropometry and biomechanics) and physiology.
- A wealth of information about human characteristics already exists in extensive anthropometric databases.
- Human information-processing models provide a means of categorising the various psychological characteristics of the human.
- Information processing has been considered here in terms of attention, perception, higher-order processing (e.g. decision making), memory and execution of action.
- With the increasing use of advanced and complex technology, issues of information processing are becoming more significant in the design of human–machine interactions.
- Within the context of human–machine interaction, it is often necessary to categorise humans into various user groups.
- Users can be classified in many ways, but probably one of the most simple (and successful) is to use a three-type definition of experienced, intermediate and novice.

3 Human–machine interaction

Man is a tool-using animal . . . Without tools he is nothing, with tools he is all.

Thomas Carlyle, 1833–4, *Sartor Resartus*, Bk 1, Ch. 5

The computer is a fast idiot, it has no imagination; it cannot originate action. It is, and will remain, only a tool to man.

American Library Association, 1964

It has already been stated that Human Factors/ergonomics is a discipline that seeks to maximise efficiency, safety and comfort by shaping the technology to the physical and psychological capabilities of the user. 'The technology' is a generic term covering all devices from simple tools through to advanced, complex systems. Although it may be possible to design very simple devices in isolation, it is not possible to do this with more advanced technology. Other influences on its use can emanate from the design of the workplace, the environment and even the activities of the organisation. Hence, the human is subject to a number of interactions: the first of these, human–machine interaction, is considered here.

Humans and tools

Homo sapiens is a tool user. From the days when we were hunter-gatherers (around 5,000 years ago), we have been making tools and using and refining them to increase our chances of survival. The progression of stone tools to copper and then iron implements is one well-known low-technology example. It could be argued that the shaping of the handle of an axe might be viewed as one of the early applications of elementary ergonomics, i.e. designing tools to aid human–machine interactions and increase efficiency. Taylor's work on shovel design outlined in Chapter 1 can be viewed as a similar application to this. Both are examples of products that are relatively simple manual tools. They tend to be used by humans singly and increasing

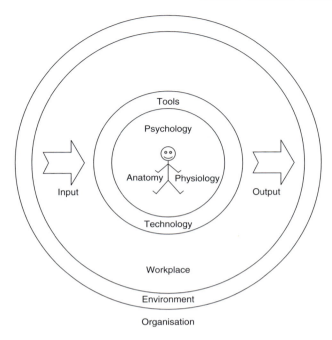

Figure 3.1   Human–machine interaction

the number of people will result in the overall job being completed faster. This type of activity (an example of mechanisation where physical effort dominates) is in contrast to the complex systems and technologies in use at the start of the twenty-first century, where automation, i.e. mental effort, supplants mechanisation (Thomas, 1969). Here, increasing the number of workers will not necessarily result in quicker completion of the job – indeed, several dozen people on a flight deck would result in chaos! However, this somewhat flippant example is somewhat misleading – increased information processing has allowed us to be more efficient in production, manufacturing, distribution and consumption. In the developed world, we have moved from an industrial-based society to the so-called 'information society' and moved from tasks requiring primarily physical effort to those needing mental effort. Correspondingly, despite their obvious differences, Human Factors attempts to cover the whole range of objects from the design of simple tools and everyday products such as chopsticks (see the ergonomic study to determine their optimum length by Hsu and Wu (1991)) to the more complex, advanced and emerging technologies. In this sense, 'machine' is a generic term being used here to cover simple tools to advanced technologies, as well as being shorthand for covering all the software and hardware in the system. This is demonstrated in Figure 3.1.

Table 3.1   Summary of controls

Primary control		Secondary control	
Simple	*Complex*	*Simple*	*Complex*
Knobs	Keyboards (sequential,	Lightpen	Function keys
Pushbuttons	chord, hybrid)	Stylus	Graphics tablet
Switches	Speech (single utterances,	Mouse	Touchpad
Levers	natural language)	Trackerball	
Pedals	Pen (optical character	Joystick	
Touchscreen	recognition, handwriting)		
	Thought		

Controls

The term 'controls' is a generic term for describing human input to machines. These can range from simple physical controls to complex modes of inputting information, some of which are still in a primitive stage of development, e.g. thought. Some devices allow direct control of the system; this usually means that operation of the control will result in an immediate change of the system state. This is in contrast to devices that result in small changes that eventually lead to changing the state of the system: moving a cursor would fall into this category. Table 3.1 shows a summary of common input devices classified according to function.

Primary controls

Simple physical controls might include knobs, pushbuttons, toggle switches, levers and pedals. Oborne (1995) stated that controls are commonly classified according to their function. This can be discrete, e.g. on or off, or continuous, e.g. increasing the volume on a radio. Human Factors issues focus on:

- Ease of use – some controls can be difficult to activate because they have too much resistance, i.e. the force-displacement characteristics, or are awkwardly positioned.
- Feedback – this provides evidence that the control is working and has been operated, but may be difficult to see, slow to register, etc.
- Dimensions – the size and shape of the control need to meet the task and human requirements.
- Location and layout – the controls should be laid out in order to meet task requirements and the user's physiological characteristics, e.g. their arm reach.
- Control–display relationships – the controls need to be compatible with the displays in terms of operation, e.g. isomorphic relations.

Corlett and Clark (1995) have comprehensively described the general suitability of a large range of simple controls for different types of operation. These include the controls listed in Table 3.1 plus rotary selectors, cranks, handwheels and footswitches.

The primary simple controls in the table also include touchscreens. These appear to be straightforward to operate but do have a number of drawbacks relating to problems of parallax, user fatigue and the greasy surface that quickly results from frequent use (see Shneiderman, 1991). Despite this, touchscreens are becoming a common feature in supermarkets and other UK retail outlets in the UK for ordering, purchasing, querying stock availability and finding out about special offers.

Primary complex controls comprise a diverse set of input devices, of which one of the most common is the word processing keyboard. The standard alphanumeric keyboard has been nicknamed 'QWERTY' after the first six letters on the top row. For a history of the development of QWERTY from the early days of the first typewriters in the 1860s, and the challenges made by other keyboards, see Noyes (1983a; 1998). Briefly, Human Factors problems relating to the design of the standard keyboard include:

- Layout – the QWERTY layout overloads the left hand (the non-preferred hand for the majority of the population) and the little fingers. Additionally, most typing involves the top row rather than the centre of the keyboard (see Noyes, 1998).
- Design – the QWERTY design slopes diagonally from the top left to the bottom right, thus making it incongruent with the shape of our hands. Further, the fact that all the keys are the same height makes it necessary to stretch the shorter fingers. These problems have been addressed in the Maltron keyboard (Hobday, 1996); this is a split keyboard with keys arranged in arcs and different heights in keeping with the natural shape of our hands. Split keyboards have also been the subject of recent investigation by Zecevic *et al.* (2000) who compared a standard keyboard with two 'segmented' keyboard designs.

Despite these problems with both layout and design, the QWERTY keyboard has become the *de facto* standard; it became an international standard in 1966 and has become documented in other standards (ISO 4169 (1979); BS 5959 (1980); ISO 9241 (1991)). It also looks as if this keyboard will dominate the market for years to come given the failures to take advantage of the many opportunities there have been to oust QWERTY with better designs and soft keyboards.

The QWERTY keyboard is a prime example of a sequential keyboard where the vast majority of keypresses involve hitting single keys. In contrast, the chord keyboards involve patterned pressing of several keys in order to achieve a single output. Hence, the letter 'A' could require two or three keys to be depressed at more or less the same time. Chord keying thus allows the number of keys to be dramatically reduced. For example, five keys allow thirty-one chords to be made (2^5-1, where '1' equals the nil response), and ten keys allow 1,023 patterns to be generated. On a one-handed chord keyboard, the addition of another key increases the number of possible chords to forty-seven, and a third key to sixty-three, and so on. Hence, it can be seen that four finger keys plus three thumb keys could cover the accepted alphanumeric set by allowing sixty-three characters to be generated. Eilam (1989) stated that if some keys act as shift keys, a relatively large dataset can be generated by a small number of keys. An extension of this is to have keys with three status positions as opposed to the binary 'on or off' approach. The ternary chord keyboard generated by Kroemer (1992) did this, and with only a relatively few keys, say one for each finger, it is possible to generate thousands of characters. The drawback, of course, is the memory component necessary to execute the different chords (Richardson *et al.*, 1987). Further, some of the chords can be physically difficult to make. For example, chords that require the fingers either side of the ring finger to depress keys but not the ring finger. As a result, chord keyboards have been used for mainly specialist applications, e.g. mail sorting (Bartram, 1986) and word processing by disabled individuals (Noyes, 1983b).

Keyboards that show characteristics of both sequential and chord keyboards were named 'hybrid' by Noyes (1983a). The ANTEL keyboard patented by Stewart and Miles (1977) is a classic example of a hybrid keyboard; it is shown in Figure 3.2. Characters are generated by both sequential pressing of individual keys, e.g. the letters 'A', 'C', 'E', etc. and chord pressing of either two or four keys, to attain the letters 'B' and 'G', for example. Unlike the traditional chord keyboards, it is not necessary to remember the patterns of keypresses necessary for the various alphanumerics. However, despite the innovativeness and advantages of this design, it has not been taken up.

It is probably worth briefly mentioning the numeric keyboards. There are two commonly used numeric layouts – the calculator design with '789' on the top row and the telephone design with the more logical '123' on the top row. Interestingly, ISO 9241 allows both layouts. The somewhat bizarre calculator arrangement probably arose from the adding machine layout where the mechanical linkages required that the higher numbers were placed at the top of the layout of keys. Over the years, many researchers have demonstrated that the superiority of the '123' layout is more in keeping with user expectations (see Conrad and Hull, 1968; Deininger, 1960; Lutz and Chapanis, 1955; Straub and Granaas, 1993).

Finally, there are specialist keyboards such as the alphabetic arrangement found in use in the airline industries, e.g. for reservations and on the flight management system, and some children's toys. There are also special function keyboards such as the concept keyboards used by some disabled

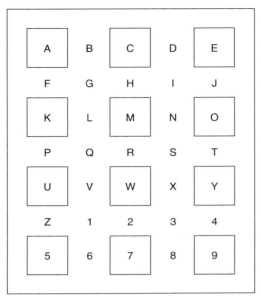

Thirty-five clearly labelled functions

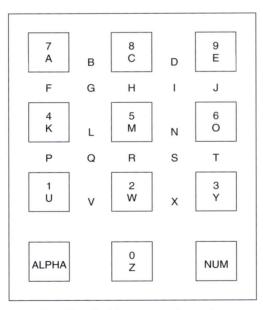

Possible calculator or computer version

Figure 3.2   Diagrammatic representation of the ANTEL keyboard layout

individuals, and specific keyboards for use in the air traffic control environment (Lam and Greenstein, 1984). Given the diversity of these special function keyboards, the dominance of QWERTY and the methodological difficulties associated with conducting keyboard experiments, it is not easy to draw definitive conclusions about their usability.

The remaining input modes in this group (i.e. speech, pen and thought) are as yet in primitive stages of development when compared with the ubiquitous keyboard. Although both speech and pen input systems are commercially available and operational, their functional capacity is limited. It probably does not need to be stated that the use of human thought for communicating with machines is in a very embryonic state, with little progress being made in successfully achieving a meaningful relationship between EEGs (electroencephalograms) and concentration on a specific item. Pearson (1999) predicts that, by 2030 or so, the technology may exist to link our brains to 'clever' computers. This will provide us with more processing power and Pearson suggests we will need to be renamed '*Homo cyberneticus*'. In contrast to these developments, progress has been made on 'talking and writing to machines' although, as already stated, functionality is restricted. When considering speech input, i.e. automatic speech recognition (ASR), one of the main difficulties arises from the detection of endpoints of words. When humans converse, they are able to take advantage of context, so the statement 'I scream' would not be confused with 'ice-cream' because the listener would relate interpretation of the meaning of the utterance to the situation. Not only are humans able to take account of context, they also tend to run words together when they talk and do not generally have a problem detecting where one word ends and another begins in their native languages. At the moment, the technology cannot take advantage of context and this, combined with the difficulty of recognising endpoints, would hinder recognition of the above statement. The result is that isolated word recognition with a relatively limited vocabulary of less than 100 items and a dedicated speaker (i.e. a speaker-dependent system) will attain good recognition performance. (The word 'item' is important here, because ASR does not necessarily relate to the recognition of words. As long as utterances are produced consistently and the technology has been programmed to accept them, any sounds, e.g. coughs, grunts, ums, etc. can be input to ASR devices.) However, the recognition of continuous speech using a natural language vocabulary of between 20 and 30,000 items and accessed by any individual (i.e. a speaker-independent system) remains a future development (Baber, 1991; Baber and Noyes, 1993; Noyes, 1993; Noyes, in press).

In conclusion, ASR technology can be successfully applied to applications that meet the first set of criteria, namely, small vocabulary, isolated word input and dedicated speakers. A further feature of a successful application might be one where mistakes are not costly. Because of the problems of misrecognition, which increase in hostile environments (see Baber and

Noyes, 1996), it is important to avoid situations where users' lives and wellbeing depend on correct recognition. The civil flight deck is one such environment and ASR is viewed very much a future development for this reason (Arbuckle *et al.*, 1998). In contrast, some industrial quality control and inspection tasks have been using ASR since the early 1970s (Martin, 1976).

Pen input shares many of the characteristics of speech input. Like ASR, character recognition of an individual's handwriting depends on a pattern-matching exercise where incoming data is matched to prestored information to select the best fit. The term 'character recognition' also covers a range of technologies from optical character readers (OCRs) that allow information given in a standard preprinted form to be input to a computer, to devices that recognise hand-printed characters, e.g. personal digital assistants (PDAs). OCRs belong to a group of input technologies that are machine-read. Other examples include optical mark readers (OMRs), bar-code readers, magnetic card readers and magnetic ink character recognition (MICRs). From a Human Factors perspective, OCRs are not of particular interest because they involve machine recognition of machine-generated characters in a special font, e.g. as found on utilities' bills. To return to pen input, many of the problems that surround the successful recognition of human speech also apply to handwriting. For example:

- Endpoint detection of characters and words – cursive, freehand, writing is particularly difficult for machine recognition. One solution is to confine the user's writing to single characters written within grid-lines, i.e. boxed input.
- Small vocabularies – recognition performance will improve with a limited character set, e.g. digits or all lower case letters.
- Dedicated users – systems that are used by one motivated, trained individual are more likely to be successful than ones used by the infamous Joe Public.

Both pen and speech technologies are subject to inter- and intra-user differences. The recognition of signatures is one example of this. Machine verification of signatures would be a useful addition to the number of personal electronic transactions that are currently being carried out. Further, the uniqueness of our signatures would enhance the security aspects in ensuring the identification of the writer. One of the difficulties, however, is inconsistency. When we produce our signatures, each is slightly different from all the others, making machine recognition difficult (Smithies, 1994). The key to successful speech recognition is also 'consistency'. As long as an individual can produce phonologically consistent utterances, machine recognition is possible. This has positive implications for disabled users because it does not matter if their speech in unintelligible to fellow humans; provided that they can form consistent vocal utterances

Table 3.2   Speech and pen input: demands that can be met

	Speech	Pen
Users	Dedicated user groups – speaker-dependent recognition	Dedicated user groups
Tasks	Use of single 'command' words (as opposed to text input)	Use of pen for pointing tasks (as opposed to text input)
Products	Small vocabularies of up to 100 items with elementary syntax and isolated item input	Personal technologies such as personal digital assistants
Applications	Most successful in non-safety-critical applications	Most successful where handwritten input is not a major component

(not necessarily words), they can successfully use a speech recogniser (see Noyes *et al.*, 1989).

One of the interesting aspects of machine recognition of activities is that new users will often have unrealistic expectations, which can hamper their interactions with the technology. For example, when our speech is mis-recognised by a fellow human, one strategy to be understood is to speak louder, more clearly and slower. Likewise, if we want to ensure our hand-writing is readable, we might resort to writing in capitals, or larger print, or both. Past experience has told us that these types of strategies usually work in human-to-human communications. However, the problem arises in that the algorithms that the technologies use for pattern recognition do not corre-spond to the ones with which we are familiar. Thus, raising one's voice or writing in capitals will have no effect on recognition rates, and indeed might exacerbate the situation. With regard to the latter, work at Bristol actually found that recognition performance was not as high with upper case text as lower case script (Frankish, 1999). In conclusion, the extent to which these recognition technologies allow 'natural' human–machine interaction must be questioned (see Gardiner and Christie, 1987; Newell, 1984; Noyes, in press). Admittedly, talking and writing are normal activities that most humans learn when young and carry out skilfully throughout their lives. Although it would seem intuitively to be a natural progression to communicate with machines in this way, the algorithms upon which the technologies operate can be significantly different from that of the human 'receiver'. Consequently, as suggested by Newell (1984), there must be more valid justifications that 'it is natural' before speech is chosen as an input mode (Table 3.2).

Secondary controls

Primary controls facilitate direct control of the system; this is in contrast to secondary controls that have more indirect control, e.g. they lead to small changes that eventually change the state of the system. In terms of secondary controls, a common feature is that these involve pointing and cursor control. These direct manipulation devices have the obvious attraction in that learning time and errors are reduced. They are classified as secondary controls because they need to be used in conjunction with other modes of input. This explains why the touchscreen that is effectively a pointing device is included as a primary control in Table 3.1. Foley *et al.* (1984) classified the tasks carried out by pointing devices. These were as follows:

- Select – the user chooses from a number of items, e.g. from a pull-down screen menu.
- Position – the user selects a position on the screen to position an object, e.g. when creating a drawing.
- Orient – the user selects a direction in a dimensional space, e.g. rotating a drawing on the screen.
- Path – the user carries out a number of 'position' and 'orientation' operations, e.g. drawing a curved line.
- Quantity – the user selects a numeric value, e.g. determining page numbers on a document.
- Text – the user enters and edits text as well as moving it. As well as inserting and deleting text, a number of more complicated tasks can be carried out, e.g. highlighting text, centring text and adjusting margins.

It is possible to complete these tasks with a keyboard, and indeed this was done in the days of character user interfaces (CUIs) and before the introduction of WIMP (windows, icons, mouse, pull-down menu) interfaces and graphical user interfaces (GUIs). Shneiderman (1998) grouped 'simple, secondary controls' according to those that included direct control on the screen, e.g. lightpen and stylus, and those that resulted in indirect control, e.g. mouse, footmouse, cat (a form of mouse), trackerball (an upside down mouse) and joystick. However, there are many variations within each category and novel designs continue to be developed, e.g. datagloves that allow direct manipulation of objects in virtual worlds.

More complex secondary controls include function keys where some learning is necessary before operation. In many ways, function keys that can be achieved via a single keystroke are shortcuts to frequent and/or lengthy operations. A special group of function keys are the cursor-movement keys. These have become important with the increase in the amount of electronic form filling and direct manipulation needed on the screen (Shneiderman, 1998). The graphics tablet is usually a detachable flat screen with a touch-sensitive surface. It is operated by a stylus or finger and uses acoustic, electronic or contact position sensing. In contrast, the touchpad tends to be a smaller device located near the keyboard and in a fixed position. It is operated by direct hand contact, with users gently rocking their fingers to attain cursor movement.

A number of experimental studies have attempted to compare input devices; one of the most well known being carried out by Card *et al.* (1978). They compared the mouse, an isometric joystick and cursor keys in a selection task on a display screen. They found that, for short distances, the cursor keys were faster than the mouse, which in turn was faster than the joystick. Empirical studies, e.g. Card *et al.*, have focused on speed and accuracy of positioning over short and long distances, error rates, learning times and user opinions. When measuring speed and accuracy, attention has to be given to the 'speed accuracy trade-off' (nicknamed SATO). Asking participants to focus on either speed or accuracy tends to be to the detriment of the other; hence, it is sometimes not easy to gain objective measures of speed/accuracy performance. With regard to objective measures, Fitts (1954) devised a law for predicting the difficulty of moving a cursor on a display. This took into account the distance (D) that the cursor has to move and the width (W) of the target. Fitts' Law stated:

Index of difficulty $= \log_2(2D/W)$

The index is a unitless value but Shneiderman (1998: 325) pointed out that it is usually measured in bits. For example, for a target 1 centimetre wide at a distance of 8 centimetres, the index of difficulty is $\log_2(2\times8/1)$, i.e. 4 bits. Fitts' Law is applicable for pointing in one dimension; it has been refined by MacKenzie (1992) to allow for two-dimensional pointing, and by Zhai *et al.* (1996) for three dimensions.

An additional group of input devices are those that have been classed as novel (allowing 'extraordinary' interaction). The British HCI Group published a special issue on extraordinary interaction in interfaces (volume 35), during the summer of 1997. Foot controls would fall into this category, although it could be argued that they have been around a long time and are not particularly novel. For example, pedals in cars, foot-operated machinery in industrial settings and dental surgeries. However, the foot mouse is an innovative input mode. It has been investigated by Pearson and Weiser (1986) and found to take about twice as long to learn to use as a conventional hand-operated mouse. However, this device may have particular benefit for users whose feet are more suitable for use than their hands. The use of the eyes to facilitate input would also fall into this category because users with severe motor impairments often retain control of the ocular muscle groups. Thus, eye movement can be used in conjunction with other modalities, e.g. positioning a pointer, selecting an item, using speech input. The use of eyetracking for disabled users is well established. Istance (1997) divided eyetracking devices into two types: those systems that provide access to bespoke software (see Hutchinson *et al.*, 1989), and those systems that allow more general purpose interaction via, for example, a keyboard displayed on the screen (see Shein *et al.*, 1991). The area of virtual reality (VR) has spawned its own set of input devices from datagloves that allow the positions of the digits to be recognised, e.g. closed fist, thumbs-up gesture, etc. and goggles that track the user's head movements. A list of various body movements that can be used as 'input devices' is given in Jenkins (1991). Another novel device is the joystring, which consists of a short T-bar that is grasped in the palm of the hand. There are a number of strings attached to the T-bar and the relative movement of these can be recognised and interpreted to allow information to be input to the computer system (Foley, 1988). A similar principle is used in the wobble-board, which comprises a flat seat that pivots at its centre. Input is achieved by moving the body around, thus making it possible for users with a mobility problem to input data to a computer (Maddix, 1990). More details about some of these and other novel input modes, e.g. speech reading, are given in Noyes and Cook (1999).

Displays

Like controls, the term 'displays' is a generic term covering output devices. In essence, there are three primary types of output: screens, printers and speech. There is little to say about printers and Shneiderman (1998: 342–3) provided a neat summary of the factors to be taken into account when considering the design features of printers. These included speed, cost, reliability and the options available in terms of the design of the character set. In the past, printer noise has been a concern, with many offices in the 1970s and early 1980s banishing the printer to its own room and manufacturers producing a range of hoods and shields to dampen the sound. As well as becoming quieter, today's printers are much faster. For example, the early printers produced about ten characters per second. These were followed by the dot-matrix printers that could generate more than 200 characters per second and also had increased functionality in that they could print graphics. Today, most office applications are supported by laser printers; speeds vary from four to forty pages a minute and the functionality and quality are high, offering a range of colours, and plotting facilities.

Screens range from simple numeric indicators, e.g. 'dials' to the generation of more sophisticated text, e.g. tables and graphics. With regard to the various sensory modes, visual and auditory screens are by far the most common. In rare instances, tactile devices that are sensed by touch, and olfactory displays of information that are sensed by smell, are used to inform users. For example, methyl mercaptan needs to be added in only tiny quantities to natural gas in order for it to be detected (Cain *et al.*, 1987). Tactile screens might include differently shaped knobs to assist in the rapid identification of controls, e.g. the tiny raised mouldings on the 'f' and 'j' keys of a typewriter to help the user find the home row. An example of an olfactory display is the noxious scent mixed with natural gas that warns of possible leaks. Some underground mines in the US also use a distinguishable odour released into the ventilation system to signal to miners to evacuate the mine. A basic aim in designing machine displays is to attract the operator's attention and, as demonstrated above, this has been done in a number of ways.

Visual screens are the most common means of conveying output information to the operator. They tend to be of two types: quantitative and qualitative. Quantitative screens are those that yield precise numerical values, e.g. speedometers in cars. In the past, circular, clock-face displays and the horizontal or vertical scales seen on radios and older stereos were widely used. However, the development of the light-emitting diode (LED) and liquid crystal displays (LCDs) has resulted in the older, quantitative, output devices being replaced by qualitative screens. These digital devices, as the name suggests, present information in the form of numbers, e.g. digital watches, whereas analogue displays show continuous information that the human has to interpret. For example, an analogue watch has continually moving hour and minute hands on a display divided into twelve sections each of 5 minutes. Hence, the user has to 'calculate' the time. Not surprisingly due to this interpretation element, analogue displays are prone to errors (Fitts and Jones, 1947; Grether, 1949; Noyes *et al.*, 1997). They do, however, have the advantage of allowing direction and rate of change to be more easily determined. This might be particularly useful in some applications, e.g. an altimeter onboard an aircraft. It should be noted that Grether (1949) carried out what has become recognised as seminal research on speed and accuracy when reading altitude from different types of display instruments.

In summary, research has shown that operators generally make more precise readings and fewer reading errors with digitally displayed information, although a loss of information can occur when moving from an analogue to a digital screen, e.g. rate of change information. And there may be some specific errors relating to reading the digits, e.g. '3' and '8', and '1' and '7' are often confused. Moreover, individuals trained to use one type of mechanical device may have difficulty adjusting to the digital output. For example, drivers used to semicircular analogue speedometers may have problems adapting to devices that display speed digitally.

The numeric indicators described above tend to be designed for very specific applications. In contrast, the most common output device is the raster-scan cathode ray tube (CRT) that is commonly found as an integral part of the visual display unit (VDU) of a computer system (Maddix, 1990). It should be noted that the term 'visual display terminal' (VDT) is favoured by some European countries, but as VDU and VDT are synonymous, the term VDU will be used here. Briefly, VDUs use the same technology as televisions, closed circuit televisions (CCTVs) and other CRT devices. An electron beam scans rows of phosphor dots; as the beam is turned on and off, so the dots either glow or remain dull. Early screens were often green because the P39 green phosphor has a relatively long decay time. In comparison, LCDs have the advantage of being flicker-free but the tiny capsules of liquid crystals limit resolution. LCDs are commonly found in laptops where their thin form does not add much weight – an important consideration in portable devices. Recent developments in desk-top publishing have led to a demand for more sophisticated screen technologies that can cope with an array of fonts, characters, and graphics. This movement has been indirectly supported by the film industry, which has witnessed significant progress in computer animation in recent times.

The development of CRT screens opened up an enormous range of possibilities for pictorial and schematic displays of information where it was possible to create more abstract, geometric forms taking information and integrating it from a number of channels. One such development was the 'object display' where information from a number of different sources could be shown on a single iconic screen (Woods *et al.*, 1981). The screen comprised a number of spokes radiating from a centre point. The length of each spoke represented the value of each parameter and, by using straight lines to join the ends of these, it was possible to create a polygon (Figure 3.3). When parameters are within 'safe limits', the polygon assumes a regular shape. Hence the operator can see at a glance from the pattern the extent to which the system is operating within limits. This single integrated screen is also replacing the need to have a number of separate dials. It has been used in nuclear power plants and certain medical applications. Although this way of displaying information appears to have clear advantages over having multiple dials, it does have a number of limitations. Petersen *et al.* (1981) found that the object display was best when the goal was to determine whether any parameter had moved outside tolerance limits. However, when trained operators were asked to report how many of the parameters were out of alignment, they performed better with the original separate meter displays. Petersen *et al.* concluded that during normal operation, object displays may be best for initial event detection, but final diagnosis may be more effectively guided by the display of discrete information.

Another example of a display screen specifically tailored for the situation is the Rankine cycle display found in nuclear power plants (Vicente *et al.*, 1996). The Rankine cycle screen is an overview display for monitoring and diagnosing the state of power plants. Studies by Vicente *et al.* have found that the Rankine leads to more accurate detection and fault diagnosis when compared to the more traditional, single-sensor, single-indicator screens currently found in nuclear power control rooms (see Goodstein, 1981). Here, screens typically consist of panels of hard-wired analogue meters. In contrast, the Rankine is conceptually very different presenting information graphically, so operators can see immediately when parameters are approaching critical levels.

In terms of Human Factors, there is a substantial body of information relating to the design of text, tables and graphics for displays, and it is impossible to do justice to this in a short paragraph. For example, Brown (1999) shows numerous tables of different presentations of text, tables and

graphs helpfully labelled 'use' and 'don't use' and Smith and Mosier (1986) have 944 guidelines on screen design. Table 3.3 is an attempt to summarise the large amount of material that is available. It should be noted that the recommendations being presented here are derived from both analytical and empirical evaluations. Issues relating to the content of the information tend to be evaluated analytically whereas issues relating to the form are more likely to need an experimental approach. Examples of analytical techniques might include usability testing and heuristic evaluations where experts judge the likelihood of a product or a system meeting specified performance criteria (see Nielsen, 1994). This is in contrast to empirical evaluations, where experiments are carried out with users specifically to look at their responses to the product or system. For a comprehensive discussion of the effectiveness testing of complex systems and the merits and shortcomings of analytical and empirical evaluations, see Pejtersen and Rasmussen (1997).

Although current display technologies are dominated by the CRT and LCD, Cochrane *et al.* (1997) suggested that, in the future, the traditional display screen would be bypassed as photons would be fired straight onto the retina of the eye. This would result in the retina being directly illuminated by photons emitted from a phosphor coating, perhaps via some sort of laser device mounted on contact lenses. Although the technique has been demonstrated successfully, there are practical problems associated with positioning the lasers. One possibility is to place the lasers on a spectacles frame to generate a head-up display.

A variation on the visual display screens described above is the auditory display of information that is generated as sound. Auditory displays range from the simple single tones found in morse code and fire bells through to the more sophisticated speech feedback systems. With regard to the former type of displays, research on their design, perceived urgency, compliance and affordance is comprehensively described by Edworthy and Adams (1996). In terms of the latter – speech generation – a wealth of information is available. Speech generation (or output) is in many ways the 'other side' of the speech recognition (input) problem. However, it is much easier to solve in that there are a number of ways of producing speech output. Bristow (1986: 3) likened the speech recognition/generation problem to a tube of toothpaste, whereby squeezing the tube to get the paste out is analogous to speech output, and trying to push the paste back into the tube is analogous to speech input. The latter, of course, is much more difficult to achieve (and may be even impossible to do perfectly).

Speech generation can range from the straightforward copying of speech onto magnetic tape through to the actual production of human speech from 'first principles'. In reality, there are very few reasons why one would want to generate totally synthesised speech and most systems will use human speech as a basis to varying degrees. There are two main approaches to generating synthesised speech. These are 'synthesis-by-analysis' and 'synthesis-by-rule'. The former takes human speech, analyses the various characteristics and

Table 3.3 Summary of screen design guidelines

Parameter	Issue	Recommendation	Researchers
Character shape	Comparison of 5×7, 7×9, 9×11, 11×15 dot matrices	9×11 dot matrix	Pastoor et al. (1983), Snyder (1984)
Character spacing	Comparison of proportional and fixed-width character sets	Proportionally faster, less error-prone and more aesthetically pleasing	Payne (1967) (research on typewritten material), Beldie et al. (1983), Snyder (1988)
Line spacing	Degree of spacing	One-thirtieth of line length	Hartley (1998)
Justification	Left hand versus right hand versus full justification	Left hand justification provides a useful starting point when reading from left to right while right hand justification makes it more difficult to read the text	Noyes and Mills (1998)
Blinking	Optimum blink rate	Not recommended	Cakir et al. (1980)
Colour	User preferences	Brightness, not colour, is the critical factor – value is primarily aesthetic but colour is used for coding, highlighting, separating and grouping; red and blue ends of frequency spectrum should be avoided	Keys (1993), Travis (1991)
Luminance	Range measured 108–163 cd m^{-2}	Task dependent	Läubli et al. (1981)
Contrast	Range 6:1 to 15:1	No significant effect on performance	Knave (1983)
Polarity	Negative (light symbols on dark background) or positive (dark symbols on light background)	Inconclusive in terms of user performance but user preference for positive polarity. Note: early displays used 'reversed video' – negative polarity – thought to reduce reflections	Radl (1980), Tapagaporn and Saito (1990)

Flicker	Dependent on regeneration rate, known to be irritating for users and can cause visual discomfort	Inconclusive because flicker depends on a number of parameters, e.g. older adults less sensitive to flicker	Grandjean (1987), Stammerjohn et al. (1981)
Cursor design	Comparison of superimposing, replacing and enhancing cursors	Inconclusive	Cakir et al. (1980)
Icons*	Good design: abstract versus concrete	Design of good clear icons is not easy (e.g. accommodating cultural differences)	Macaulay (1995), Rogers (1989)
Menus	Consideration of what items to include and how to group them	Groupings should be consistent with other parts of the application, and may be alphabetical, by category, or frequency of use (separating opposite items such as 'save' and 'delete')	Hill (1995)
Help	Hard copy versus online	Hard copy is frequently preferred but online is suitable for quick reference material, although it should not normally exceed one screen	Hill (1995)
Hypertext	Navigation (the user can easily become lost), omitting pages unintentionally, and printing	Recommended routes through the text, and having different levels of access, e.g. a superficial versus a fuller description	Noyes and Mills (1998)
Animation and video	The addition of motion to images	No real recommendations – this reflects the 'newness' of the area	

* The latest icons are known as emoticons. These are ways of expressing emotions commonly used in computer communications on the Internet, e.g. :-) = happy = ☺, :-(= sad = ☹, :-D = said with a smile.

then regenerates it in a digitised form. It is only speech synthesis-by-rule that actually produces speech totally from linguistic and acoustic parameters. Although the latter will allow greater flexibility in that speech can be output according to the current situation, there is still a problem with obtaining good prosody. The monotonic computer-generated robotic-sounding voice that results is not very popular with the listener, who finds it unnatural. However, unnaturalness may not mean the speech is unintelligible – just that more effort needs to be put into comprehension. This also results in synthetic speech being harder to remember than natural speech (Waterworth and Thomas, 1985). In conclusion, the two main Human Factors issues pertaining to generated speech are naturalness and intelligibility (see Greene *et al.*, 1986; Keller, 1994). For applications of speech synthesis, see the work carried out by Alastair Edwards (Edwards, 1991).

Stimulus–response compatibility

An important consideration when designing controls and displays is their stimulus–response compatibility, i.e. the extent to which the controls map onto the displays. In a well-designed product, the location or movement of a control response should map onto the location or movement of the stimulus or display (Fitts and Seeger, 1953). Norman (1988) highlighted the importance of this design feature in his text *The Psychology of Everyday Things*. An everyday example of stimulus–response compatibility is the mapping of the burner controls onto the burners found on hobs in most kitchens. Ideally, the spatial mapping should be the same for the controls and the burners, as shown on hob 1 in Figure 3.4.

This work stems from Chapanis and Lindenbaum (1959) and their now classic work on control–display relationships where they found that incompatible displays resulted in 7.25–8 per cent errors whereas the compatible arrangement did not incur any mistakes. The study has been repeated a number of times with reliable results (Hsu and Peng, 1993; Osborne and Ellingstad, 1987; Payne, 1995; Ray and Ray, 1979; Shinar and Acton, 1978). There are two aspects to this type of compatibility: one, location compatibility, where the response needs to be physically close to the stimulus, and two, movement compatibility, where the direction of movement is congruent between the control and display. An example of movement compatibility relates to the expectation we have for controls that move clockwise to result in displays that move in the same direction.

A further simple example is the light switch. It only needs a row of three identical light switches on a wall relating to a centre light and two wall lamps, for a user to have to make a conscious effort to remember which switch operates which light. If the switches were arranged in the same canonical arrangement as the lights, spatial compatibility would be preserved and stimulus response transformations would be minimal. This would be to the advantage of the user. Unfortunately, designers often favour banks

Hob 1 – good mapping

Hob 2 – poor mapping (the author's hob!)

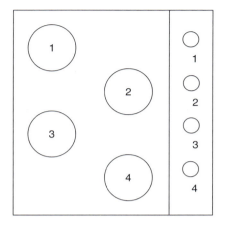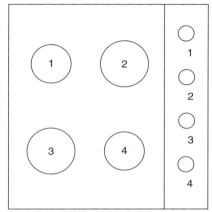

Figure 3.4   Mapping controls onto displays

of identical switches, as found in many nuclear power control rooms. Although these examples relate to spatial compatibility, they demonstrate a principle that can be applied to other types of compatibility, e.g. cultural and cognitive mappings. Cultural compatibility relates to the extent that designs adhere to population strereotypes. With regard to the light switches mentioned above, 'up' indicates 'off' in Europe, and pushing the switch down turns it on. However, this use is not world wide and is reversed in the US. A further example relates to the use of colour (Courtney, 1986). In western society, the colour 'red' is associated with danger, and signals 'keep away'. This is in contrast to 'green' that conveys safety. Traffic lights certainly keep to this association with red meaning 'stop', and green informing motorists that they can 'go'. Another example relates to warning messages on the civil flight deck, where red signifies the highest level of urgency followed by amber. In terms of design, it is important that these population stereotypes are not violated, as this will cause unnecessary confusion to the human operator. Cognitive mappings, on the other hand, relate to the extent that designs match aspects of our higher order processes within the context of stimulus and response. For example, the number of auditory warnings that we can differentiate needs to be taken into account when designing industrial warning systems such as those found on the civil flight deck.

Interactions

The development of the information society has had a number of implications for human–machine interactions. In the days when simple tools dominated the workplace, the human was firmly in control of when and how they were used. This situation began to change in the 1930s as equipment became more advanced and the question of the degree of automation arose. The philosophy of the early 1950s (which perpetuated into the 1960s and 1970s) was to automate systems as fully as possible. This view was articulated by Birmingham and Taylor (1954), who proposed that 'he [Man] is best when doing least'. Hence, the trend at this time was firmly towards the automation of human–machine interactions and complete automation, i.e. the replacement of all human activities by machines, was the goal. It was not only the increasing complexity and sophistication of machines that had led to automation, but also the fact that, in many situations, this led to greater efficiency. For example, in aviation, automation resulted in a more efficient use of fuel (Lerner, 1983). However, one of the ironies of automation, as pointed out by Bainbridge (1983) in her now classic text, is that designers tended not to automate those tasks that were too difficult or complex. These were left for the human operator who often was 'out of the loop' in terms of having good situational awareness and understanding of the system when things went wrong. Hollnagel (1999) referred to this as the 'left-over' principle. A second reason for automation is as a reaction to accidents – following a major incident there is often pressure to introduce automation to prevent repetition of the accident.

One of the spin-offs from increased automation in manufacturing is that maintenance has become more difficult. Helander (1995: 171) stated that in order 'to maintain an automated piece of equipment or a robot, an operator needs knowledge of electronics, hydraulics, pneumatics and programming'. This is also the case with the computerised systems on civil aircraft, which, in some parts of the world, maintenance personnel have declared are too complex to maintain. Consequently, it is important to ensure that the equipment is well-designed to facilitate fault diagnosis and maintenance checks. In the past, it could be concluded that insufficient thought has been given to designing systems for maintainability. This has important implications for the prevention of accidents and incidents, because it is now realised that maintenance errors make a significant contribution to them. Although there has been an increasing use of automatic test equipment (ATE) and diagnostic aids (Kemp *et al.*, 1995), these have not always led to improved fault finding. Coppola (1984) gave an example from avionics where, out of 12,000 trouble indications, 85 per cent were false alarms and 6 per cent were confirmed problems. This was deemed to be typical of machine fault finding, i.e. a large number of false alarms and a small number of actual problems, which result in a lot of people hours being invested in maintenance work.

A further important issue relating to automation is trust, because humans have a tendency to place trust in the machines and the decisions emanating from them; the reader is referred to work by Lee, Moray and Muir on this topic (Lee and Moray, 1992, 1994; Muir, 1989, 1994; Muir and Moray, 1996).

Case study: trust in automation – trust and allocation of function in human–machine systems (from Lee and Moray, 1992)

Research suggests that the allocation of activities to humans or machines may be in part determined by the amount of trust that the operators place in the automation (Zuboff, 1988). A study has been carried out that considered the changes in trust during the operation of a semi-automatic process control simulation. Nineteen participants took part in the study that required controlling a simulated orange juice pasteurisation plant. The goal was to produce as much juice as possible in a set time by controlling temperature and flow rates. Performance was measured by dividing the total input by the amount of input flow with a bonus for achieving high rates above 90 per cent. Safety was also taken into account with the plant shutting down if the input vat emptied. The simulation had provision for both automatic and manual control and participants had to demonstrate competence in the ten training trials before taking part in the fifty trials comprising the main study.

To investigate trust, a fault of varying magnitude was introduced into one of the three subsystems where a pump failed to respond as it should. In addition to this transient fault, a chronic fault was also introduced into the last twenty trials. At the end of each trial, participants were given feedback about their performance and completed four questions relating to their subjective feelings about the predictability and reliability of the overall system. These measures had been hypothesised by Muir (1989) to relate to the different dimensions of trust. It was found that participants lost trust in the system when the faults appeared. Likewise, their performance degraded, although it did recover. In the case of the transient fault, the loss of trust appeared to be approximately proportional to its magnitude. Like performance, trust was recovered, although in the case of more severe faults, this was not so instantaneous. Lee and Moray drew a number of conclusions from this study:

- Performance – operators were quick to adapt to the changing situation induced by the faults and to recover and maintain their performance.
- Trust – their trust in the system also returned to former levels after the faults, but this change was slower than their performance recovery.
- Fault – unlike trust, performance was not affected by the magnitude of the fault.

It was suggested that trust depends on the overall system performance, as well as on the extent to which the system components appear to operate normally.

Table 3.4   Example of a Fitts' list approach

Function	Humans	Machines
Speed	Can work fast for short bursts, limited reaction times, comparatively slow, e.g. measured in seconds	Can work fast for long periods of time, much faster reaction times, e.g. up to the speed of light
Accuracy	Can be extremely accurate but, again, difficult to sustain over periods of time	Can maintain high standards of accuracy over long periods of time
Repetitive actions	Soon tire, subject to learning, fatigue and boredom	Excellent at repeating actions in a consistent manner
Attention span	Poor, especially when required to sustain attention over long periods	Not an issue – if programmed to monitor, will continue to do this *ad infinitum*
Perceptual skills	Excellent, especially at pattern detection and interpretation	Poor (unable, for example, to carry out simple tasks such as edge detection)
Memory	Selective, impressive in that unprompted instant retrieval of items is possible, not always reliable, versatile and innovative	Completely reliable in that all items stored in memory can be accessed quickly, limited (but extremely large) capacity, formal structure
Decision making	Tend to use heuristics ('rules of thumb'), good at inductive reasoning when need to draw on past experience	Rule-based approach, good at deductive reasoning, poor in new situations
Intelligence	Excellent	Limited

In the 1950s, the approach to systems' design was primarily one of considering the attributes of humans and machines. This constituted a simple approach in that a relative comparison of humans and machines was conducted and function was allocated according to the strengths of each (Fitts, 1951). For example, humans are better at decision-making tasks that rely on previous experience, whereas machines excel at monotonous, repetitive jobs that need to be conducted over long periods of time. This allocation of function approach has subsequently been referred to as the 'compensatory' principle and is exemplified in Table 3.4, which gives an example of a Fitts' list.

The Fitts' lists later became known as MABA–MABA ('Men [sic] Are Best At – Machines Are Best At') lists (Moray, 1999b) and they have continued to become more elaborate over the years as technology has changed (Berry and Houston, 1993). However, it is perhaps time now that we referred to them as the more politically correct HABA–MABA (Humans Are Best At – Machines Are Best At) lists.

This type of approach is not popular these days; there are several reasons for this (Table 3.5). In the first instance, the distinctions are somewhat

Table 3.5   Some disadvantages of the 'list' approach

1. Some functions have to be performed by humans because machines cannot do them, and *vice versa*
2. There will be some functions where no rationale for differential allocation is obvious, i.e. they might be carried out by humans or machines or both
3. It implies that tasks that machines do well need to be assigned to them, leaving the remainder for the humans
4. Direct comparison of attributes suggests that machines and people have opposite capacities. Obviously, this is not the case
5. Some functions must always be performed by the human operator, e.g. the control for aborting operations
6. Some functions may be allocated to humans to make their jobs more interesting
7. Technology changes faster than the lists
8. A list does not cover all the reasons why the human might be allocated a 'machine' function
9. Being skilled at a task is only one facet/dimension
10. Humans have a need to work and feel valued
11. Humans are unique in that they have an emotional component
12. Humans could have a preference to interact with other humans rather than machines

simplified and sterile. As pointed out by Chapanis (1965), machines evolve faster than lists such as those described above, and human performance can be modified and improved to a certain extent through training and experience. Thus, the approach is an over-simplification of the distinctions between humans and machines. Further, it provides a sterile approach, e.g. because a machine can complete a task more efficiently than a human, this does not mean that the functionality should be allocated to the technology in this instance. There are other reasons why humans may be given a job, just as there are reasons why the machine might be given a task that has nothing to do with the relative strengths and weaknesses of the human or the machine. Some activities may just be unacceptable for a human to do, e.g. checking out unexploded bombs. Further, humans are unique in that we have an affective component and this may provide a primary reason for allocating function to us. Take the operation of a toll booth. This can be carried out by having a human worker collect payments or automatically via a coin-operated barrier. The latter may be more efficient in terms of reliability, costs and consistency of performance. However, the former may be more useful for those occasions when drivers fail to have the correct change, omit to follow the correct procedure for negotiating the toll barrier, or simply prefer to interact with a fellow human than a machine. The preference for interacting with a fellow human has been indicated by studies of the use of bank automatic teller machines (ATMs) and automated telephone enquiry systems (Hone *et al.*, 1998). A further scenario is demonstrated by the fact that we still have humans sitting at the front of civil aircraft when there is no reason today why the technology could not control the flight of the aircraft from the ground. However, it is unlikely that passengers would be happy embarking upon a pilot-less flight. There may, of course, be sound reasons for this: at least the flight deck crew has an incentive to get home whereas the computers do not! A further reason for the demise of this approach is that it works primarily on comparing humans to machines, whereas many human–machine activities are complementary (Jordan, 1963). As Singleton (1989: 35) pointed out 'A man without the support of machinery is physically weak and informationally slow. A machine without human guidance is inflexible and highly limited in recognition and learning facilities'. In summary, it can be seen that allocation of function according to the relative strengths and weaknesses of humans and machines is a limited approach that will rarely work on its own. However, to be fair to Paul Fitts and others in the 1950s, this was seen very much as a starting point upon which allocation of function activities could be built (Wulfeck and Zeitlin, 1962).

This simple comparison approach has been superseded by a more integrative one that takes into account the set of tasks to be achieved by the system and enables the designer to weigh-up the value of function allocation in terms of total system operation (Price, 1985). As a result, flexible allocation of function is possible. This might take into account the skills and traditions of the workforce (liveware), specific detail relating to the design of the software, hardware and environment, and issues of safety and reliability. Moreover, system design is a dynamic and iterative process and it may be that during appraisal of the design, further consideration has to be given to the human–machine interactions and the allocation of function (Singleton, 1989). Allocation of function need not, and indeed should not, be decided beforehand but should take place according to the dynamics of the application and the interactions. Hollnagel (1999) referred to this as 'complementary' allocation. For a good review of the historical development of the allocation of function concept, see Singleton (1974).

Although the dominant philosophy up until the 1970s was to automate systems and procedures as much as possible, the 1980s witnessed a change in approach. One of the primary reasons for the automation of human–machine interactions was to safeguard against the humans' propensity to make errors. Although this could be viewed as a 'sledgehammer to crack a nut', removal of operators from direct contact with machines was seen as a way to avoid accidents arising from human error and thus increase safety and productivity. The problem, of course, was that humans were never totally divorced from machine operations even if their only function was control of the abort button in a nuclear power plant. Moreover, they were always involved in decisions relating to the design, development, operation and maintenance of systems. Hence, removal of the operator did not remove the opportunity for error, it actually placed a greater load on the designer to predict the operating characteristics of the system. The reliability of complex software systems provides a classic example of this where it is often impossible to ensure that the software is bug free. Given that humans will always make errors, a more enlightened approach witnessed recently has been to design taking this into account. This has resulted in the concept of the 'error-tolerant' system (Billings, 1997), i.e. designers take into account human fallibility and design systems accordingly. This approach also allows the benefits of having humans working in conjunction with machines to be realised, as combining the activities of both often results in exceeding the performance of either (Sanderson, 1989).

In conclusion, the preferred approach today is to think in terms of a symbiotic relationship whereby humans and machine work in conjunction, i.e. human–machine co-operation (Hoc, 2000). The various levels at which this might occur were summarised by Sheridan (1997) in his chapter on supervisory control. Automation is thus viewed as a continuum of levels rather than a two-state 'all or nothing' system. At one extreme, the human assumes full manual control, while at the other, the machine controls all aspects of its functioning. In between are various levels of supervisory control. At the highest levels, it is not possible for the human operator to over-rule the machine, e.g. the flight envelope protection evident in the A320 aircraft (Parasuraman and Riley, 1997). Since the 1980s there have been many advances in our understanding of human information processing but, as Moray (1999b) pointed out, little research has been done on locating the optimal level of human–automation co-operation. This remains a challenge for the next decade.

Designing for humans

Central to the Human Factors approach is the concept that we design primarily for the human, i.e. we adopt a 'user-centred design' (UCD) approach, as opposed to a 'system-centred design', an 'organisational-centred design' or a 'socially centred design' approach (Stanney, Maxey and Salvendy, 1997). In the system and organisational approaches the human is considered as another resource that has to be optimised in order to meet the goals of the operation. In the UCD approach, the users' roles and responsibilities are viewed as fundamental to ensuring the success of the operation and are given priority in the design process. Very simply, the rationale is to design to enhance human abilities, to support human limitations and to meet the subjective, affective component that is unique to humans. This final attribute is important; it is more than just aesthetics but extends to encompass a design that is enjoyable to use and free from frustration and irritation. The UCD approach is embedded in the concept of usability – a term defined by the International Organisation for Standardisation (ISO 9241, 1997) as 'the usability of a product is the degree to which specific users can achieve specific goals within a particular environment; effectively, efficiently, comfortably, and in an acceptable manner'. In many ways, the word 'usability' replaces the frequently mentioned term of 'user-friendliness'. However, there is much debate about the exact meanings of the terms UCD, usability and user-friendly, and the reader is referred to Noyes and Baber (1999) for a fuller discussion.

Usability is an important topic in design and, hence, in Human Factors. This is exemplified in the number of publications on the topic – see the books by Jordan (1998), Jordan *et al.* (1996), Kirakowski (2000), Nielsen (1993), Rubin (1994), Trenner and Bawa (1998) and Wiklund (1994), to name but a few. There are many ways of measuring usability but it is generally recognised that usability encompasses the ease in which the product/system can be used (both during training and operational use, i.e. its learnability), its effectiveness in allowing the user to achieve his or her goals, and its likeability. This final point reflects the subjective component and whether or nor the design is pleasing to use. It is frequently stated that the ultimate test of usability is whether people use the design. If there is an alternative or if use is optional, users will 'vote with their feet' and might not bother to use the product or system. Standard usability paradigms tend to focus on the quality of the system rather than on the quality of the interaction. It may be that we have to start rethinking this approach as more and more people expect to have pleasure from their interactions with products and systems. Bill Green and Pat Jordan have been particularly active in this field and in facilitating the move from usability based approaches to pleasure-based approaches to design. Looking to the future, the 'quality factor' will undoubtedly increase in importance, as people will no longer tolerate using products that do not please them.

Case study: usability – usability of retail websites (from Thompson, 1999)

An increasing amount of electronic commerce is being carried out via the Internet but, in contrast to other human–machine interfaces, there are relatively few Human Factors guidelines to aid the WWW designer. Further, when individuals use the Web, they will form a mental model based on their previous experiences and knowledge of similar activity (Johnson-Laird, 1983). In the case of Internet shopping, it is hypothesised that users will bring with them a pre-existing mental model of conventional shopping and that the closer websites conform to this model, the more likely users are to rate them highly.

A study was carried out to assess users' models of real-world shopping and compare these to their models of Internet shopping. It was conducted in a number of stages. These were: (i) task analysis of users' reports of a typical sequence of actions they would follow from entering a shop to purchasing an item; (ii) heuristic evaluations of websites to locate any specific difficulties with the sites being trialled; and (iii) users' perceptions of ease of use of the websites. The results lent support to the hypothesis that the closer the match between the users' existing models of shopping and the ones they developed when shopping on the Internet, the higher they rated the design of the website. This has a number of implications for WWW design.

Apart from the natural world, we live in a world that is designed by us. In essence, all the objects and artefacts designed by humans should meet our basic requirements in terms of usability. Of course, when we start to look around, we do not have to look far to realise that many of the everyday products that we use are poorly designed. Norman (1988) in his now seminal text on the design of everyday things gave the example of doors. When we approach a door there should be enough cues on the fascia of the door for us to know how to open and close it. But in our everyday lives how often do we all attempt to push doors that need to be pulled open and vice versa? We still have smooth, round door handles that provide us with no clues about which direction they move in! Table 3.6 lists some well-designed everyday objects; Table 3.7 lists some poorly designed items. The tables were compiled as the result of a brainstorming exercise carried out with two classes of MSc Organisational Psychology students. It can be seen that 'ease of use' features frequently amongst the design characteristics.

Norman and Draper (1986) drew attention to the importance of mental models in the design of products and systems. Although there is a lack of agreement about what exactly is meant by a mental model, it has been defined as a representation that we form of the world (Sasse, 1997). In the case of systems, we construct a working model to explain the way in which the system behaves. This model may be incomplete and insufficient to explain how the system works but provides the individual with enough information to allow successful interaction. It may also be totally inaccurate. For example, a person may use a computer to achieve their desired goals but have little or even no understanding of how the system works, e.g. the 'skilled user' as defined earlier in this chapter. Norman and Draper suggested that one of the reasons that we have poor designs is because the mental (user) model that we build when using a device does not match the system model developed by the designer when planning the product/system. The 'further apart' that these models are in terms of correspondence, the more likely the user is to have problems and difficulties when using the product or system. Hill (1995: 23) described this as the 'gulf of execution'. Good design needs to bridge this gulf and ensure that the system and user conceptual models match as much as possible because it is thought that, the more accurate the user model, the more usable the system will be. Some ways of overcoming this mismatch are given in Table 3.8.

Table 3.6   Well-designed everyday products

Well-designed tools	Well-designed systems	Features of good designs
Ball-type screwdriver 1906 mechanical sheet clippers Octopus diving equipment Jug kettle Drinks can	Apple Macintosh computers EPS (electronic point of sale) supermarket systems Laptop computers	**Ease of use:** able to tilt to make operation easier, easy to list and pour, easy to fill, gauge to show water level, easy to open, positive (body) support, easy to operate and keep hands free, comfortable, don't notice, simplicity – no redundancy, flexible, provides good feedback, easy storage, resilient, well-balanced, short training time, good anthropometric fit, adjustable – accommodates use by children through to adults, fits well with clothing, minimises opportunities for errors, easy to correct mistakes, no previous knowledge necessary, easy to hold, easy to read, fast, quiet operation with short-cut procedures **Safety:** no trailing leads, electrical hazards minimised, handle position avoids scalding, non-toxic **Portability:** light, light proof, flat pack – easily portable, carrying case – put over shoulder, lightweight **Environmental:** reusable material, ring pull not detachable (on some soft drinks cans) and so cannot cause litter problems, can cope with considerable range of temperature, can cope with pressurised contents, heated automatically, durable, self-renewable, biodegradable **Automatic functions:** energy saving, switches off automatically **Flexibility:** variable height, adjustable hardness/softness, allows user mobility **Compatibility:** with accessories and other systems, standard quantities, obviousness of which switch controls which function, compatibility between robustness and length of time required to use, compatibility between claimed and actual use **Size:** large smooth design space, small **Maintenance:** self-cleaning **Aesthetics:** neat and good-looking **Cost:** value for money

Table 3.7   Poorly designed everyday products

Poorly designed tools	Poorly designed systems	Features of poor designs
Metal tin opener Straight wheel spanner Strimmer – garden tool Video recorder	Directory enquiries Getting drinks in theatre intervals Some cars	**Ease of use:** lack of variety in fittings, pull-start – mechanically very difficult, physically too much unlikely information needed, no consistency of identifying marks or position, buttons are too small, plastic flap to protect falls off, barcode doesn't work, words under buttons not clear, need to lie flat on stomach in order to read, instructions useless, time clock – no memory if turned off and needs to be reset, no mechanism for spring/autumn time changes, slow speed – cannot be played on normal only, not meant to be portable – connectors not robust enough – should have been over-designed, digital display too small – cannot see readout or state of device, lack of adaptation, unnecessarily complex (e.g. automatic oven – eight steps and five knobs to set), ambiguous, uncomfortable, too much force needed, difficult to hold and operate, too complex, confusing cues for operation, mode of operation not obvious, two-handed operation required when one hand would be preferred, takes time to work, uniformly shaped controls make operation difficult **Environmental:** corridors too narrow and claustrophobic, maze-like internal structure, no natural light, poor ventilation, badly lit small display **Safety:** cannot poor water without burning hand as lever conducts heat, slippery soles on highheeled shoes, no support for ankles, very breakable, dangerous, accident-prone, ill-fitting parts **Health:** shoes that damage feet – corns, bunions, crossed toes, disrupt balance, shortening Achilles tendon, poor anthropometric fit **Flexibility:** not adjustable, no adaptability by system, no facility for sudden large numbers **Maintenance:** difficult to clean, collects dust/dirt in recesses, complex to claim **Aesthetics:** poor decoration

Table 3.8   Some recommendations for the design process

1.	A large number of methods exist for facilitating the design process. These include direct methods (where the users have contact with the actual product) and indirect methods (where the users report their experiences and views on using the product). Noyes and Baber (1999) reported over twenty methods
2.	Some of these methods are specific to Human Factors, e.g. heuristic evaluation and usability testing, and some are commonly used elsewhere, e.g. questionnaires and interviews
3.	Human Factors can be applied throughout the design lifecycle from the initial development of the product/system through to operation, maintenance and decommissioning. However, it is generally recognised that the earlier in the design process that Human Factors are applied, the greater the benefits (Monk *et al.*, 1993)
4.	An iterative approach works best where design issues are revisited throughout the lifecycle. This provides an opportunity for designs to be assessed and modified a number of times, resulting in better designs because the users have had a greater input to the design process
5.	A large number of design guidelines already exist – the 944 guidelines for display screen design developed by Smith and Mosier (1986) have already been mentioned. It is suggested that, initially, designs are developed to take account of recognised guidelines, e.g. compatibility, simplicity, predictability, reversibility, redundancy of operations, graceful degradation
6.	In addition, every product will have specific features that need to be addressed through the design process, e.g. reversion techniques, error correction, feedback mechanisms, customisation
7.	A number of phases encompassing different assessment methods are recommended, as demonstrated by Noyes *et al.* (1996a)

Key points

- Controls can be categorised according to whether they are primary or secondary, simple or complex.
- The development of some control modes is still in a primitive state, e.g. large-scale 'natural language' speech and handwriting recognition systems, and thought.
- A wealth of information exists on display screen design guidelines.
- Technological developments in computing have opened up a range of possibilities for display design relating to specific applications.
- Stimulus–response compatibility is an important component of good designs.
- Humans have characteristics such as flexibility and adaptability, as well as emotional attributes, that need to be taken into consideration when determining allocation of function.
- The first approach to allocation of function was to automate any functions that could be automated and leave the rest to the human operator – the left-over principle.
- The Fitts' and MABA–MABA lists provide starting points for the allocation of function of human and machine activities but carrying out

a direct comparison is rarely an optimum way of allocating function –
the compensatory principle.

- The current approach to automation is to have a symbiotic relationship
  where the activities of the humans and machines complement each
  other – the complementary principle.
- The optimum level and balance of human–machine activities between
  the two extremes of fully manual to fully automatic has yet to be
  determined.

4   Work environments

In manufacture and in handicrafts, the worker uses a tool; in the factory, he serves a machine.

Karl Marx, 1867, *Das Kapital*

The life-efficiency and adaptability of the computer must be questioned. Its judicious use depends upon the availability of its human employers quite literally to keep their own heads, not merely to scrutinise the programming but to reserve for themselves the right of ultimate decision. No automatic system can be intelligently run by automatons – or by people who dare not assert human intuition, human autonomy, human purpose.

Lewis Mumford, 1970, *The Myth of the Machine*

One of the components of both the SHEL (software, hardware, environment, liveware) and the user-centred design model is 'environment'. In its narrowest sense, this covers the immediate environment of the user, i.e. the workspace, but can be extended to encompass a number of social and organisational issues, e.g. job design and management structure. Work environments defined here will be interpreted broadly to take into account physical, social, cultural and organisational factors, although this chapter will focus on physical parameters. It is correspondingly also possible to interpret 'work' very broadly in the sense that it 'can be any form of meaningful activity – running a home, bringing up children, voluntary, sheltered or paid employment' (Herbert, 2000: 25). However, the main premise being suggested here is that it is impossible to consider Human Factors and ergonomic issues in isolation, e.g. the design of the human–machine interface alone. It has already been established in Chapter 3 that human–machine interactions will be influenced by a number of environmental and other factors. Therefore, we cannot consider workplace design, for example, without taking into account the attitude of the organisation to flexibility in catering for individual needs. Further, the design of work environments also has important implications with regard to performance, comfort, safety and the reduction of hazards. These are covered in Chapter

6 on Occupational Health and Chapter 7 on Safety, where the legislation relating to the work environment is reviewed in the section on regulations.

Workspace

Physical considerations

One area in which many advances have been made in recent years is the human factors speciality of engineering anthropometry – the measurement of the physical characteristics of the human body and the development of equipment designed to fit the characteristics of the user. Anthropometry has an important role to play in workspace design in terms of both static and functional measurements.

In terms of design, it is often not possible to design to accommodate all the population. For example, doorways would need to be designed to allow the tallest adults to walk through them, and chairs would need to withstand the weight of some of the heaviest people around. Grieve and Pheasant (1982) contrasted the anthropometric characteristics of the smallest adult female in the population with the tallest adult male. They surmised that the male would be over one-third taller, over twice as heavy and up to five times as strong. This illustrates some of the difficulties of designing for all of the population.

One way of designing to cater for extreme individuals is to have adjustable equipment. As an example, Shute and Starr (1984) carried out a study investigating the effects of adjustable furniture on computer users. They found that there were many benefits to having adjustable equipment. When this is not possible, the usual approach is to design for 90 per cent of the population. Given that most human characteristics assume a normal, bell-shaped, population, the majority of individuals will fall in a range whose width is 1.64 standard deviations above and below the mean, i.e. from the 5th to the 95th percentile. As an example, 90 per cent (+ or – 1.64 standard deviations) of Northern European males will have heights falling in the range 1.64 to 1.85 metres (Bridger, 1995). The corresponding range for females is 1.51 to 1.72 metres. Hence, designing for 90 per cent of the population can be optimal in terms of the cost benefits – allowing the design to accommodate the extremes would be expensive for the relatively few people that will benefit. A general rule is to design at the maximum or minimum dimension according to the anthropometric unit, e.g. designing a doorway to accommodate the 95th percentile, or a reach measurement at the 5th percentile. However, it should be noted that there will be some situations where it is necessary to cater for the 100th percentile. For example, it may be necessary to design for the heaviest users in order to ensure the equipment is robust enough to withstand the heaviest weights, as in the case of parachutes.

Data for a large number of anthropometric variables exist. It can be seen from these data that designing for the mythical 'Mr or Ms Average' will not always work, primarily because there are very few individuals who are 'average' on several dimensions. Tall people do not necessarily have long legs, long arms, etc. Hence, the average person probably does not exist and designing according to the 50th percentile may not result in an optimal design. There will be occasions, however, when designing for the average may be the most appropriate approach. Sanders and McCormick (1987) quote the example of designing supermarket checkouts for the average person as being the most expedient design. As the action of paying for goods is not a safety-critical task, people who are very tall or very short will be inconvenienced by the height of the checkout, but the poor design will not create a life-threatening situation for them. However, it is generally recognised that designing for the average person should be considered only after the use of adjustable equipment (clearly not feasible in the case of supermarket checkouts) and designing for extremes and 90 per cent of the population have been discounted. It should also be noted that there will be some aspects of the workspace that do not need to take into account anthropometric data, e.g. the height of a room.

A more recent concept is that of 'universal design', where designs take into account the needs of disabled people. It is thought that if designs accommodate this group of users, they will also cover the rest of the population, e.g. positioning lift controls at a height that can be reached by wheelchair users. Universal design comprises a philosophy whereby disabled users or older adults are not considered as special subgroups who require Human Factors solutions different from the rest of the population. Designing to accommodate these groups will result in general rather than specific improvements. Rabbitt (1993) commented that if you improve design for older adults, you also make improvements for younger people. This is similar to the adage of the Centre for Applied Gerontology: 'Design for the young and you exclude the old; design for the old and you include the young'.

The design of the workspace needs to take into account user characteristics (e.g. anthropometric measurements, clothing thicknesses, fitness, eyesight, handedness) as well as task characteristics (e.g. the scheduling and nature of the work) and environmental aspects (e.g. illumination levels). An underlying consideration in all human activities is cost; uniformity in some designs may reflect this, e.g. tools designed for right-handed use. Hence, anthropometric considerations can be secondary to costs. However, the emphasis here is on physical considerations and the workspace needs to be ergonomically designed ensuring that the users can attain and maintain good working postures. Figure 4.1 demonstrates some of the factors that need to be taken into account in workstation design.

One approach to enable good working posture is to develop a workspace envelope – sometimes referred to as a kinetosphere. Roth *et al.* (1977) used a workspace envelope to demonstrate the functional arm reaches for the 5th percentiles of males and females. It comprised a bird's eye view of the person

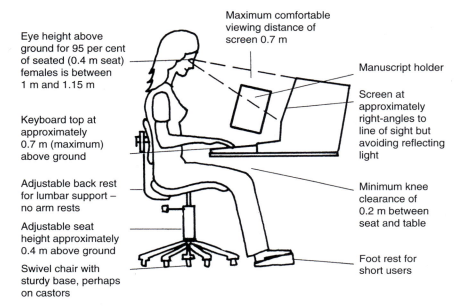

Eye height above ground for 95 per cent of seated (0.4 m seat) females is between 1 m and 1.15 m

Maximum comfortable viewing distance of screen 0.7 m

Manuscript holder

Keyboard top at approximately 0.7 m (maximum) above ground

Screen at approximately right-angles to line of sight but avoiding reflecting light

Adjustable back rest for lumbar support – no arm rests

Adjustable seat height approximately 0.4 m above ground

Minimum knee clearance of 0.2 m between seat and table

Swivel chair with sturdy base, perhaps on castors

Foot rest for short users

Figure 4.1   Workstation dimensions diagram (from Cakir *et al.*, 1980; reprinted with permission from IFRA, Darmstadt, Germany (later reprinted by Wiley, UK))

with their head representing the centre of the circle. Within this circle, their unrestrained and restrained (i.e. when the shoulders were in a fixed position) arm reaches could be drawn. These traces could be constructed for a number of different seat positions. Hence, the three-dimensional space envelope could be constructed to show the limits of arm reach for the population under consideration. It could also be used for other anthropometric dimensions. There have been a number of published studies relating to workspace envelopes of the seated person (see Damon *et al.*, 1966; Kennedy, 1964; NASA, 1978). Often, the studies involve military applications, e.g. the arm reaches of individuals when strapped into aircraft seats.

The most recent approach is the use of computer-aided design packages that allow interactive anthropometric models to be manipulated onscreen and various body dimensions to be tried out within the constrictions of a particular workspace. For example, various arm lengths could be tried out on a mannequin in a vehicle cab to look at the effects on ability to reach the controls. One of the more well-known is SAMMIE (System for Aiding Man–Machine Interaction Evaluation; Figure 4.2), developed at Loughborough University of Technology (Case and Porter, 1980; Porter *et al.*, 1998). Others include Jack and COMBIMAN (COMputerized BIomechanical MAn Model) (Badler *et al.*, 1990; Karwowski *et al.*, 1990). For a review of eighteen computer-based anthropometric models, see Porter *et al.* (1995).

Figure 4.2   Example of SAMMIE display (reprinted with permission of
SAMMIE CAD Ltd.)

Psychological considerations

Research has shown that the physical layout and design of a work setting,
the amount of work space available and the type of furnishings can all
affect worker behaviour. The design of the physical aspects of the workplace can create certain psychological conditions, e.g. feelings of privacy or
crowding and of status and importance, or the converse – perceptions of
anonymity and unimportance. Logically, it would be expected that work
settings designed to allow social interactions between workers typically
have positive influences on job satisfaction, given that this has been stated
as the primary reason why people go to work. This is in contrast to work
settings that are crowded and/or allow too much socialising and too little
privacy and so do not allow people to be as productive in their work as they
might be in a quiet, self-contained workspace. A study that attempted to
consider the interactions of a number of physical characteristics of the
working environment and psychological considerations was carried out by
Oldham and Fried (1987). They attempted to assess the effects of four
workspace characteristics on the attitudes and behaviours of 109 clerical
employees (of whom 93 per cent were female) from nineteen offices in a
large university. The four measures were:

1. the number of workers in an office, which constituted the measure of crowding
2. the measured seating distance between workers, another index of crowding
3. the number of enclosures or partitions surrounding each individual workstation
4. office darkness.

The results showed a link between these four variables and the rates of employee job dissatisfaction and turnover. For example, when the office was perceived as dark and crowded, workers tended to be dissatisfied and were more likely to leave than workers who were not exposed to these conditions.

Several research studies have compared traditional offices (i.e. closed, cellular designs where individuals work in private office spaces) with open-plan offices (i.e. landscaped designs where workers are often in large, open-plan, rooms with partitions) (see Brookes and Kaplan (1972); Hundert and Greenfield (1969); Marans and Spreckelmeyer (1982); Zeitlin (1969)). The concept of the open-plan office, or Bürolandschaft, is thought to have originated in Germany (Brookes, 1972). Results have indicated that open-plan offices facilitate communications amongst individuals as well as allowing easy access to a variety of different groups within the organisation. However, the open-plan office has been shown to have a number of disadvantages – lack of privacy and control over personal space with an increase in the number of distractions and interruptions (Nemecek and Grandjean, 1973). Anecdotal evidence from personal experience of working in an open-plan office suggests that the telephone was one of the most irritating aspects of the office, in terms of having to listen to people continually talking to callers. Outcomes include an increase in job dissatisfaction and negative effects on work behaviour. However, the psychological effects of the physical layout of the workspace are complex and will be dependent on the characteristics of the organisation, as well as on workers' attitudes and previous experiences.

One area of interest in the design of the workplace is that of aesthetic factors. In the 1950s and 1960s it was thought that certain types of music and colours would have a positive effect on work performance. The management of some industries began to pipe-in background music for the workers, or had the walls painted in colours that they thought would encourage the work ethic. For example, reds, yellows and oranges are usually considered to be 'warm' colours and stimulating, whereas the blues and greens are 'cool' colours suggesting restfulness and cleanliness. Despite the interest at this time, there has been little sound evidence clarifying the effects of these aesthetic factors on performance at work (Kwallek and Lewis, 1990). However, it is realistic to hypothesise that factors such as music and an aesthetically pleasing environment might have positive effects on work behaviour. Aesthetic factors affect employees' perceptions of the work environment and this in turn might encourage them to produce more work, as no one wants to work in a shabby, run-down environment. A pleasant work setting could increase worker satisfaction and convey the message to the workers that the management 'care' about the quality of their surroundings. However, too lavish a work environment might result in employees feeling that the organisation is spending too much money on furnishings – expenditure that could be better spent on employee wages and benefits.

A further aspect of the psychological aspects of the workspace envelope relates to the so-called personal space – the acceptable distance from which to communicate with other people in a given situation. (For an excellent overview of personal space, see Oborne (1995) and a chapter by Bechtel (1997: 163–84)). Every individual has a three-dimensional space that encapsulates them. This personal space is regarded as being exclusive to us and we are unhappy when individuals whom we feel have no rights to do so invade it. As an example, this may be the stranger who stands too close. Argyle (1975) stated that the origins of this come from our basic instincts to protect our territory and the threat that we feel when people, especially those not known to us, move in too close.

The study of personal space is referred to as proxemics and has its foundations in the work carried out by E.T. Hall (1959, 1966, 1976). Hall (1966) described a number of personal spaces ranging from the intimate, to the personal, the social and the public. The intimate distance is in the region of 0–45 centimetres and we only allow individuals who are known and liked by us to invade this personal space. Hall stated that this zone is typified by close physical contact; an unwanted intrusion might imply a threatening situation. The next zone comprises the personal distance. This has been described as a buffer between the zone reserved for intimate contact and the social zone for more formal occasions. The personal distance (45–120 centimetres) is reserved for friends who are known and liked. At this distance we are particularly vulnerable from being attacked and, hence, it is important that only individuals recognised as being friendly are allowed to enter it. The third zone is the social distance (1–3.5 metres). This is the one in which most formal social interactions take place, e.g. talking to people at a works party or conducting business. It is recognised that when people work together on a frequent basis, the social distance will reduce. Hall (1966) suggested that this was to allow work colleagues to be able to move into each other's personal distance without appearing rude. The outer zone comprises the public distance (3.5–7.5 metres). This is the distance at which strangers feel comfortable. However, it is violated in certain situations, e.g. travelling on crowded underground trains. There are also a number of exceptions when individuals do not conform to the recognised norms of personal space. Examples include children, who appear to have smaller personal space zones and will certainly invade the intimate zone of people they know. Children's personal space has been shown to increase with age (Smetena *et al.*, 1978). Females have been shown to have smaller zones (Liebman, 1970; Phillips, 1979) as do couples who are mutually attracted to each other (Allgeier and Byrne, 1973). However, generalisations such as these need to be qualified and gender on its own is not a good predictor of personal space needs (Gifford, 1987; Severy *et al.*, 1979). Further, Fukui (1983) found that patients with different mental illnesses had varying personal space distances. For example, it has been reported that schizophrenics have larger personal space zones (Srivastava and Mandal, 1990). There are also marked cultural differences between countries, e.g. countries in the Middle East and India have smaller distances while North Americans and Northern Europeans tend to have larger distances (Smith and Bond, 1993; Sommer, 1969; Watson, 1970). Status is also an important variable, with higher status individuals being given more space (Patterson and Sechrest, 1970). Hence, personal space is an important aspect of workspace design. As an example, Sinha and Sinha (1991) carried out a study of infringements of personal space in the workplace. Participants carried out a series of simple and complex cognitive tasks: these comprised letter cancellation tasks. Participants were given sheets of paper on which the letters of the English alphabet were printed in a random order. In the simple task, participants had to cancel all the vowels, while in the complex task they had to cancel all the consonants intermingled between two vowels. Both tasks lasted for a period of 10 minutes. It was found that performance on the complex task was degraded when workers' personal space was violated. In summary, we use personal space (or interpersonal distance) as a means of conveying our relationship with others and of regulating our social interactions.

Design of furniture

A wealth of information exists relating to the design of furniture for both standing and sitting postures (see Bendix and Hagberg, 1984; Mandal, 1982). As an example, consider horizontal work surfaces. In general, it is recommended that adjustable equipment is used wherever possible, the arms should be in a relaxed posture and excessive flexing of the spine should be avoided. Finer precision work, e.g. making jewellery, will require a higher work surface than work requiring exertion of pressure, e.g. ironing (Grandjean, 1981). Ayoub (1973) provided recommendations for work surface heights for three different types of task – precision work, light assembly work and heavy work – for standing males and females. These values ranged from 109–119 centimetres for males carrying out precision work to 78–94 centimetres for females doing heavy work. On some occasions, it is useful to allow the person the option of sitting or standing and there are some types of stools that allow this.

An area that has attracted a lot of attention from Human Factors is that of chair design. This is probably not surprising given that three-quarters of workers in industrial countries have sedentary jobs (Reinecke *et al.*, 1992). One of the ironies of chair design concerns the fact that the 'best design' will probably be the chair that allows us to fidget. The human body is built to move. Prolonged static mechanical loading is detrimental to us – the blood flow to the muscles is restricted, the chemical balances become disturbed and waste metabolic products accumulate. This is exemplified by the fact that we find it difficult to stand still for more than a few seconds but can walk for hours without ill effect. Pheasant (1997: 59) suggested that fidgeting is the body's 'defence against postural stress'. This leads to the concept of comfort. Physiologically, comfort could be considered as the absence of discomfort, because the peripheral nervous system does not transmit positive feelings of comfort. Therefore, comfort could be viewed as state of mind that arises when we have no feelings of discomfort. Comfort is an interesting concept in that it is usually measured in terms of discomfort. Further, we cannot tell either by observation or direct measurement the level of comfort that the person is experiencing. The only means of assessing comfort is for the individual to report on how comfortable they are; usually some form of questionnaire is used to attain the required information. Some of the initial work on the subjective measurement of comfort was carried out by Shackel *et al.* (1969) and Corlett and Bishop (1976). One of the most well-known of the 'comfort' questionnaires is the Nordic Questionnaire (see Dickinson *et al.*, 1992; Kuorinka *et al.*, 1987). As a final comment, it is interesting to note that *Homo sapiens* can assume over 1,000 different resting positions – all of which are comfortable (Hewes, 1957).

Case study: chair design – design of school furniture (from Knight and Noyes, 1999)

In the developed world, schoolchildren spend a significant amount of their time at school in a sitting position. Storr-Paulsen and Aagaard-Hansen (1994) calculated that 8- and 9-year-olds were expected to sit fairly still for more than 60 minutes in any 90-minute period. As school-aged children might spend 30 per cent of their waking hours at school (Linton *et al.*, 1994), the design of their school furniture is of considerable importance. In terms of chair design, there are essentially two basic and quite different designs: the traditional chair with variants of backward sloping/horizontal seating, and the higher, forward-sloping seating favoured by Mandal (1993) and others. The latter was termed 'Chair 2000'. Knight and Noyes compared these two designs by studying children's on-task and sitting behaviour over a 4-week period. Chair fit anthropometric measurements were also taken with a group of children aged nine and ten.

Experimental results supported previous findings in that there was a modest 2 per cent increase in the frequency of on-task behaviour with the introduction of Chair 2000. It was also found that Chair 2000 resulted in a lower frequency of non-standard sitting and this has some interesting implications with respect to classroom management and orthopaedic considerations. Given that 62 per cent of the children in this study reported that they experienced back pain 'sometimes' or 'more often', and 9.5 per cent experienced it 'very often', this could be of considerable concern, especially given the relatively young age of the participants. One of the messages from this research study must be that we need to pay more attention to the design of our school furniture.

In conclusion, a number of points about furniture need to be taken into account when considering optimum designs for human use. In the first instance, there is no single set of principles that can be applied to cover all types of seating. Second, the nature of the task will mean that, in some applications, one advantage will have to be traded for another. For example, when considering seating, the type of seat will relate to the reasons for sitting. The seat design should allow the user to vary posture as well as providing support and stability. A large number of recommendations for furniture dimensions exist: for example, Grandjean *et al.* (1969) provided a range of dimensions of seats for reading and resting activities.

Physical parameters

Lighting

Definitions

Most tasks require vision and hence illumination has a major role to play in ensuring good levels of performance. There are several definitions associated with the measurements of light, e.g. measures of quantity and intensity. However, three of the most common include:

1. Illuminance – this is a measure of the total luminous flux falling on a surface given that some of the light striking a surface will be absorbed and some reflected. Illuminance is measured in units such as lux or lumen per square metre and is often denoted by the letter 'E'. A typical value for office work would be in the region of 500 lux. The range of illuminance values is from 50 lux (e.g. outside environments where detail of the surroundings is not required) to 2,000 lux (e.g. some inspection tasks of extremely fine detail).

2. Contrast – this is the relationship of an object's luminance to its surround, e.g. the ratio of character luminance to background luminance.
3. Reflectance – the reflection characteristics of surfaces can be measured in terms of the direct and the indirect reflectance. The former provides a measure of the luminance of the image that can be seen as directly reflected on the surface of the screen. The indirect or diffuse reflectance provides a measure of the luminance of a surface when light falls on it, e.g. if the surface is completely matt.

Colour

Our judgement of colour is dependent on the luminance of the object being observed. For example, reds often appear more yellow and blue–green colours become bluer as the luminance increases. There appears to be little benefit for increasing luminances to aid colour identification other than for older people, who demonstrate a marked improvement in colour matching performance as illumination levels are increased to 1,200 lux (Boyce and Simons, 1977). Changes in colour vision occur with age as the lens in the eyes tends to yellow with time. This particularly affects discrimination of colours in the blue–green range. When considering the use and application of colour, it is also worth noting that a number of the population is colour defective. Pokorny *et al.* (1979) stated that between 6 and 10 per cent of males and between 0.5 and 1 per cent of females had colour-defective vision. A final point concerns the extent to which coloured illumination influences our thermal comfort. Fanger *et al.* (1977) carried out a study where individuals read in two environmental conditions, namely, 'warm' red light and 'cold' blue light. Participants were asked to state their colour preferences and it was found that there was a small but significant preference for the red light but at a lower ambient temperature, i.e. participants felt slightly warmer in the red light condition. However, Fanger *et al.* (1977: 17) concluded that 'the effects of coloured lighting on man's preferred temperature is so small that it is of no practical significance'. Further, it is generally recognised that having lighting of differing colours in the same room produces an annoying twilight effect and is best avoided (Cakir *et al.*, 1980).

Flicker

The increasing use of luminous sources in our visual environment has led to concerns about flicker, i.e. rapid fluctuations of the light level that can annoy and irritate the observer. Howarth (1995: 455) cited flicker as being 'the major identifiable complaint arising from the temporal variation of VDUs'. Our sensitivity to flicker is dependent on a number of factors. It should also be noted that objective measurements of flicker are not straightforward and require specialist equipment and personnel. In general, the larger the stimulus the more sensitive we are to it, particularly when the stimulus is in the periphery of our visual field. The contrast of colours on a VDU screen makes them more susceptible to flicker, e.g. dark characters against a bright background as opposed to lighter characters on a darker background. One of the remedies for reducing flicker in this situation is to turn down the overall screen luminance. However, this can result in decreasing character discriminability, which can adversely affect overall task performance. In the longer term, increasing the refresh rate of the screen (defined as 'the reciprocal of the time required to produce a full screen image' (Shneiderman, 1998: 337)) may provide the solution. Manufacturers focus on trying to reduce flicker by altering the properties of the phosphor. Older screens are more likely to exhibit flicker, although older people are less able to detect flicker (Cakir *et al.*, 1980). Frequencies around 60 Hz are generally taken as being the maximum detectable under 'normal' lighting conditions, although frequencies as high as 90 Hz can be detected in appropriate conditions (Howarth, 1995). Epileptics are particularly sensitive to frequencies at around 10 Hz and hence, there is a possibility that flicker can result in seizures. At the other end of the spectrum, we cannot perceive flicker with frequencies over 100 Hz, although there is evidence that our visual system is responding to the flicker. It could be concluded that there is still much to be found out about the effects of flicker and high frequencies on our visual system.

Glare

Glare occurs when one part of the visual field is brighter than the level to which the eye has become adapted, i.e. when the range of luminances is too great. There is no internationally agreed unit for glare but it is known to create problems in the working environment. Glare is commonly described as being of two types – disability glare and discomfort glare. Both types can arise from direct or indirect glare. Direct glare occurs when the light appears directly from the light itself as in a badly positioned light, while indirect glare arises from very bright reflections from polished or glossy surfaces, e.g. VDU screens. Because the eyes tend to be drawn to the brightest point of light, the so-called phototropic effect, glare can result in impaired human functioning. Disability glare, as the term suggests, is where the glare seriously disrupts vision even if only on a temporary basis. Lukiesh and Holladay (1925) distinguished three types of disability glare: (i) veiling glare, resulting in situations with poor contrast, e.g. in the mist; (ii) dazzle glare, where the individual is momentarily 'dazzled', e.g. when we emerge from a dark building into the sunlight; and (iii) blinding glare, where the effect is more sustained, e.g. driving along a wet road that is directly exposed to the sun. This last type of glare creates difficulties particularly for older people and partially sighted individuals (Christie and

Fisher, 1966). Discomfort glare has a different physiological origin to disability glare because it relates to the actions of the muscles that control the iris of the eye. It results in annoyance and physical discomfort but the origins of subjective complaints associated with this type of glare are not known (Megaw, 1992). A glare index known as the British Glare Index was developed by Petherbridge and Hopkinson (1950) to measure the levels of glare that were acceptable to the individual. One of the problems with using this index is the amount of variability in our responses to glare, as there are often other aspects of the environment or situation that influence the extent to which we tolerate the glare. For example, a study by Hopkinson *et al.* (1941) reported an interesting finding when they compared glare levels from artificial lighting and exterior windows. They found that participants did not report that the high levels of glare from exterior windows were causing discomfort when they were interested in what was happening outside. This exemplifies the subjective element in our responses to glare.

Glare is a major complaint among VDU operators (Stammerjohn *et al.*, 1981). However, since the publication of the Stammerjohn study it has become less of a problem now with the advent of treated computer screens that reduce reflectivity. Other practical ways to reduce glare include reducing the luminance of light sources by either diffusing the light (unshielded fluorescent lights should be avoided) or having movable lights under the control of the user. Light sources should not be placed either immediately behind or in front of the operator as these can produce direct and reflected glare (Tattersall, 1992). VDUs should be positioned at right angles to natural light coming in through windows and artificial light from fluorescent lighting. One of the worst situations is to have high luminance reflections of the strip lighting in the room present on the screen. Screen filters on VDUs, and shades and blinds on windows with tinted glass may also be useful. Cakir *et al.* (1980), in a field study of direct and reflective glare, ranked the three most common types of glare shield according to subjective preference. The result was as follows: prismatic pattern shielding, grid (or louvre) pattern shielding and smoked glass shielding. The former two are preferred because they result in a more favourable light distribution. Two further suggestions to help reduce glare include the use of non-gloss paint and the avoidance of bright metals.

Performance

The relationship between lighting conditions and performance is not straightforward (Megaw, 1992). In any environment, the amount of light falling on a surface will depend on the:

- luminous intensity of the light sources
- distance of the sources from the surface

- angles of the sources to the surface
- number of original and reflecting sources in the immediate environment.

Other factors to take into consideration will include the overall illumination levels, the size of the object being viewed, the contrast between the object and its surround and the colours in the environment. Further, there will be individual differences relating to the observer as changes in the visual system occur as we age or as result of malfunction. From about the age of ten, all visual functions are subject to deterioration although to some extent these losses are counterbalanced by the fact that, with increasing experience, less information is needed in order to recognise objects. More specifically, between the ages of twenty and sixty, the visual acuity of a normally sighted individual is reduced by about 25 per cent, sensitivity to glare increases with age, while the ability of the eye to detect very small differences in luminance also decreases. Research has shown that the difference between individuals in the age ranges twenty to thirty and sixty to seventy is very great. For example, the average 60-year-old will require three times as much light as a 20-year-old to see the same object (Haigh, 1993). Finally, the ability of the eye to adjust or accommodate diminishes very rapidly with age.

There have been a number of experimental attempts to measure the effects of illumination on work performance, beginning with the Hawthorne studies in the 1920s (see Roethlisberger and Dickson, 1939). An experiment carried out by Weston and Taylor (1926) was typical of the type of studies being conducted at this time. They gradually increased the illuminance levels from 14 to 265 lux in a room of typesetters and measured the corresponding output of the workers at half-hourly intervals. They found that work production increased, but the subsequent publication of the Hawthorne studies and the so-called Hawthorne effect have opened these results to question. However, what is worthy of comment is the way that general lighting levels have increased over the decades. Today, it is unlikely employees would be expected to work in illumination levels of 14 lux. In fact, the trend since the 1950s has been towards higher illumination levels in our shops, homes and workplaces. For example, the IES (Illuminating Engineering Society) recommended 100 lux for office work in 1936; by 1984 the CIBS (Chartered Institute of Building Services) was recommending 500 lux (CIBS, 1984). This has implications with regard to setting standards and providing guidelines because the illumination levels of 20 years ago would be considered inadequate today (Howarth, 1995). *↳ How does light fatigue factor?*

As well as these field studies, there have been a number of laboratory-based studies where greater control over the experimental variables can be facilitated. A typical laboratory study was conducted by Hughes and McNelis (1978), who took a group of experienced office workers and gave them a pencil and paper task where they had to locate target numbers on worksheets containing large groups of numbers. Correspondingly, the lighting levels were varied and the task took place over 2 days and under three different illuminances: 538, 1,076 and 1,614 lux. It was found that performance in terms of speed and accuracy was best under the highest illumination level. Other studies (see work by Smith and Rea, 1976, 1978, 1979, 1982) have not been so definitive in their findings with some results indicating little or no improvement with higher illumination levels.

In terms of drawing a general conclusion, it might tentatively be suggested that increasing the levels of illumination results in smaller and smaller improvements in performance, and benefits are more apparent in older members of the population. We also know that the visual system deteriorates with age and, although some of these changes are slight, designers need to take this into account when designing equipment to be used by older adults. For a comprehensive guide to the design of lighting, see Tregenza and Loe (1998).

Case study: lighting – car window tinting and visual performance in elderly and young drivers (from Burns et al., 2000)

Tinted car windows may compromise road safety because they hinder the rapid detection of low contrast, unilluminated targets. We know there is a general decline in visual functions and speed of cognitive processing with age and so any effects are more likely to be greater in older adults. In Australia, the regulatory authorities have agreed that windows to the front of the car should have 75 per cent visible light transmittance, decreasing to 35 per cent at the rear of the vehicle. The key question is whether this level of tinting is appropriate for all sectors of the population.

Thirty participants (eighteen older and twelve young adults) performed a recognition task under two illumination levels (daytime and twilight) and three visible light transmittance conditions (63 per cent, 32 per cent and 20 per cent). It was found that under optimal viewing conditions, i.e. daytime, the level of visible light transmittance did not affect the inspection time of either age group and it could be concluded that the tinting of car windows will not affect driver performance. This finding supports previous research findings. However, in twilight elderly drivers showed deterioration in performance as the visible light transmittance decreased from 63 per cent to 20 per cent. Younger adults also showed a decrease in performance across the three levels of visible light transmittance but it was not as marked. A second experiment was carried out with a further twenty-six participants (thirteen older and thirteen young adults) to consider high and low contrast targets in three visible light transmittance conditions

(100 per cent – no window, 81.3 per cent and 35.1 per cent). It was found that there was no significant difference when viewing in the 100 per cent and 81.3 per cent conditions, but the elderly participants were detrimentally affected by the reduction in visible light transmittance to 35.1 per cent. Although elderly participants showed a range of individual differences with performance not being consistent across participants, this may have implications when considering the drafting of legislation. The conclusion drawn from this experimental work is that the level of tinting should not be reduced to 35 per cent as this deleteriously affected the elderly participants. However, it should also be borne in mind that older adults do modify their behaviour and often avoid driving at night and during the rush-hour (Ernszt and O'Connor, 1988).

Recommendations

The level of illumination required for a particular task will be 'determined by the complexity and visual difficulty of the task, the average standard of eyesight of those concerned, and the level of visual performance expected' (Cakir *et al.*, 1980: 174). It is not easy to be prescriptive because some visual tasks may be effectively carried out at 50 lux. However, this is a comparatively low illuminance and provides quite a gloomy atmosphere, so the usual recommendation for working environments is set at a minimum of 200 lux. At the other end of the scale, 1,000 lux has been recommended for large offices and similar workplaces – the argument being that this will match the level of illuminance outdoors from natural light. It should also be noted that some very exacting visual tasks of extremely low contrast and tiny size may require illumination levels in the 10,000 to 20,000 lux range (Kaufman and Haynes, 1981).

With respect to VDU operation, suggestions for illuminance levels of VDU workstations range from 100 to 1,000 lux, representing a very wide span of lighting. Field studies have shown that VDU operators turn down the lighting levels corresponding to the range 300 to 500 lux. Consequently, Cakir *et al.* (1980: 176) made the following recommendation: 'VDT working areas should be illuminated with 300 to 500 lux illuminance with the best possible glare shielding to safeguard against both direct and reflection glare'. Reflections can be reduced with the addition of screen filters. Common ones include micromesh filters that allow only light parallel to the holes in the mesh to pass through, hoods (sometimes quite spectacular hoods built by the operators) and shields placed between the light source and the screen. These observations imply that individuals prefer to have dimmer lighting levels in their working environment. To address some of these issues, the Illumination Engineering Society (IES, 1984, 1987) has provided the following guidelines for illumination levels for interior lighting. They recommend that before deciding on an appropriate illumination level for a visual task, four questions should be asked:

1. Are the reflectances or contrasts unusually low, e.g. having to select dark objects from a dark, matt background?
2. Will errors have serious consequences?
3. Is the task of short duration?
4. Is the area windowless?

Temperature

Definitions

Humans are homeotherms. Thermoregulation of the human body maintains deep body 'core' temperature at around 37°C, i.e. within a narrow range of between 36.1°C and 37.2°C. The body continually strives to maintain a state of equilibrium by balancing heat loss with heat production. If the body loses heat, vasoconstriction reduces heat loss to the environment. Conversely, if the body becomes too hot, vasodilation of the blood vessels takes place in order to increase heat loss from the body's surface. The outer limits of the range that the body can tolerate are around 35 and 42°C. Fairly small amounts of deep body cooling can lead to hypothermia; clinically, a state of hypothermia can be said to exist when the body's core temperature falls to about 35°C. Below this temperature, the body's regulatory processes become seriously disrupted, although there have been cases of individuals surviving core temperatures of 28°C. Interestingly, a temperature of 9°C has been recorded in an artificially cooled patient who went on to make a full recovery (Lloyd, 1986). At the other end of the temperature spectrum, findings are not so clear. Acclimatisation plays a greater role in the extent to which we can tolerate body temperature increases. However, despite this, Grandjean (1981) recommended that the core temperature (as measured by a rectal thermometer) should not exceed 38°C. Further, it should be noted that there tend to be large differences between the core and shell temperatures: this can be up to 4°C in 'normal' environmental conditions when the body is at rest, but may be 20°C, or more, in the cold.

Thermal environments are commonly categorised into hot, neutral and cold, where 'neutral' represents moderate conditions. It is now recognised that six primary factors affect how individuals respond to thermal environments: air temperature, air velocity, radiant temperature, humidity, clothing worn and the intensity and level of the activities of the humans in the environment (Parsons, 1995). These factors have been integrated into a single index to allow different environments to be assessed for comparison purposes. A number of instruments exist for measuring air and radiant temperature, velocity and humidity. Again, these can be combined into various thermal indices. In contrast, subjective methods have to be used to gauge thermal comfort, i.e. measures of how satisfied we are with our thermal environment. A number of comfort indices have been developed (see ASHRAE, 1985; Rohles, 1974; Youle, 1990). In essence, these tend to be fairly simplistic: for example, the Bedford scale rates thermal comfort on a 7-point scale from '1 = much too cool' to '7 = much too warm', while the ASHRAE scale has a range from '−3 = cold' to '+3 = hot'. However, our understanding of the interaction of the variables determining thermal comfort is still somewhat limited, and the concept of thermal comfort is an elusive one. It is known to be subject to individual differences (possibly as a result of varying metabolic rates), the nature of the work being performed, the clothing being worn and even the season of the year (Sanders and McCormick, 1987).

Performance

Cold environments result in a decrease in the body's temperature. As the environmental temperature drops, the human's protective response is to shiver, which increases the body's rate of metabolism. Other reflexes include inhibition of sweating, vasoconstriction and pilo-erection. Frostbite is a threat especially to the extremities. Physical performance is affected by the cold as manual tasks become impossible to carry out. The ability to move the fingers particularly suffers as the extremities are cooled and manual dexterity is reduced as shell temperatures fall below 20°C (Enander, 1984). The V-test devised by Mackworth (1953) is often used to measure manual dexterity. Participants have to discriminate the two separate edges of a wooden V-shaped tool, and increases in the gap width indicate loss of sensitivity. Other tests of manual dexterity include reaction time and visual-motor tracking tasks. In contrast to manual dexterity, cognitive perform-ance does not always appear to degrade significantly as the ambient temperature drops (see Ellis, 1982). Examples of cognitive tasks that have been used in research include mental arithmetic, paired-associate learning and subjective time estimation. It is generally agreed that cold leads to discomfort resulting in information processing tasks becoming difficult, e.g. vigilance is reduced at a core temperature of around 36°C. This is primarily because the person becomes distracted and finds it difficult to concentrate on the cognitive task.

Hot environments cause the temperature of the body to rise. In physio-logical terms, if the deep body temperature increases to about 42°C, the onset of heat stroke (hyperthermia) resulting in collapse can be very sudden. The effects of heat stress on our ability to carry out physical work have been well-documented. In general, physical performance degrades as body temperatures increase, i.e. we find it increasingly difficult to carry out physical tasks as we become hotter. An exception to this is simple behaviour, e.g. reaction times and time estimations that do not appear to be particularly sensitive to heat (Bell *et al.*, 1982). Interestingly, some manual performance tasks may benefit from taking place in a warmer environment (Meese *et al.*, 1984). Likewise, increases in core temperature are associated with a decrease in cognitive functioning (see Hancock, 1981). More demanding cognitive tasks follow a general form whereby performance tends to degrade as the temperature increases until a point is reached where performance is impossible. In contrast, ambient temperature has been shown to have only a slight effect on mental tasks requiring little cognitive effort (see Grether *et al.*, 1971). Much of the research in this area has been laboratory-based, often taking place in environmental chambers that can be thermatically controlled. Hence, findings may not be representative of the situation in the field because the effects of acclimatisation are not being taken into account. Further, the motivation of experimental participants might not mirror those individuals carrying out physical and mental tasks in a hot natural environment.

Case study: temperature – effects of heat and hydration on firefighters (from Stirling and Parsons, 1999)

Fighting fires places high physiological demands on firefighters, and this is especially the case with trainees who will be exposed to extreme heat several times a day during practice sessions. As part of intensive training, they will be required repeatedly to enter 'fire houses', i.e. buildings with controlled fires. Many of the stressors, e.g. high temperatures and heavy physical work, to which firefighters are exposed are unavoidable. However, hydration is one aspect that can mitigate the effects of heat exposure and, up to a point, can be controlled.

A study has recently been published that considered the effects of hydration state on nineteen male trainee firefighters. Physiological measures were taken throughout two training sessions taking place on separate days: these included oral temperatures, sweat measures and urine samples. Drinking and eating patterns were also recorded prior and during the training as were subjective measures of thermal sensations, thirst, nausea and dizziness. It was found that firefighters did not demonstrate excessive rises in body temperature and that they consumed enough fluid to remain in fluid balance. However, it was recommended that they drink more liquid during heat exposure, i.e. advocated drinks such as water, juice, squash, flavoured drinks with less than 8 per cent carbohydrate and milk as opposed to caffeine (tea, coffee, cola and chocolate), alcohol, carbonated drinks, oral rehydration solutions and carbohydrate–electrolyte beverage concentrations (Nevola, 1998).

Recommendations

There are complex relationships between the effects of temperature on physiological aspects on the one hand and psychological aspects on the other. It does not need to be stated that if the environment is sufficiently extreme in terms of heat or cold, the internal temperatures of the humans in it will move outside of the usual levels of tolerance. Until the extremes of temperature are reached, it is quite difficult to predict reliably the effects of increasing or decreasing core temperatures on manual and cognitive performance (Parsons, 1995). Although performance will be impaired as ambient temperature changes, effects will be moderated by individual differences, e.g. level of motivation and physical activity, proficiency at the task, degree of acclimatisation. Thermal comfort is an important factor. Although the resultant sensations of comfort depend both on the environmental conditions and individual factors, there are a number of variables that will affect thermal sensations. These include age, gender, circadian rhythms and colour (see Fanger *et al.*, 1977).

There are a number of national and international standards covering thermal comfort and environments; for example, ISO DIS 11399 (1993) provides a general presentation of standards relating to the ergonomics of the thermal environment. For office environments in the UK, it is recommended that the temperature should be maintained in the range 21–23°C. Further, the relative humidity should not fall below about 50 per cent and should not be subject to wide variations during working hours. A recommended value is 50–55 per cent (Cakir *et al.*, 1980). Humidity is important because changes in the thermal environment can affect an individual's comfort; 'dry air' has been found to be a common complaint among computer users.

A further environmental feature related to temperature concerns the air quality in terms of the levels of negative and positive ions. These can occur naturally, e.g. warm dry winds will bring positive ions while rain and water features increase the density of negative ions. Ions can also be generated artificially by machine. High concentrations of negative ions are thought to have beneficial effects, i.e. they are associated with increased sense of wellbeing, energy and alertness, resulting in better cognitive performance. In contrast, positive ions are associated with more negative effects, e.g. irritability, depression, loss of energy and insomnia. Our understanding of ions and their influence remains incomplete (see Farmer, 1992, for a comprehensive review of ion studies) but a study carried out by Tom *et al.* (1981) did provide some evidence for the beneficial effect of negative ions.

A final highly topical area related to air quality is that of air pollution. In recent times, chemical pollution has become 'more widespread, more intense, and much more complex' (Cassidy, 1997: 102). This is due not only to increases in industrial waste but also to our greater use of transport. Indoors, one of the greatest pollutants is tobacco smoke. It is generally accepted that chemical pollution has a number of adverse effects on humans, animals and the natural environment. For a review of air pollution and behaviours, see Horvath and Drechsler-Parks (1992). These effects can affect both our physical and psychological wellbeing (see studies by Bunnell and Horvath, 1989; Palinkas *et al.*, 1993; Potasova and Arochova, 1994; Veitch and Arkkelin, 1995).

Noise

Definitions

Sounds (and noise) are a constant feature of our environment and it is rare to experience total silence. Whether sounds are interpreted as noise can depend on the listener. Smith and Jones (1992: 1) stated that the term 'noise' has at least three meanings. These are sounds that are:

- Unwanted – sound that we do not wish to hear for whatever reason.
- Variable – sound varying in intensity and frequency both at random and with regularity.
- Interfering – sound that interferes with or masks other sounds.

These types of sounds could be classed as noise with the proviso that noise is situation-specific, i.e. a sound in one situation might or might not be a noise in another. Likewise, the listeners will exhibit individual differences; pleasant sounds to me might be noise to you. The first definition does cover this with noise being an unwanted sound. This was the definition favoured by Kryter (1985) who defined noise in terms of its effects, e.g. 'audible acoustic energy that adversely affects the physiological and psychological well-being of the listener'. This fits with the definition of 'unwanted sound'. The subjective component of noise is often assessed via questionnaires and surveys. Kryter (1985) generated some scales for measuring annoyance in units of noys.

Sound is transmitted in the form of pressure waves of air. The intensity of sound/noise is measured in the unit of decibels (dB), which relate to a logarithmic scale of the ratio of the energy of the sound and a referenced energy standard. Table 4.1 gives a range of typical noise levels. Humans can actually hear some sounds below the zero dB level because we can detect the movement of air that these infrasounds generate.

In addition to the decibel measurement of the intensity of sound, frequency of noise is measured in hertz (Hz). The human ear is sensitive to noise frequencies between 20 and 20,000 Hz. Most speech occurs at frequencies between 300 and 700 Hz and, interestingly, we are less sensitive to lower frequencies, i.e. below 1,000 Hz.

When considering noise, duration is also an important consideration. Noise of a very short duration is termed impulse noise, e.g. a door

Table 4.1 Some examples of noise levels

Source of noise	Typical noise level (dB)
Rocket launch	180
Jet aircraft at take-off	140
(Note: threshold of pain	130)
Loud music	120
Punch press at 1 metre	110
Inside an underground train	100
Lathe	90
Inside a noisy car	80
Inside a quiet car	70
Ordinary conversations	60
Normal office	50
Quiet home	40
Public library	30
Soft whisper	20
Ticking watch	10
Threshold of hearing	0

slamming, whereas longer sounds are labelled impact noise. Noise can also be intermittent occurring with or without regularity.

Performance

Noise can have both a physiological and psychological effect on the listener. However, the interaction between the two effects is complex. If we return to Smith and Jones' (1992) definition, the sound might be merely unwanted, creating a psychological effect but no physiological effect. Likewise, variable or low decibel sounds resulting in no auditory impairment could be viewed as irritating and a source of annoyance. Conversely, a person might not interpret the sound as a noise, although it might be loud enough to be creating auditory impairment. When performance is measured, again the results can be conflicting. The noise could be loud enough to change the physiological state of the listener, and they might also find it very annoying, but there might be no change in physical or cognitive performance. Hence, it could be concluded that the effects of noise on human performance are complex because of the number of influencing factors involved. One such factor is control. Research has shown that having control over the noise tends to diminish its adverse effects (Jones and Chapman, 1984). Other factors include the nature of the noise, the type of activity or task being attempted, the characteristics of the listener and the background conditions. Further, individuals can adapt to continuous background noise and this has important methodological implications (Haslegrave, 1995).

Many of the early experimental studies considering the effects of noise on performance took place within the workplace. Methodologically, these types of studies are difficult because of the number of possible confounding variables over which the experimenter has no control. This, combined with the so-called Hawthorne effect, makes it difficult to draw well-founded conclusions from some of the studies carried out in applied settings. Following the problems associated with these early field studies, there has been a shift towards laboratory-based work in a more controlled environment. Ethically, there is a problem presenting very loud sounds to human participants because of the risk of auditory damage; Smith and Jones (1992) noted that some of the early studies used noise levels that would be viewed as unacceptably high today.

Some reviews have indicated that noise does not interfere significantly with human performance (Kryter, 1970); some have even showed a performance improvement (Gawron, 1982) while others have been more specific and generated a list of the possible effects of noise (Broadbent, 1979). For example, noise reduces the efficiency with which we can monitor and change our performance, if necessary. In this sense, it makes us less flexible and inhibits our ability to change. It seems that a vital component of our reactions to noise is the nature of the task. For example, Sanders and McCormick (1987: 467) listed the following findings:

- With the exception of short-term memory tasks, the level of noise needed to demonstrate effects is quite high, e.g. 95 dB and above.
- Performance in simple routine tasks often show no changes when the person is exposed to noise, and some can show an improvement.
- The detrimental effects of noise are usually associated with tasks that need to be performed continuously for relatively long periods of time without rest breaks.
- Likewise, cognitive tasks requiring high levels of concentration and application can be degraded by high background noise.

Recommendations

It has not proved possible to develop a single theory of noise and performance because the effects of noise are dependent on a number of factors. Broadbent (1979) concluded that the effects of noise on performance *can* be defined, but within the context of being dependent on the type of noise and the task being performed. Jones and Davies (1984) also highlighted the importance of individual and group differences. This makes the generation of recommendations difficult because the overall picture can be complex and confusing. Despite these problems, a number of international standards have been developed for assessing environmental noise. These provide the sound levels at which prolonged exposure is thought to be damaging to the human auditory system (see ISO 1999, 1990).

In terms of reducing noise, this can be done by either limiting the noise at its source or along its path or at the point of reception, i.e. when heard by the human. For example,

- Remove (or mask) the source of the sound – noise is often produced by vibration in an industrial setting and damping the amplitude of the vibrations can reduce the noise.
- Low frequency noise is perceived as being less irritating than high frequency – this may be a consideration when purchasing equipment that is know to be noisy.
- Mufflers may be useful in reducing higher frequencies.
- High frequency noises are easier to deflect than lower frequencies in that they tend to be more directional – adding sound absorption materials to the building can lead to a substantial reduction in ambient sound levels.
- Providing the listener with hearing protection devices, e.g. muffs or direct insert devices, may be a useful option. However, there may be a certain reluctance on the part of the listener to wear these protective devices correctly, or even to wear them at all (Casali and Park, 1990; Gasaway, 1984).

Finally, in some situations the only solution might be to remove the human from exposure to the noise. The difficulty being that at this point in time irreversible damage may not be evident, e.g. workers exposed to the high levels of noise emanating from the bottling plants of many production industries might not suffer hearing problems, such as tinnitus, until several years later.

Vibration

Definitions

Vibrations have been defined as 'mechanical oscillations produced by regular or irregular movements of a body about its resting position' (Bonney, 1995: 541). Characteristics of vibrations include their magnitude, direction, duration, frequency (i.e. repetition rate, measured in hertz) and amplitude (i.e. distance from the resting position). Vibration is frequently linked to noise because it often generates it and, like noise, it can result in a number of detrimental effects on the individual. However, it should also be noted that mild vibration, such as that experienced when sitting in a car or on a train can be quite pleasant, as well as reassuring the traveller that the mechanics of the vehicle are operating correctly. Griffin (1990) stated that these 'good vibrations' had been advocated for improving the joint mobility of athletes and people suffering from arthritis.

Performance

The human system is a complex set of hard and soft tissues; some structures with more elastic properties will vibrate at a natural frequency while others will absorb and effectively dampen the vibration. When the body is subject to vibration, a range of problems from mild discomfort through to permanent injury can result. Its effects can be localised, e.g. vibration of individual fingers as found when operating some hand tools, through to whole body vibration. They can also be cumulative, building up with repeated exposure to the source of the vibration.

The most well-documented vibration effect is that of 'white finger' or Raynaud's disease, first described by the French physician, Maurice Raynaud in 1862. Continual vibrating of the hands in the 50–100 Hz range can initially result in tingling or numbness of the fingers; if the person persists in exposing the hand to vibration, the effects of blanching will begin to occur. Bonney (1995) stated that these will be particularly noticeable in the morning and when the hands are cold. Eventually, the fingers will become less sensitive to touch, pain and temperature and will begin to lose their dexterity, as well as being painful. The term 'white finger' is used because the fingers will eventually become drained of blood as the nerves and blood vessels become damaged, and the hand will appear whiter in hue. Because the soft tissues of the hands have been damaged through being subject to vibration, there is no cure, although Riddle and Taylor (1982) noted that, in the early stages of the disease, withdrawal of exposure to the vibration did result in some remission. It is also worth pointing out that 10 per cent of the population could exhibit the white finger symptoms at any one time, even though they have not been exposed to the effects of vibration (Griffin, 1982). This, coupled with the fact that Raynaud's disease tends to result after long exposure to the vibrating source, perhaps 5–10 years, means that diagnosis is often difficult.

Another disease arising from hand tool vibration is Dart's disease (Helander, 1995). This arises from vibrations around 100 Hz, and the symptoms are different to Raynaud's disease in that the hands become blue as blood pools in them. However, the associated feelings of pain and loss of dexterity are similar.

The other main type of vibration that has been studied is 'whole body' vibration, as this is of particular interest to the transport industries and has been shown to result in detrimental health, comfort and performance effects. A lot of research has been carried out on vehicle drivers and pilots. For example, National Aeronautics and Space Administration (NASA) conducted a comprehensive survey of aircraft ride comfort with over 2,200 experimental participants acting as passengers (Leatherwood *et al.*, 1980). Likewise, Griffin *et al.* (1982) carried out a series of studies on whole body vibration. Physiological effects emanating from whole body vibration have been well documented: giddiness, motion sickness, abdominal pain, visual disturbance, speech difficulties and muscle tension. In contrast, there is little evidence to suggest that cognitive processing is affected, the problem being, of course, that it is quite difficult to carry out fine motor tasks because of the unsteadiness of the body and the difficulty in focusing on the task, because of the oscillations of the eyes. As Griffin (1992) pointed out, both these effects are occurring outside of the body. Hence, studies looking at the effects of vibration on cognitive performance have to be carefully designed to ensure that the input/output means are not masking the true effects (Griffin, 1990; Sherwood and Griffin, 1992). Visual performance is particularly sensitive to vibrations in the frequency range 10–25 Hz. Poulton (1978) concluded that vibrations between 3.5 and 6 Hz could actually improve performance in vigilance tasks because they increased the level of alertness of the individual. It could probably be concluded that performance on fairly simple cognitive tasks is not affected by vibration. Griffin (1992) argued that this could also be the case for more complex tasks but designing experimental studies to confirm this is difficult. Further, there are wide individual differences in subjective responses to whole body vibration and research by Oborne *et al.* (1981) indicated that it is not easy to determine the causes of these differences.

Recommendations

Human performance is more susceptible to the lower frequencies, i.e. in the range from 0.5 to 100 Hz. Below 0.5 Hz, motion sickness might be the only symptom, whereas above 100 Hz, the neuromuscular system will be detrimentally affected. International Standard ISO 5349 (1986) provides information relating to the acceptable limits of vibration in terms of time of exposure and various frequencies. Given the primarily negative effects of vibration, this standard also covers technical recommendations for reducing the level of vibration at its source.

Environments and performance

Environments can be considered in terms of their physical and psychological effects on an individual's health, comfort and performance. It should be noted that only the main environmental aspects have been considered here, and that there are others, e.g. the effects of gravitational forces. The emphasis here has been on performance issues and particularly those relating to physical activities and cognitive processing. The area of engineering anthropometry, i.e. the measurement of the physical characteristics of the human body, has made considerable advances in the last couple of decades. This has enhanced our understanding of how to design equipment to fit the characteristics of the user and, in this respect, a tremendous amount of time and energy has gone into developing functional and comfortable seats for various workstations from offices to vehicles for transportation purposes. However, it should be noted that although workspaces must be designed for functional efficiency, their characteristics must also be aesthetically appealing to the user. As an example, Cassidy (1997) demonstrated the importance of personal space and the consequences when it is violated.

Given that vision for most people is the dominant sense, it follows that illumination is an important aspect of the working environment. Megaw (1992) concluded that there is a general acceptance that once lighting levels are above certain thresholds, an individual's reaction and response to illumination is a complex process. As the Hawthorne studies demonstrated, measuring human performance is not straightforward. This is certainly the case when combinations of stressors are considered, e.g. the effects of noise and vibration on performance (see Sandover and Champion, 1984; Seidel *et al.*, 1988). Further, certain levels of some physical parameters can actually enhance human performance, e.g. warmth and low levels of vibration.

Key points

- The environment can be considered in terms of its physical and psychological characteristics and the interactions of these on human performance.
- The range of anthropometric dimensions of the population can often be accommodated with the use of adjustable equipment. Alternatively, designing for 90 per cent of the population, the extremes of the population, the mythical 'average' person, and employing the universal design approach, are all commonly used methods in design.
- The construction of workspace envelopes is a useful aid for facilitating design in three dimensions; the most recent approach is the employment of computer-aided design packages.
- The aesthetics of the working environment can also affect human performance, e.g. the amount of personal space – the invisible, three-dimensional 'bubble' that surrounds and moves with us.
- A tremendous amount of ergonomics research has gone into furniture design and, in particular, chair design. This has resulted in the generation of a large number of recommendations for the dimensions of furniture used in the workplace.
- In terms of the physical design of work environments, a number of standards exist. It is generally recommended that illumination levels should be between 300 and 500 lux; temperatures should be in the range 21–23°C with relative humidity around 50 per cent and little air movement; noise levels are tolerable up to around 70 dB; and vibration should be minimal, i.e. less than 5 Hz. However, there are several other factors to take into consideration, e.g. the nature of the task, issues relating to comfort and individual differences.
- As the Hawthorne studies demonstrated, the measurement of the effects of the working environment on human performance is not always straightforward due to the large number of factors that can influence human–environment interactions.

5 Organisational issues

So there he is at last. Man on the moon. The poor magnificent bungler! He
can't even get to the office without undergoing the agonies of the damned,
but give him a little metal, a few chemicals, some wire and twenty or thirty
billion dollars and vroom! there he is, up on a rock a quarter of a million
miles up in the sky.
> Russell Wagner Baker, 1969, *New York Times*

The bigger the organization, the fewer the jobs worth doing.
> Sir Antony Rupert Jay, 1967, *Management and Machiavelli*

The use of 'machines' always takes place within an environment and it can
be seen from the Noyes and Baber (1999) model that this extends to
encompass organisational issues. Certainly this is the case with the traditional workplace although the extent to which 'organisational issues' could
be applied to the increasing use of tools, technology and computers in the
home is debatable. Chapter 4 focused on the physical aspects of the
working environment; this chapter will extend this definition of environment to consider some of the organisational issues that can influence
human performance in the workplace. Again, it must be remembered that
the Human Factors/ergonomic approach is to consider the 'whole', and it
would be unwise to focus on the design of human–machine interactions
without reference to the larger picture.

Organisations can be defined as 'collectivities of parts that accomplish
goals more effectively when organised in a larger structure' (Muchinsky,
1997: 246). This definition implies that several groups of people will be
working together to achieve a common goal as determined by the nature of
the organisation. The 'group' aspect is important because, in the past,
human interactions with technology have tended to focus on the individual
and the social aspects of human–machine interaction have often been
ignored. This is particularly true of research in the experimental sciences:
take, for example, the human information-processing model described in

Chapter 2. This focuses very much on individual cognitive processes such as decision making and memory when carried out by a single person. It could be argued that, more recently, the shift has been towards groups, e.g. team working, and social and sociological processes. It is perhaps also worth mentioning the recent trend towards teleworking, where individuals work from home with the aid of a computer and a telephone (UK Government Survey, 1998). In the UK, it is estimated that around 350,000 employees work from home (IRS, 1999), and this number is expected to increase over the next decade or so as employees realise savings in workplace overheads and productivity improvements of up to 20 per cent (see Huws, 1993).

Organisation theory

Although organisations in one sense have been around as long as people, their formal study could be considered to be a relatively 'new' activity, and some date the beginnings of this as recent as the 1950s (Davis and Powell, 1992). Beginning with Max Weber's work on bureaucracy, there have been a number of theories put forward to describe organisations. However, it should be noted that these are not actually 'theories' in the true scientific meaning of the word but rather descriptions of organisations in terms of their design, function and performance (Pugh, 1966).

Historically, we can divide organisation theories into three main categories: classical, neoclassical and systems. Classical organisation theory was the earliest and focuses on the structural relationships within the organisation (Fayol, 1949; Follett, 1942; Weber, 1947). Taylor's principles of scientific management as discussed in Chapter 1 are sometimes considered to be a classical theory. Classical theory included the view that organisations have four basic components. These are:

1. a system of differentiated activities
2. people
3. co-operation towards a common goal
4. authority.

The emphasis is on the relationship between people and their jobs. Appropriate analysis of these key aspects when determining the structure of the organisation would enable us to predict the success of the organisation in attaining its goals. Four principles emerged from classical organisational theory (Scott *et al.*, 1981):

1. Functional – organisations should be divided according to work demands, i.e. into units that perform similar functions.

2. Scalar – organisations can be viewed as having vertical chains of command, with each level being accountable to only one level above.
3. Line/staff – work functions are either 'line', with primary responsibility for meeting the goals of the organisation, or 'staff', i.e. supporting the activities of the line workers.
4. Span-of-control – organisations will have flatter structures when managers have a large number of subordinates to oversee. Hence, there will be fewer levels between the top and bottom of the organisation.

Classical organisational theory is today viewed as dated and old-fashioned, primarily because organisations are much more complex than the four basic principles suggest. However, it did lay the foundations for the later neo-classical theories. These claimed that there were a number of shortcomings associated with the classical principles and attempted to overcome these by applying results from behavioural research and, in particular, studies of individual differences. For example, the line/staff distinction is not always clear-cut and it will be hard to tell whether some jobs include primary line responsibilities or supporting staff activities. The job of a sales person in a production industry would be an example of this conflict in work function. Although sales would not be viewed as a line function, because it is secondary to the goal of the organisation in producing the product, it is critical to the success of the organisation. Hence, this particular job does not fit into the principles of classical theory.

Recognition of the complexity and dynamics of organisations led to the systems approach. 'Systems theory' describes the nature of the organisation's interaction with the environment, and the development and life of the system in dynamic terms (Boulding, 1956). Briefly, the nature of the system results from the continual adaptation to both internal and external demands, changes in one component of the system affect other components (because they are linked through their exchange of objects such as information) as well as the system as a whole. The roots of systems theory lie in the biological sciences (Kast and Rosenzweig, 1972) and parallels with living organisms are immediately apparent.

Systems theory suggests that organisations are made up of five major components:

1. Individuals.
2. Formal aspects of the organisation, e.g. the various jobs that provide the structure of the system.
3. Small groups.
4. Status and role, e.g. jobs confer different status and roles upon their holders.
5. Physical setting, i.e. the external environment in which the organisation exists.

The theoretical foundation underpinning much of the thinking on human–machine system design is general systems theory. There are two primary exchange processes – inputs and outputs and, within a component, an internal conversion process occurs between input and output. Both the human and the machine have internal conversion processes. All these dynamic processes exist in the human–machine work system. Input to the human is conveyed by the machine's displays, output devices and the environment with each type of input having a corresponding output. This output from the machine provides information to the human. However, the feedback loop is two-way because the machine receives information from the output of the human – a feature that has yet to be exploited by computer designers. A final point concerns the human–machine system's vulnerability to 'go wrong'. A system such as this only performs well when the interactions between its components are effective. Mistakes and accidents occur at the interfaces between the components. When designing the system, special attention needs be given to strengthening these links between components, i.e. the human–machine interface. In terms of the human, consideration of their needs and capacities can improve the system by making these links stronger. These aspects are discussed in more detail in Chapter 6.

Unlike the two earlier theories, systems theory is deliberately vague. It does not specify the level of detail found in, for example, the span-of-control principle of classical theory. The complexity of organisations demands that we consider them at a conceptual rather than an actual level and general systems theory does try to do this. However, all three theories are restricted in that they attempt to seek an optimum design for all organisations in all situations. Further, there has been little testing of these theories. Ashmos and Huber (1987) even went as far as stating that the overuse of systems theory had actually been detrimental to any value that the theory might have had. A more recent approach is to take a contingency approach in which various situational variables are stated. For example, Woodward (1965) suggested that an organisation's effectiveness depended on technology and the level of its complexity. More recent research places further emphasis on the interaction between the organisation and technology. Mintzberg (1979) proposed 'technical systems theory', which considers how technology determines the structure of the organisation. A variation on technical systems theory is the 'sociotechnical systems theory' pioneered by the Tavistock Institute in the UK. According to research carried out by Trist and others in the British coal mining industry, the technological and social aspects of work were found to influence productivity and attitudes (Trist *et al.*, 1963). Finally, a theory that began to emerge in the 1980s was 'culture theory'. Here, the organisation is viewed as a culture that shares knowledge and values and evolves slowly over time (Peters and Waterman, 1982; Sheridan, 1992; Wilkins and Dyer, 1988). Again, parallels with biology and the lifecycle of living organisms can be seen.

Design of work

Job design

Jobs vary according to a number of characteristics, one of which concerns how specialised they are. When division of labour is highly specialised, jobs are narrowly defined, e.g. the simple, repetitive actions that are often required on a production line. Jobs like these are often referred to as 'low-technology jobs' (Bridger, 1995) and are characterised by being relatively simple and easy to learn and carry out by workers who need few skills and little motivation. In contrast, some jobs are not highly specialised and involve a variety of activities, e.g. an academic's job that involves teaching, research, administration and management; these types of jobs would be classed as 'high-technology jobs'. The issue of job redesign is particularly relevant to highly specialised jobs such as those described by the production line example. These jobs are simple in design and operation but, although this may lead to efficiency in the short term, workers may suffer from fatigue and boredom. Ironically, the simplicity of some jobs may actually be detrimental. One solution might be to make the jobs more complex. This might include introducing greater task variety and more 'ownership' in terms of participation and responsibility in the planning and execution of the work. This can be achieved by job rotation where workers rotate through a small number of similar jobs perhaps on a weekly basis. Job rotation has the benefit of increasing task variety.

Berry and Houston (1993) defined job redesign as a motivational change programme. They gave examples of five particular theories that might lead to increased worker performance. These were:

1. Needs–hierarchy theory (e.g. Maslow, 1954) – providing workers with more opportunity to satisfy higher level needs.
2. Goal-setting theory (e.g. Drucker, 1954) – providing workers with more opportunity to set their own goals.
3. Two-factor and expectancy theories (e.g. Herzberg, 1966; Vroom, 1964) – increasing the intrinsic satisfaction of the work itself.
4. Equity theory (Adams, 1965) – workers bring 'inputs' to a job, i.e. qualifications, experience, etc., and gain 'outputs', i.e. money, status, recognition, etc. When output is seen as being equal to (or exceeding) input, workers feel the exchange is fair; hence, the goal is to increase outputs.
5. Reinforcement theory (e.g. Luthans and Kreitner, 1985) – providing workers with more feedback and knowledge of results about their performance resulting in positive gains and rewards.

Although a little dated now, it is interesting to note that Katzell *et al.* (1977) found that 103 motivational change programmes had been reported in the literature between 1973 and 1977. Hence, applications of motivation theories in the workplace have been clearly demonstrated. It is probably also appropriate at this point to highlight some issues relating to worker performance that may provide indicators that all is not well in the workplace. In the UK, the Health and Safety Executive (1999: 4) listed the following:

- Accidents involving staff, contractors or visitors where 'human error' is given as a cause.
- Occupational health reports of mental or physical ill health.
- High absenteeism or sickness rates.
- High levels of staff turnover.
- Low level of, or changes in, compliance with health and safety rules.
- Behaviour or performance issues identified in risk assessments.
- Complaints from staff about working conditions or job design.

The basic premise upon which motivational change programmes work is to make jobs more 'motivating', i.e. more intrinsically satisfying and interesting for the worker in the hope that this will increase (or maintain) their productivity. This is often referred to as 'job enrichment'. Basically, there are two primary ways of enriching jobs and these fall under the umbrella of 'job enlargement'. Jobs can be enriched by horizontal enlargement, where tasks are added to increase variety and reduce repetition, or by vertical enlargement, where workers take greater responsibility for the planning, execution and output of the job. Other ways of designing jobs include having autonomous work groups who take responsibility for the complete production of a product from start to finish – this is in contrast to having responsibility for just one aspect. These work groups have been shown to increase motivation, the quality of the finished product and job satisfaction. However, the distinctions between job enrichment and enlargement are blurred and some view them as different entities in theory although very similar in practice. For example, in programmes of job enlargement, jobs are combined or restructured so workers can experience each other's jobs. Lawler (1969) found that job enlargement did not improve productivity but it did enhance the quality of the work generated. Campion and McClelland (1991) added to these findings by suggesting that redesigned jobs can provide more satisfaction and less boredom. However, the costs included increased training requirements and skills. In contrast to job enlargement, job enrichment involves restructuring jobs in order to make them more challenging. McEvoy and Cascio (1985) provided some evidence for the effectiveness of job enrichment as a means of making jobs more stimulating. Regardless of their specific definitions, the evaluation of the effectiveness of job enrichment and enlargement programmes is not easy. The relationship between job design and employee performance can vary as a function of individual differences, task attributes and the difficulties associated with the choice of measures of performance (which could include productivity, employee turnover, absenteeism, lateness, and occupational stress). Further, it may be necessary to monitor the effects over time; a single reading might give a false impression.

Despite the problems of evaluation, job redesign programmes are a popular choice for increasing worker motivation. Research has tended to concentrate on job characteristics in order to locate those task attributes that lead to a change in performance. One of the most well-known of these studies led to the development of the Job Characteristics Model (Hackman and Oldham, 1976). This model sought to explain how job design influenced attitudes and worker behaviour by describing jobs in terms of five core dimensions:

1. Skill variety – the number of skills required by the job.
2. Task identity – the extent to which the job allows completion of the final product as opposed to contributing to a part of the design or production process.
3. Task significance – the more global aspects relating to the job's significance in a wider context.
4. Autonomy – the extent to which the job allows the worker to be autonomous.
5. Task feedback – the extent to which workers receive information about their performance.

The model used these five core dimensions as a means of assessing three psychological states:

1. Experienced meaningfulness of work – this arose from core dimensions 1–3: skill variety, task identity and task significance.
2. Experienced responsibility for outcomes of work – this arose from core dimension 4: autonomy.
3. Knowledge of results from work – this arose from core dimension 5: task feedback.

High scores on each of these three states will result in good worker performance outcomes. Hackman and Oldham (1976: 256) listed these as 'high internal work motivation, high quality work performance, high satisfaction levels, and low absenteeism and turnover'. They hypothesised that individuals scoring high on the five core dimensions would be those with a need of personal growth and development. To quantify this, they developed an equation for generating the motivating potential score (MPS).

MPS = (Core dimensions 1 + 2 + 3)/3 × Core dimensions 4 + 5

Individuals score each of the five components and, because they are multiplied, low scores or zero on any of the five dimensions will result in a

low MPS, i.e. the job fails to motivate the individual. The Job Characteristics Model has been used extensively. For example, Fried and Ferris
(1987) reviewed over 200 studies that had used the model. They drew a
number of conclusions relating to job characteristics that included the
following:

- Jobs do have a number of characteristics but it is not easy to be
  definitive about how many or which ones.
- The relationship between job characteristics and psychological states of
  the worker is tenuous.
- Performance outcomes do seem to be related to job characteristics.

A great deal of research effort has gone into locating job and task characteristics. One of the difficulties arises from the need to ask workers how
they perceive their jobs and this introduces a strong subjective component.
Spector (1992) pointed out that perceptions of job characteristics will be
influenced by attitudes, mood, current disposition and feelings.

Work organisation

Given the interest in job redesign as a means of improving worker performance, the question remains of how work can be optimally organised to
ensure the workforce performs well. This includes consideration of issues
such as shift work, flexitime, and work breaks. There are some organisations
that need to operate around the clock, e.g. heavy industries with production
lines that are costly to shut down and start up, and services industries that
'care' for the population. Although the '9 to 5, Monday to Friday' work
model remains popular in the developed world, a large number of people
work shifts. Muchinsky (1997) estimated that around one-quarter of the
American workforce had 'non-traditional' working hours. Similar estimates
have been made for the UK and Scandinavia (Monk and Folkard, 1992;
Reilly *et al.*, 1997).

Research studies have indicated a wide variation in workers' degree of
satisfaction with traditional hours and shift work. For example, Wedderburn
(1978) found that 18 per cent of British steelworkers liked working shifts very
much, in contrast to 8 per cent who disliked it very much. Zedeck *et al.* (1983)
supported this finding by concluding that one-third of their sample liked shift
work and would prefer not to change to traditional work patterns.

One of the many problems of working shifts is adjusting to the change in
lifestyle; this is especially evident when working night shifts (Folkard,
1987). Working during the night can result in physiological problems as the
body's 24-hour circadian or diurnal cycle is disturbed. The word 'circadian'
comes from the Latin with *circa* meaning 'about' and *dies* the 'day', while
diurnal is from *diurnus*, translated as 'of the day'. They are reinforced by
time markers often referred to as zeitgebers (from the German *Zeit*

meaning 'time', and *geber* meaning 'giver'). Night working can lead to gastrointestinal upsets and even cardiovascular disorders (see two studies of heart disease in shift workers carried out by Knutsson *et al.* (1986) and Wolinsky (1982)). For this reason, evening shifts are preferable to night shifts. Night working can also lead to social problems as domestic relationships become strained and leisure activities are difficult to pursue. Frost and Jamal (1979) found, not surprisingly, that shift workers participated in few activities outside of the workplace. However, it has been suggested that shift work could lead to fewer social problems if communities catered for workplaces that needed to operate 24 hours a day throughout the year. Certainly, the developed world is moving towards providing services that are 'open' longer, and it is likely the Internet will extend this further. The physiological problems that arise from shift working, e.g. fatigue, sleeping and digestive upsets, are probably not so easy to overcome as the social difficulties. Physiological problems are likely to be exacerbated when workers rotate across shifts as opposed to working fixed shifts (Barton, 1994). Further, worker alertness and performance will be determined by circadian effects, the amount of preceding sleep and the length of time since the last sleep period (Miller, 1999). There seems no obvious solution to this problem other than to recruit individuals who prefer shift work, and to provide appropriate training for shift workers and their families to alert them to the difficulties. Helander (1995) suggested that about 20 per cent of the population will have extreme difficulties adjusting to shift work and will probably never make a successful transition to working in this way. It would seem a sensible idea to try to locate these individuals at the selection and recruitment stage.

Research has indicated that adjustment to some patterns of shift work rotation are easier than others, e.g. forward rotation (from day to afternoon to night) as opposed to backward rotation (from day to night to afternoon shifts; Knauth and Kiesswetter (1987)). However, Duchon *et al.* (1989) dispute this in their study of shift work and conclude that there was no significant benefit of forward as opposed to backward rotation. A more recent study by Totterdell *et al.* (1995) may help explain these findings. They studied recovery from work shifts in a sample of sixty-one shift nurses. Over a 28-day period, participants kept a sleep diary, completed self-ratings of mood and work satisfaction and carried out serial-choice reaction time and memory search cognitive performance tasks. Totterdell *et al.* found that certain factors influenced recovery, such as the quality of the non-work time, e.g. whether this was taken as leisure or spent carrying out effortful activities such as domestic chores and personal maintenance tasks. Also, some shift workers forced themselves to keep going in order to ensure they would be able to sleep. This may help explain the counterintuitive finding that some performance measures were worst at the end of the rest day than they were at the end of the night shift. In terms of worker performance during night work, one might expect to have some degradation in quality and/or output due to the physiological difficulties and social concerns that we know these workers have. The research literature seems to support this, with evidence that night workers are less productive and make more mistakes (Gannon *et al.*, 1983; Rogers *et al.*, 1989; Wilkinson *et al.*, 1989). However, research on shift workers has indicated that there may be social reasons why they volunteer to work night shifts in the first instance and comparisons with day workers may not be fair.

Case study: shift work – effects of age and habitual physical activity on shift work (from Reilly* et al., *1998)

Shift work is known to disturb circadian rhythms. It is thought that with age we are less able to tolerate these circadian shifts and therefore, older workers will have more health-related problems than younger workers. Further, it is hypothesised that habitual physical activity may influence circadian rhythms (Redlin and Mrosovsky, 1997). A study has been carried out to determine the effects of age and habitual physical activity on the adjustment and tolerance to shift work.

Twenty male shift workers (nine having a mean age of 23.4 years and eleven with a mean age of 48.9 years) were divided into active and non-active subgroups as determined by the Physical Activity Questionnaire (Lamb and Brodie, 1991). A battery of measures was taken: these included oral temperatures, grip strengths, peak expiratory flows, arousal and rhythm characteristics as well as completion of the Standard Shiftwork Index (Barton *et al.*, 1990). Three shifts (morning, afternoon and night) were assessed over a 5-day period and measurements were taken every 2 hours. It was found that younger shift workers had higher amplitudes in their circadian rhythms and faster adaptations to shift work. Despite these higher amplitudes, younger people had more difficulties in adjusting to the morning shift. Participants with a higher level of physical activity also showed higher amplitudes, but not faster adaptations, to shift work. As a result of the findings from this study, it is suggested that older individuals should be scheduled to work morning shifts rather than night shifts, because it was during the night working that the younger adults performed consistently better. Physical activity was found to have no effect on shift work performance.

One variation on the traditional 40-hour working week spread over 5 days is to compress this into four 10-hour work shifts. This is sometimes abbreviated to '4/40', i.e. 40 hours over 4 days. Generally, this compressed work model has received positive reviews with workers benefiting from the 3-day break, and with no loss in performance (Latack and Foster, 1985). The drawback is the level of fatigue that results from the longer shifts. This was particularly evident in one study on nurses, who were working in excess of 10-hour shifts (Breaugh, 1983). However, Duchon *et al.* (1994), in their study with underground miners, recommended the move from an 8-hour to a 12-hour shift. They found the workforce supported the longer working day and that physiological measures, e.g. oxygen consumption and heart rate, did not show indications of physical fatigue. However, the 12-hour shift workers were lodging on-site and it is thought that this influenced the findings, in that participants were reporting longer and better quality sleep. It is therefore not possible to draw general conclusions from this study. In conclusion, the compressed work schedule 4/40 seems to offer a number of advantages but caution needs to be exercised concerning other models, such as 5/60, where worker performance has been shown to be affected by fatigue (Rosa and Colligan, 1988).

Another variation on the traditional model is to have 'flexitime' where workers choose their arrival and departure times outside of a designated core time, say 10 a.m. to 3 p.m., when everyone is expected to be present. The advantage of flexible working hours is that it provides individuals with some autonomy over their work schedules and allows them to fit in to some extent with social and family commitments. As long as workers arrive before core time, lateness can be eliminated because work begins at the time of arrival. In general, flexitime has been received positively. Employees like it because it enables working parents to drop-off and collect children (who traditionally have a shorter school day), it relieves the pressure on people to travel during the 'rush hour' traffic, as well as giving workers more control over their work schedules. This last point was particularly evident in a study carried out by Narayanan and Nath (1982), who compared the impact of flexitime on two groups of workers: lower level and professional employees. The lower level workers particularly benefited from the introduction of flexitime, whereas it made little difference to the professionals other than to formalise a working relationship that they already had with the organisation. In a review of flexitime, Dunham *et al.* (1987) concluded that it did not usually affect worker performance although it was not evident that it led to any improvements. In terms of negative effects of flexitime, there is little reported in the literature other than the difficulties associated with team working where members of the team are working different work schedules. However, comprehensive lists of advantages and disadvantages of flexitime have been compiled by Tepas (1985) and Kogi (1991). The author's own experience of working in two organisations operating flexitime echoes some of the disadvantages; planning meetings was sometimes a problem because they always needed to take place during core time. Further, some employees always seemed to be waiting for the start of core time to make contact with colleagues, because they argued that

Table 5.1   Summary of recommendations for work organisation (based on Kroemer *et al.*, 1994: 329)

1.	Whenever possible, work should follow our natural circadian rhythms
2.	Work during daylight hours is preferable to night work; at night, high illumination levels of 2,000 lux or more should be maintained
3.	Evening shifts are preferable to working a night shift
4.	If shift work is unavoidable, it is better to have a worker permanently on the same shift, or ensure that the worker returns to day work after only one shift cycle
5.	Compressed weeks are appropriate for some jobs and result in no performance loss
6.	The optimal length of the shift and the frequency and duration of rest breaks are dependent on the nature of the job

it was a waste of time to try to do so during flexitime. Hence, it could be implied that flexitime results in poorer communications within the organisation and with contacts outside.

The traditional 8-hour day is usually punctuated by two short breaks either side of a longer meal break. However, the demands of some jobs will mean that either more frequent rest breaks are needed or shorter work cycles. For example, jobs that require high levels of vigilance may need more frequent rest breaks, e.g. air traffic controllers. It is generally recognised that the recovery value of having several short breaks is greater than having a few longer breaks (Kroemer *et al.*, 1994). Moving off-task is also preferable to taking breaks and remaining in the vicinity of the location of the work. Wickens *et al.* (1998) cited the example of helicopter flights by the Army, where the night flights impose a greater workload on the crew and hence night duties need to be shorter. In conclusion, the frequency and duration of the rest breaks in the job will be dependent on the type of work being carried out. A summary of the recommendations from Kroemer *et al.* (1994) is given in Table 5.1.

Performance-shaping factors

Several factors are known to affect worker performance. These range from intrinsic to external variables and are summarised in Table 5.2. Several of the environmental stressors were discussed in Chapter 4; the interest here is on those internal factors that shape performance and how jobs can be designed and work organised to accommodate them. Of particular interest are fatigue, vigilance and workload.

Fatigue

Fatigue has a strong subjective component – we may be feeling tired until invited to do something exciting, when our fatigue will suddenly disappear! Further, we all react differently when tired. For example, in studies of pilot

Table 5.2 Summary of factors that influence performance (adapted from Christensen and Talbot, 1986)

Psychological, Psychosocial and Psychophysiological	Environmental
Fatigue (physical/mental)	Immediate environment
Vigilance	Temperature
Workload	Noise
Cognitive abilities, e.g. decision making	Social, e.g. lack of privacy
Limits of performance (perceptual/motor)	Work–rest cycles
Motivation	Shift change
Emotions/moods	Desynchronisation of body rhythms
Attitudes	Hazards
Personality variables	Stresses
Social skills	Boredom
Human reliability	
Communications	

fatigue, Bartlett (1943) noted that some individuals when tired became aggressive and irritable while others responded by withdrawal and inertia. However, recent progress has been made in the measurement of fatigue with the Fatigue Component Analysis Spreadsheet (Miller, 1999) and the Swedish Occupational Fatigue Inventory (SOFI; Åhsberg *et al.*, (2000)). Prior to these, there were few reliable measures of fatigue and early results from testing SOFI look promising. Although little is known about fatigue in terms of its exact nature and causes (Åstrand and Rodahl, 1986; Kroemar *et al.*, 1994), it can affect performance in the workplace. It is thought that fatigue results from the costs of effort and performance as indicated by the perceptions of the workers, reduced task performance and behaviours associated with sleepiness. Miller (1999) divided fatigue into three categories according to cause: circadian, acute and cumulative. Circadian fatigue results from diurnal effects, acute fatigue results from a single work period while cumulative effects develop over time when inadequate rest is taken. Consequently, fatigue and its effects are often confounded with feeling tired because of a lack of sleep. Because fatigue can also lead to injury, it is important that the work environment is designed to take this into account. A person who appears to be suffering from fatigue may in fact be bored by the work, poorly motivated to do the job well and, hence, easily distracted.

Grandjean (1968) suggested that there were four types of fatigue – muscular, mental, emotional and skills – and proposed that the latter manifested itself as a decline in performance, possibly in speed and accuracy of response, lack of attention to detail, not noticing something in the environment. As Singleton (1989: 161) pointed out 'paradoxically, although the perceptual field narrows in the sense that there is increasing "tunnel vision", there is also a greater awareness of task irrelevant stimuli, such as feelings of discomfort'. The response in terms of job design will be different for each type of fatigue. For example, muscular fatigue may mean that the job has to be totally redesigned, perhaps introducing different procedures that provide rests between exertions or the use of equipment to prevent the person becoming tired. Mental fatigue may indicate basic intrinsic problems with the nature of the work itself that might have to be addressed or attempts made to make the work more stimulating and challenging. Emotional fatigue resulting from intense stress has often been found to arise from factors outside of the work environment (Muchinsky, 1997). As a fictional example, Kanki (1996) described Captain A, an airline pilot, who started his working day feeling fatigued and upset by recent events in his family life. His First Officer interpreted this fatigue and preoccupation as arrogance and hostility. This increased the general stress levels of the flight deck crew, thus providing a potential threat to overall job performance in flying the aircraft. Counselling may provide a solution here, and indeed, the crew resource management (CRM) training programmes popular in the aviation and shipping industries are designed to address this type of situation. Finally, skills fatigue may mean that workers have to be closely monitored and moved off-task if necessary. For example, transport researchers have been considering the possibility of 'fitness for duty' testing of long-haul lorry drivers (Miller, 1996). In conclusion, fatigue in the workplace should always be taken seriously as it may prejudice worker performance and lead to a compromise in safety.

Vigilance

Some tasks demand that workers remain vigilant, i.e. that they remain alert in order to maintain good performance. Tasks that require vigilance have a number of common features. For example, changes to be detected are small and perhaps irregular, making detection difficult. The situation may require low arousal and the task may be monotonous. As discussed in Chapter 1, vigilance became of interest during World War II when radar operators were required to monitor radio pulses that were either reflected onto screens or by changes in auditory signals. It was found that operators were unable to sustain visual attention on a target for more than 15–20 minutes without a decrease in vigilance performance. In some jobs where vigilance is needed, performance can be severely degraded. Wickens *et al.* (1998) cited the example of assembly line inspectors who could miss between 30 and 40 per cent of targets (although they gave no information about the task or the conditions under which it was being carried out). In the medical, transport and defence industries, there would be some jobs where this performance level would not be acceptable. The classic work carried out by Mackworth (1950) demonstrated that vigilance performance could be improved by shorter working periods, having breaks, the provision of feedback and, in the short term, by taking amphetamines. Given how poor humans are at locating low frequency targets, one solution might be to send 'dummy' targets past the operators in order to increase their general level of arousal. However, interventions such as this will probably increase the hit rate as well as the number of false alarms. The relative costs of this will need to be considered within the context of the specific application. Davies and Parasuraman (1982) put forward six theories to explain vigilance but, like organisational theories, much of this work is descriptive and does not help particularly to suggest remedial actions to cope with the performance decrement experienced in particular vigilance tasks. In terms of general recommendations, once it has been established that a task has a vigilance component, the work schedule may have to be reorganised to ensure short work periods, i.e. less than an hour. Training individuals to recognise the problem may also be helpful in conjunction with the application of Human Factors to the design of the interface, workplace and environment.

Workload

There are two basic types of workload: physical and cognitive (or mental) workload. Both types can be measured using objective and subjective methods, although given the nature of physical and cognitive workload it is more usual to measure the former with objective techniques and the latter by subjective means. The assessment of workload is generally based on a resource model where there is a limited resource available to complete the task of which a certain percentage is demanded by the task or job. A brief description of each type of workload is given here.

Physical workload

Physical workload relates to the amount of energy expended by an individual when carrying out an activity. There are obviously limits to the amount of energy that workers should expend and jobs need to be designed to take this into account. Physical loads are greatly influenced by the time over which they have to be sustained, and workload measurements take this into account. We can withstand our maximal workload for only a few minutes and this is very different from a workload that can be endured over several hours. Physical workload is measured by aerobic capacities; these are calculated by measuring the oxygen consumption and heart rates of the person doing the job. For example, healthy young Army recruits would have aerobic capacities in the range, 45–55 ml of O_2 consumed per kilogram of body weight per minute (Sharp *et al.*, 1988). Aerobic capacities are subject to a number of individual differences, e.g. age, gender, level of fitness, training, general health and genetic factors. Hence, any recommendations for physical workload need to take these factors into account. As an example, the National Institute for Occupational Safety and Health (NIOSH, 1981) provided guidelines that recommended that workers should not work over an 8-hour shift at more than 30–40 per cent of their short-term work capacity. Likewise, strenuous work taking up to 70 per cent of a worker's aerobic capacity should not be carried out for more than 30 minutes (Rodgers, 1997). In conclusion, there are standardised methods for measuring physical workload and guidelines such as NIOSH (1981) that provide help in determining what physical workload an individual could safely endure over a specific working period.

Work involving physical exertion can also be measured via self-rating scales, e.g. the Borg RPE (Ratings of Perceived Exertion) Scale (Borg, 1985). This scale requires individuals to rate their perceived physical effort on scales of 6 = 'no exertion at all' to 20 = 'maximal exertion' representing the heart rate range of 60–200 beats per minute. It was first developed by Borg in 1960 and was subsequently modified in the 1980s. The attraction of this type of paper-based measurement is that it is non-invasive and requires no specialist equipment. It may also be particularly useful in cases where individuals have unreliable heart responses to direct physiological measurement perhaps because of illness and/or medication. In the workplace, the RPE scales have been used to only a limited extent (Kilbom, 1995). This is primarily because of the other influences relating to this subjective measurement, e.g. overall impression of exertion might affect the rating, as well as individual differences, e.g. experience and motivation.

Cognitive workload

Cognitive (or mental) workload can also be measured by subjective means, e.g. estimates of workload, and objective methods such as EEG activity, blink rate, pupil diameter, heart rate and galvanic skin responses (Kramer, 1991; Tsang and Wilson, 1997; Wierwille and Eggemeier, 1993). Wickens *et al.* (1998) suggested that, in general, physiological measures of workload correlate with other measures such as the subjective ones. These are often paper-based, where a person is simply asked to rate their feelings of workload on a scale, e.g. the Modified Cooper–Harper (MCH) Scale (Wierwille *et al.*, 1985). For example, the MCH scale of task difficulty asks the following questions:

- Is mental workload level acceptable?
- Are errors small and inconsequential?
- Even though errors may be large or frequent, can the instructed task be accomplished most of the time?

However, because workload is a multidimensional construct, many researchers feel that it is better to rate it on several scales. Two of the more well-known subjective workload scales – the NASA TLX (Task Load Index) and the SWAT (Subjective Workload Assessment Technique) do this. The NASA TLX (Hart and Staveland, 1988) has six rating scales – mental demand, physical demand, temporal demand, performance, effort and frustration. The SWAT (Reid and Nygren, 1988) requires respondents to rate workload on one of three levels (high, medium and low) relating to three scales – time load, mental effort load and psychological stress load. These two workload scales have been shown to be highly correlated with the modified Cooper–Harper scale (Kroemer *et al.*, 1994). One of the ironies of subjective workload measurements is that they do not always relate to people's performance (Andre and Wickens, 1995). By definition, they are subjective, but there does seem to be a more complex relationship occurring between actual and perceived workload and its effects on performance. As an example, the author's research with a Bakan vigilance task (Leggatt and Noyes, 1996) indicated that the source of workload was emanating not from the amount of work as measured by correct responses but from the number of false alarms. It was found that those individuals who had a significant number of false alarms reported the highest workload as measured by the NASA TLX. Further, dissociation is an important aspect of workload assessment and it is recognised that workload will often increase as overall performance increases. One explanation for both these results is that subjective measures of mental workload ascertain how much cognitive effort is invested in a task. This might include resource investment and the demands on working memory (Yeh and Wickens, 1988). In the Bakan vigilance task, this relates to the added workload associated with the number of false alarms, whereas in the case of overall performance the extra effort indicates the higher workload. The interesting point being that the demands and nature of a task could remain the same but the individual, for whatever reason, might be more highly motivated to complete it on some occasions. They will then invest more effort and correspondingly report higher cognitive workload levels when undertaking the same activity.

Interactions of fatigue, vigilance and workload

High workload levels will lead to fatigue, which will eventually result in degradation in performance. Orasanu and Backer (1996) stated that the effects of fatigue from high workloads can be cumulative and that performance will become affected over time. This can happen in a relatively short time; Haslam (1985) reported a loss of cognitive performance within 24 hours. In contrast, physical performance takes longer to degrade as fatigue sets in. As already mentioned, there is the confounding problem of tiredness occurring through loss of sleep, so the person is suffering sleep loss rather than general body fatigue. When individuals are fatigued as a result of sleep deprivation, tasks requiring a high level of vigilance seem to be the first to suffer (Horne *et al.*, 1983). This is especially true of visual tasks. When we become tired and sleepy, increases occur in the number of eye blinks and closures (including 'microsleeps', where we nod-off briefly). Tasks that do not have enough stimulation to maintain a high level of awareness are particularly vulnerable, e.g. night driving.

The nature of some vigilance tasks might result in the individual having a low-workload, i.e. 'underload' (Melamed *et al.*, 1995). Take, for example, civil aircraft flight deck crew. On a long haul flight, they will be subject to long periods when they essentially do little more than monitor displays and the current flight situation. However, if a malfunction occurs, the crew will be subject to a cacophony of alerts and warnings and will move suddenly from a low-workload (underload) situation to high workload. Although the level of workload has changed significantly, and it could be envisaged that this change (as well as the low-workload situation) is tiring, research has indicated that maintaining high vigilance in a low-workload situation is equally fatiguing (Hancock and Warm, 1989).

In summary, the nature of the task is a major factor in determining the level of workload. Vigilance tasks can cover the range of workloads from underload, when the operator is monitoring a safe situation, through to high workload, when careful decision making is required. The interaction between fatigue and vigilance is an interesting one. When tired, we find it more difficult to maintain good vigilance levels, especially with low-workload tasks. However, low-vigilance tasks without a lot of interesting material or motor activity may result in operator tiredness and be just as fatiguing as the high-workload situation. The above discussion has focused on the individual; a final point concerns team performance. It is well established that in high-cognitive-workload situations, teams do not perform well: they suffer from problems of communication and degradation in job performance (Urban *et al.*, 1996; Xiao *et al.*, 1996).

Fitness to work

Although work can be designed and organised to fit the worker, there is a need to ensure that individuals have a certain number of physical and cognitive skills in order to demonstrate their fitness to work. When a person is working under stress, it is known that various physiological parameters will change, e.g. heart rate will increase, as will levels of certain hormones in the blood. There is a need, therefore, to ensure that workers are physiologically fit and able to cope with the demands of the job. This includes all individuals covering a range of abilities and individual characteristics, as there may be some jobs that are eminently suitable for special groups such as older workers or disabled people. A further consideration is the worker's attitude to work. For example, a person may be physically able to carry out a job that is well within their cognitive capabilities but they may lack the motivation or the incentive to do it. At a superficial level, this person is fit to work but the lack of motivation may seriously disrupt, even inhibit, their ability to complete the job.

Having said that we do have a number of objective ways of measuring physiological work demands such as work capacity, so the amount of physical effort in terms of energy expenditure can be quantified. This allows some gauge of the amount of physical effort needed and, hence, how fit the person needs to be to do certain jobs. These physiological measurements have usually been applied to workers who have a high physical workload, e.g. Kukkonen-Harjula and Rauramaa's (1984) study of lumberjacks. A more recent study is that of Rayson *et al.* (2000) who have carried out a validation of the British Army's new Physical Selection Standards for Recruits (PSS(R)). The PSS(R) comprises measures of body mass, body fat and fat-free mass, static lift strength, back extension strength, dynamic lift strength, pull-ups, static arm endurance and a fitness test. Scores on these successfully predicted the outcomes of four military tasks (a single lift, carry, repetitive lift and loaded march) in 75 per cent of recruits. Thus, the PSS(R) tests were deemed to be a valid predictor of job performance.

There are a number of ways of assessing cognitive skills and knowledge, e.g. a job may require a graduate with a professional qualification gained through having a minimum amount of experience. However, we do not have similar means of reliably assessing (or predicting) attitudes and feelings, so even if a person appears keen and committed when they first carry out the job, they may soon become bored and uninterested, and their performance may suffer accordingly. Likewise, the development of fatigue may be more prevalent in some individuals, i.e. people who have a low level of motivation and interest in the job. Paradoxically, individuals presenting obvious physical or cognitive disabilities may appear not to be 'fit to work' but, when given the opportunity, they may prove to be some of the most conscientious and dedicated workers. In this context, fitness needs to be differentiated from health (Reilly, 1991). A person is healthy when they demonstrate no evidence of disease; ironically, some of the fittest athletes can actually be unhealthy in that they subject themselves to a tough training regime that results in injuries, as well as often being susceptible to colds and viruses. This is particularly important when considering job prospects for specific groups such as older adults or disabled users.

The UK has been referred to as having a 'greying society'. By 2031, it is predicted that one in four people will be of retirement age; this is compared to a ratio of one in six in the 1970s. This has important implications, especially for the workplace. Not only will people want to work for longer because they are healthier and living longer but, economically, the country will need these older individuals to work. Therefore, it can be seen that the assessment of both the person and the job is not straightforward when considering fitness to work issues. In Human Factors terms, there is a need to ensure that the job can be safely and efficiently carried out by the largest number of workers (Bridger, 1995). If it is not possible to accommodate some of the special groups of workers, e.g. older adults or disabled people, then it is important that the minimum level of fitness required for the job is specified.

Organisations and worker performance

Organisations exist in order to make products, be these goods or services, and it is the provision of these that is the formal goal of the workers. In essence, organisations need high productivity and low costs to improve/ ensure their chances of survival. Many studies of organisations have considered their designs in relation to work performance. Performance-shaping factors considered in this chapter have included fatigue, vigilance and workload. It should be noted that much of the work on the design of organisations in relation to performance has been descriptive rather than evaluative research. The relationships between structural, functional and technological factors and performance are complex and, increasingly, this is being recognised in the literature. Organisations are dynamic entities with varying internal, external and environmental demands and influences. Berry and Houston (1993: 512) summed this up in the following statement: 'Increasingly, we are treating the organization as an open system composed of a network of social and technical entities that are intricately woven into the surrounding environment'.

Organisations have a number of statutory obligations in respect of the health and safety of their workers and, if they are to retain an efficient workforce, have also to attend to their welfare. It is important to ensure that the 'fitness' levels of the workers match the demands of the job on both an individual level, in terms of worker wellbeing, and on an organisational level, i.e. with regard to productivity. Indeed, this is what organisations should continually struggle to do – optimise the fit between the worker and workplace.

In terms of solutions, there are three main generic approaches: selection, training and design (Huey and Wickens, 1993). In the first instance, selection and recruitment procedures should result in only the fit applicants being chosen. However, the message from the preceding section is for selectors to look very carefully at candidates, in order to differentiate between fitness and health, and at more subjective aspects such as motivation and willingness to work. Once applicants are in post, the provision of training and associated opportunities is the main route for ensuring the fitness to work of employees. In the aircraft industry, there is an expression that it is easier to 'fix the human than bend the metal', i.e. in the aftermath of an accident, it is easier to retrain the worker than redesign the workplace. This is primarily due to the expense of retrofitting aircraft and the fact that the majority of civil aircraft accidents are thought to be due to human error. In addition to training opportunities and motivational change programmes, organisations can also offer a number of support measures for employees, e.g. health screening, medical check-ups, sports centres.

Careful consideration of the design and scheduling of work will contribute to the effectiveness of the person–organisation fit. Job design that encompasses job enlargement, enrichment and rotation focuses on changing the components of the job, while scheduling focuses on the optimum arrangement of work–rest periods and the need to avoid excessive workloads, both physical and mental. In essence, there is a need to ensure the demands of the job are within, the capabilities and limitations of the workers. Errors arising from fatigue, vigilance and workload demands need particular consideration when designing jobs. However, the organisational responsibilities discussed so far have focused on the individual worker and the job. It is also necessary for organisations to take a longer view in terms of their development, i.e. how organisations need to grow and change in order to become more effective. The topic of organisational development is a considerable one and its evolution has been charted by Mirvis (1990). It encompasses the development of strategies, structures and processes at an organisational level in order to improve overall effectiveness (Huse and Cummings, 1985).

Key points

- Early organisational theories included the classical and neoclassical schools.
- One of the popular organisational theories has been general systems theory, which views organisations as living organisms that need to develop and adapt to survive.
- More recent theories include technical systems theory, sociotechnical theory and culture theory.
- Job redesign and motivational change programmes may be warranted when there is a need to enhance the job to increase worker performance and productivity.
- Job enrichment and job enlargement are two ways in which jobs can be redesigned to make jobs better for the workers.
- The traditional '9 to 5, Monday to Friday' work model is the normative model in the developed world.
- Shift work has physiological and social implications for workers; some patterns of shift work are easier to adjust to than others and these should be adopted whenever possible.
- Despite the subjective nature of fatigue, it should always be taken seriously in the workplace because of the implications for safety.
- Maintaining vigilance is not easy for humans and jobs that have a vigilance component need to comprise short work periods interspersed with rest breaks.
- Workload has both physical and psychological aspects and can be measured using objective and subjective methods.
- Fitness to work encompasses a number of physical, cognitive and attitudinal aspects and needs to be differentiated from health.

6   Occupational health

I suppose that even the most pleasurable of occupations, that of batting baseballs through the windows of the RCA Building, would pall a little as the days ran on.

James Grover Thomas, 1945, *The Thurber Carnival*, 'Memoirs of a Drudge'

One of these was called Procrustes or the stretcher. He had an iron bedstead on which he used to tie all travellers who fell into his hands. If they were shorter than the bed he stretched their limbs to make them fit; if they were longer than the bed he lopped off a portion.

Thomas Bullfinch, 1796–1867, *The Age of Fable*

The work environment can present a number of dangers, or hazards, to workers – a hazard being defined as 'the potential to cause harm' (Pheasant, 1997: 117). In extreme situations, these hazards could seriously affect the health of the workers and, in some circumstances, they might even be life threatening. An important goal of Human Factors psychology is to protect the worker by attempting to design work environments that remove health hazards and thus prevent accidents and incidents in the workplace. In this context, British psychologists work closely with the Health and Safety Executive.

To understand hazards in the workplace, it is important to consider their sources. Some of these dangers will emanate from the workers themselves, e.g. tendencies for individuals to engage in risky or dangerous behaviour perhaps as the result of fatigue and/or stress. In Chapter 5, stress was mentioned on a number of occasions and, indeed, job stress is a primary area of concern. Smither (1994: 472) gave the example quoted by the American National Defense Council that 'as many as 10,000 Japanese work themselves to death every year'. Occupational stress is therefore an important aspect when considering health and safety issues in the workplace. Further, some hazards will stem from errors in human–machine system design while others will be caused by conditions of the work environment that may harm the workers' health and create work-related disorders, even diseases. For example, throughout the world many thousands of workers are exposed to silica dust and asbestos in their industrial environments, and hundreds of thousands to cotton dust in textile mills (Bechtel, 1997). In the developed world, isocynate exposure is a problem with the SWORD (Surveillance of Work-related and Occupational Respiratory Disease) scheme recording 138 cases of occupational asthma per year due to iso-cynates (Waterman, 1999). Other contemporary issues relate to the intro-duction of computer technologies and include work-related repetitive strain injuries, radiation effects, facial and visual problems arising from screen-based work, postural problems, e.g. back pain, sick building syndrome and pollutants.

Hazards in the workplace

Many tasks in the workplace, especially those that are machine-paced such as on industrial production lines, can result in excessive use of a body part. Repeated use of any part of the body can eventually lead to an overuse disorder, e.g. the 'white finger' injuries described in Chapter 4. This type of injury can be caused by the cumulative effect of repeated actions that on their own would be of no consequence or harm. The widespread intro-duction and use of computer technologies has drawn attention to overuse disorders and the focus here is on this hazard in the workplace. The number of workers using computers for their daily activities continues to grow from 10 per cent in 1980 to over 50 per cent of the working population less than 20 years later (Anshel, 1998). A recent job advertisement for professional ergonomists mentioned that 50,000 people in Washington state alone suffered from work-related musculoskeletal disorders (source: e-mail query to ergonomics mailbase, 3 July 2000). Given the number of people working with new technologies in the developed world population, it is reasonable to conclude that the effects of computers are considerable primarily because they affect large numbers of people. Further, Violante and Kilbom (2000) stated that work-related musculoskeletal disorders are the leading cause of worker impairment, disability, compensation costs and loss of productivity.

There are several terms to describe overuse disorder: for example, occu-pational overuse syndrome, musculoskeletal disorder, work-related dis-order, repetitive stress or strain or motion injury, rheumatic disease or cumulative trauma disorder (Putz-Anderson, 1988). Probably one of the better-known terms is 'repetitive strain injury' (RSI), which has attracted much media interest. In the US, the equivalent term is 'cumulative trauma disorder', while the Japanese and Scandinavians prefer 'occupational cervicobrachial disorders'. Other terms used include 'neck and limb dis-örders' (Kuorinka and Viikari-Juntura, 1982) and 'neck and upper limb disorders' (Wallace and Buckle, 1987). In the UK, the favoured term is probably 'work-related upper limb disorders', which is abbreviated to WRULDs (Health and Safety Executive, 1990). Concerns about RSI and its effects on health have arisen as greater numbers of the population use computers. Indeed many of the current occupational health concerns are associated with the use of computer technology.

The introduction of computers to the workplace has been relatively recent, given that the first PC was only launched in 1978 (see Chapter 1): the growth in the number and use of computers has been phenomenal since then. This has had several implications for users, the tasks being carried out and the overall application. First, the profile of the user group has changed from being a small group of highly trained experts to a wide range of individuals from the general population who are attempting to use the technology with no prior training. Further, user support is patchy, with hard-copy manuals often not available (e.g. in academia there is often only one set of manuals for every ten computers purchased) and on-line help systems that are frequently inadequate, poorly designed and a source of frustration for the user (Reeves *et al.*, 1996). The outcome is that far greater numbers of people are using computers and, of this population, only a small fraction will have any training. Second, computers provide access to a greater number of facilities in the workplace and the days of having a PC only for word processing activities are long gone. The computer now allows access to the Internet, with its enormous wealth of information, communications anywhere in the world via electronic mail and the capability for sophisticated calculations and analyses that 25 years ago would have involved visiting a mainframe computer and leaving punch cards to be batch-processed overnight. Although it is a bonus to have this amazing capability only a few key presses away, it does mean that the user does not physically have to move from the seat of their chair. Maintaining this fixed posture is a problem for *Homo sapiens*, who is designed to move and not to stand or sit still (Grieco, 1986). Hence, in physiological and mechanical terms, the idea that a constrained posture should be maintained for periods of time is unacceptable. Eason (1984) suggested that the jobs demanding these highly constrained postures may be the cause of the increase in health hazards associated with computer use. Consequently, it is suggested that jobs that result in the user being highly constrained need to be designed to have flexibility built into the workspace, e.g. adjustable furniture. Further, by law, frequent rest breaks or natural breaks providing alternative tasks should also be scheduled that allow the user to move away from the site of the computer. It is also true that applications, like tasks, have become broader. Take, for example, the newspaper industry. Up until the late 1970s, newspapers were produced according to the 'hot metal' approach, whereby metal alphanumerics were punched out from heavy, grease-laden machines to be arranged in wooden trays in the format in which the newsprint would eventually appear. This all took place in an industrial environment that quickly changed to that of an office, with carpets and rubberplants, when newspapers began to be typeset on the computer screen. The contrast between the two environments is significant and, although there were many benefits from the use of computers in this application, the workforce viewed the introduction of new technology negatively. They were forced to move from working in a familiar, industrial-type environment to that of an office. Further, the extra capability afforded by the computers in being able to allow the whole of the newspaper to be set on the screen resulted in the workers having to undergo extra training in, for example, touchtyping. Consequently, there was much discontent and stress associated with the introduction of the new technology. A further 'fear' of computer technology emanates from its monitoring capabilities; some workers are on piece-rate payments and paid according to number of keystrokes made. Knowing that the time spent on-task can be calculated (as well as details relating to the user performance) can be a further source of stress.

Use of computer technology

Repetitive strain injury

RSI is not new: Tichauer (1973) referred to the symptoms in office clerks described by Bernadino Ramazzini nearly 300 years earlier. Ramazzini (1713) thought the problems presented by the workers were caused by repeated movements of the hands, a fixed body posture and the mental stress of the job. Interestingly, Ramazzini's thoughts could equally apply if stated today. In essence, RSI is a condition brought about by doing the same activity over and over again, and it can occur in any repetitive task masquerading under titles such as tennis elbow, housemaid's knee, writer's cramp, gamekeeper's thumb and trigger finger. The term RSI covers a portmanteau of conditions (e.g. tenosynovitis) and complaints (e.g. aches and pains in the hands and then the arms, sometimes accompanied by burning sensations). RSI is thought to occur in the soft, connective tissues, especially the tendons and their sheaths, and it used to be common to use the term for specific identifiable injuries (such as tenosynovitis) rather than for the more general presentation of symptoms that has become recognised more recently as RSI (Keisler and Finholt, 1988; Mullaly and Grigg, 1988). Common sites for RSI are in the hand–wrist area of the forearm (the 'carpal tunnel') and at the base of the neck or back. More recently, some researchers have suggested that RSI might be peripheral nerve pain (Quinter and Elvey, 1993). The nervous system runs throughout the body and contains numerous connections and interconnections. Therefore, activity at one point will influence and interfere with movement at another. One view put forward is that damaged nerves in one part of the system can contribute to chronic pain of the sort found in sufferers of RSI. Therefore, damage to the back could manifest itself in wrist and forearm discomfort. In the case of the hand and wrist, the grip might become affected and the individual might have no strength and find it difficult to hold cups or similar objects.

RSI has attracted a lot of media interest (Pearce (1995) reviewed 371 press cuttings on WRULDs) and accompanying controversy about its clinical definition and symptoms, and whether such a debilitating disease can result from computer use (Arksey, 1998). The origins of the RSI phenomenon lie in Australia (Hocking, 1987). A nationwide journalists' dispute in 1980 over the introduction of computer technology has (retrospectively) been suggested to have influenced the significant level of publicity this subject received in the Australian popular press. RSI was seen as a three- (or five-) stage disease, beginning with a pain or discomfort in the arm and ending in a crippling injury. For example, Kroemer *et al.* (1994) described a continuum of symptoms resulting from repetitive work from normal fatigue experienced at the end of a day's work through intermittent discomfort, persistent pain, the need for medical intervention and, finally, disability. However, the concept of RSI was finally challenged in the Australian law courts in 1986 – the jury decided that the plaintiff was not injured as claimed.

Despite the growing realisation in Australia that RSI was an unscientific and unhelpful concept, the phenomenon has been imported to the rest of the world. There is evidence that medical professions in other countries have used the term RSI when diagnosing upper limb disorders among keyboard operators. In the UK, the rising interest in RSI was demonstrated by the increase in the number of legal cases as reported by the Banking, Insurance and Finance Union. Pearce (1998) argued that this may be due to an increase in reporting rather than an increase in the number of incidences. Prior to the publicity given to the Australian RSI phenomenon the majority of ergonomists and professionals involved in occupational health and safety would have considered the risk of a permanent, musculoskeletal injury arising from the use of a computer keyboard as far-fetched. Moreover, diagnosis of RSI is frequently inaccurate because sufferers often rely on subjective reports to describe many of the conditions associated with RSI. Accurate diagnosis is important because of the need to establish that the condition arose as a result of the work being carried out. It is now thought that working on computers may simply unmask previously latent conditions as many musculoskeletal problems have been shown to be transient and self-limiting (Pearce, 1986).

The impact on the parts of the body from repeated movements is well-documented, what is not recognised is the connection of RSI to occupational work patterns (Pheasant, 1992). Brian Pearce, a leading expert in this field, has described RSI as a facile acronym that describes a phenomenon rather than a condition. The Health and Safety Executive supported this view in their publication on WRULDs (Health and Safety Executive, 1990) with a footnote that explained that the term RSI is medically imprecise and not accurate. It is generally recommended that the term 'work-related upper limb disorders' be used when referring to pain or discomfort experienced by keyboard operators. The solution to the problem seems to be to stop using parts of the upper body as soon as they begin hurting, i.e.

to listen to the signs that the body is sending (Veijalainen, 2000). This obviously applies to all activities, not just ones related to technology. In 'normal', healthy people, symptoms and injuries should simply not occur; this may account for the other explanations, such as fatigue, malingering and mass hysteria, that have been proffered for the symptoms (Bammer and Martin, 1988; Caple and Betts, 1991; Pickering, 1987).

Case study: use of non-keyboard input devices – health risks from mice and other non-keyboard input devices (from Hastings et al., 2000)

Non-keyboard input devices (NKIDs) include mice, trackballs, joysticks and touchscreens, and there has been increasing concern since the 1980s that these have health implications for users (Abernethy and Hodes, 1987). To begin to assess the extent of the problem, a survey of IT and Health and Safety managers is currently being conducted. For the initial part of the survey, 128 managers from 102 organisations responded. It was found that the mouse was the most frequently used NKID, with 95 per cent of organisations reporting its use in conjunction with word-processing activities. A total of 38 per cent reported mouse-associated problems including 'pain and discomfort in the fingers, hands and wrists after prolonged use' (Hastings *et al.*, 2000: 314). Skin infections were given as a problem relating to the use of joysticks and touchscreens.

The questionnaire survey was followed up with twenty-five user observations, diaries and interviews from a sample of five organisations. Observational data was collected on posture and workstation set-up with video recordings being made onsite. This is to be used primarily to assess the amount of time spent using NKIDs. In terms of mouse use, 36 per cent of interviewees reported pain and discomfort that they had not had before using this input device; this included 'weakness in the wrists and stiffness and discomfort in the hands and wrist after using the device for long periods of time' (Hastings *et al.*, 2000: 315). The authors intend to follow-up these findings with some laboratory-based experimental work.

Radiation effects

Radiation occurs naturally from the earth's magnetosphere, solar flares and cosmic activity, but there are also man-made sources, e.g. computers generate a considerable amount of radiated energy. This is in the form of the visible light that is needed to produce the characters on the screen. Like all radiation, this is undetectable by the human operator but it does mean the computer user is exposed to a continuous source of radiation. This exposure has raised a number of concerns. In the past, these have included consideration of the effects of the radiation given off from computers relating to the user, their fertility and the unborn fetus.

When considering the effects of radiation from computers, VDUs give off much less radiation than natural environmental sources and levels are well below those considered harmful by the National Radiological Protection Board. In fact, more X-ray radiation would be received from a person sitting at a comparable distance, because the human body is slightly radioactive. Cox (1984) carried out a comprehensive survey for the British Health and Safety Executive that involved measuring different types of radiation, e.g. X-ray, ultraviolet A, visible and infrared, microwave/radio frequency, from over 200 different types of VDU. He found that the measured radiation emissions were much less than the limits for continuous occupational exposure given in many national and international standards, and this was in a position close to the VDU with all brilliance and contrast controls set at their maximum. Cox concluded that the radiation emitted from a VDU does not pose a hazard to computer users either in the long or short term.

Concerns relating to the use of VDUs by pregnant women were raised initially in Canada, when the *Toronto Star* suspected that a 'higher number than average' of their female VDU operators were giving birth to children with abnormalities. However, closer analysis of the numbers involved indicated that the four cases fell within those expected on the basis of statistical chance (Pearce, 1984). A study reported in the *Guardian* described a study carried out by Ros Bramwell and Marilyn Davidson at the University of Manchester Institute of Science and Technology, which concluded that pregnant women did not appear to suffer adverse effects from using VDUs (Bowcott, 1990). Lewis *et al.* (1982) and Nielsen *et al.* (1989) found no evidence supporting the increased occurrence of spontaneous abortion in VDU users. Likewise, McDonald *et al.* (1988) could not provide any evidence of serious malformation in the offspring of VDU users, while Nurminen and Kurppa (1988) similarly found no support for low birth weight or fetal death around delivery. However, Tribukait *et al.* (1986) found that pregnant mice, when exposed to radiation emitted by a VDU, produced an increased number of malformed fetuses. As mouse and human physiology are similar, it was thought that this finding might provide some evidence relating to the effects of VDU radiation on humans. However, the general conclusion reached is that there is no evidence to suggest that either the user or the unborn child is at risk from full-time working at a VDU. To quote Smith (1987: 245) 'most experts agree that the biological effects of VDU radiation are inconsequential to health'. Marriott and Stuchly (1986) supported this by concluding that the shielding of VDTs was not justified. In conclusion, there is no supporting evidence that radiation from a computer is a threat to physical health (Purdham, 1980).

However, there may be psychological problems arising from the perceived threat of radiation. If a female employee is concerned, she should express her fears to her employer because the anxiety itself may cause problems, especially if she has had previous miscarriages and/or difficult pregnancies. Hence, difficulties may arise from the way in which the VDU is used rather than from the VDU itself. This was a view expressed by Mackay (1987), who concluded that there was unlikely to be any threat from irradiation on the alleged reproductive hazards of VDUs.

Facial rashes

Outbreaks of facial rashes have been reported by a very small number of VDU operators, who have complained of itching skin or redness of the face and/or neck (facial erythema) when working at a VDU (Rycroft and Calnan, 1984). For example, during the winter of 1979, there were rumours of Norwegian operators becoming sunburnt at work (Tjønn, 1984). The question is whether these facial conditions were caused by working at a VDU. There were a number of pertinent facts surrounding the cases in Norway. For example:

- The rashes developed after less than 2 hours of work at the VDU and usually began with a feeling of itching followed by the appearance of redness.
- In most cases, the rashes disappeared within a few hours of leaving work and only a few individuals needed more than 18 hours to recover.
- All reported cases took place during the winter months.
- The working environments were dry, with relative humidities around or well below 40 per cent.
- All rooms had synthetic carpets with a substantial amount of static electricity.

Various experiments were conducted to try to reduce skin reactions in these cases. For example, glass shields were placed in front of the VDU, floor coverings were replaced with antistatic carpets and aquaria with electrolyte liquids were connected to the surface of the screen in order to ground any static electricity. All these were applied with some success. In addition, provocation tests were carried out to try to simulate the workplace environment. However, no rashes appeared with the workers when taking part in the provocation tests, whereas a positive result was attained in the actual workplace, i.e. the rashes appeared. Attempts were made to explain the skin problems in terms of the low-frequency magnetic field emanating from the VDU, but this link has not been substantiated (Swanbeck and Bleeker, 1989). It was concluded that the facial rash was occupational contact dermatitis caused by airborne dust particles and exacerbated by the build-up of static electricity around the VDU and the dry atmosphere of the workplace. Further, it was also thought that the skin complaints probably arose in people who had sensitive skins and represented only a small percentage of the population. This is probably supported by the tiny numbers involved: approximately forty in Norway and four cases in London. In conclusion, it is now generally accepted that there is no link between VDUs and the development of facial rashes (Lidén and Wahlberg, 1985). When rashes do appear in computer users, it seems that features of the environment need to be addressed, i.e. the amount of synthetic material/covering and the relative humidity (Berg, 1989).

Visual problems

One of the concerns associated with the growth of VDU usage has been eyestrain. A study carried out by NIOSH in 1994 (cited in Anshel, 1998) indicated that 88 per cent of the 66 million people who worked on computers for more than 3 hours a day complained of eyestrain, i.e. nearly 60 million individuals. Eyestrain is a term used to describe a wide range of symptoms. People might talk about eye discomfort, visual fatigue or eyestrain (asthenopia) all described as 'subjective visual symptoms or distress resulting from the use of one's eyes' (National Research Council Committee on Vision, 1983: 153). They might describe symptoms of tired eyes, blurred vision, slow refocusing, double vision, colour distortion, irritation, watery eyes, soreness and sensitivity to light (photophobia), which might be accompanied by headaches. Hence, when considering visual problems associated with the use of new technologies, there is a wide range of symptoms and a problem of objective definition. These have now been grouped under one term to become collectively known as Computer Vision Syndrome (Sheedy, 1992). We also know that eye complaints arise from many types of working conditions, the question is whether the incidence of eyestrain is higher amongst VDU users because they have been using computers.

When investigating eyestrain and related eye problems, a difficulty arises because of the prevalence of eye disorders in the populations of the developed world. Studies have suggested that eyestrain affects about one-third of the working population and a large number of people have non-corrected eye defects, e.g. one survey showed that more than 50 per cent of all West Germans had eye defects needing correction. This can make analysis of the situation difficult because eyestrain is a common occurrence and checking the vision of any group of individuals will result in some needing corrective treatment, regardless of whether they are VDU users. A further problem arises where impairments in visual ability already exist as some individuals may experience heightened awareness of any visual difficulties that they may attribute to VDU use.

Several researchers have concluded that using a VDU makes no greater demands on the visual system than many other activities encountered in a work situation (Muter *et al.*, 1982; Nordqvist *et al.*, 1986). However, many studies indicate that VDU users report more eye-related problems than non-VDU operators (Collins *et al.*, 1991; Dain *et al.*, 1988). One explanation put forward by Udo *et al.* (1991) is that working with VDUs places a considerable strain on the visual system and that individuals could have 'hidden' vision disorders that do not cause symptoms when working on less demanding, visual tasks. In a relaxed position, when we look ahead but do not focus on a particular object, the resting position of binocular vergence is about 1 metre from the pupils (Jaschinski-Krusza, 1991). If the eyes are continually forced to concentrate on a target that is not at the person's natural resting position, this might become effortful. For example, Tsubota and Nakamori (1993) found that the blink rate decreases to about one-third during VDU use and this can lead to dry and irritated eyes. Research has indicated that symptoms arising from eyestrain resulting from VDU use are reversible, although they may persist for more than a few hours. For example, one study found that for thirty workers a work period between 2 and 4 hours on a VDU induced a temporary myopia (Watten and Lie, 1992). Luberto *et al.* (1989) also found that 20 per cent of VDU workers had a nearsighted tendency towards the end of their work shift. Long-term effects are more difficult to monitor but, given the transitory nature of short-term effects, this looks promising in terms of VDU operation having any more permanent effects upon eyes or eyesight. In conclusion, visual problems and computer use have attracted a lot of interest. This is primarily due to the fact that visual symptoms are thought to occur in 75–90 per cent of VDU workers (Anshel, 1998). However, there is little evidence to suggest that VDUs can damage the eyes or exacerbate existing eye defects. However, it is recommended that special attention should be given to individuals who wear spectacles. Workers who wear glasses prescribed for reading at a closer distance may need an alternative pair for VDU work. If their usual glasses have bifocal or multifocal lenses, they may have to adopt an uncomfortable posture at the computer workstation.

A further issue has been the question of whether VDU use increases the risk of cataract formation. In the early 1980s, radiant energy cataracts were observed in a number of VDU operators (Zaret, 1984). Cataracts are a disease of the lens of the eyes indicated by opacities in the epithelial structure. They are thought to be a normal part of the ageing process as they are common in older people – 40–50 per cent of 50- to 60-year-olds show some opacity of the lens. Estimates of the normal incidence of cataracts in younger people in the 30- to 50-year age group is also as high as 20–30 per cent (Grandjean, 1984). However, radiant energy cataracts are unusual in young people and the question arose of whether they had been exposed to radiant energy in the workplace and, if so, had this arisen from using VDUs. One of the difficulties in addressing this question is that there are many different types of cataract and, while small opacities might not be perceived by individuals, medium and large opacities can produce visual impairments. Further, there is a congenital tendency for some individuals to develop cataracts, and this can happen over a considerable period of time. There were also a number of aspects relating to the American operators that made it difficult to draw meaningful conclusions about the effects of using VDUs. For example, only a small number – ten individuals – were affected and there is a lack of ophthalmologists trained in defining and categorising different cataracts, particularly the radiant energy type. In conclusion, there is probably insufficient evidence to suggest that there is a link between VDU use and the formation of cataracts in the eyes. This view is reinforced when considering the large number of young computer users who have not developed cataracts.

Postural discomfort

The maintenance of fixed and forced postures whilst working on a VDU and focusing on the screen for long periods of time can lead to postural discomfort. This has become a major concern for office workers (Liao and Drury, 2000; Sauter *et al.*, 1991). Stammerjohn *et al.* (1981) stated that muscle strain, back and neck aches are common complaints of VDU users. The screen itself may be adding to the situation, with reflections and glare from windows and lighting, greasy fingerprints resulting in blurred images, flicker and high contrast and brightness levels. The workplace may be poorly designed and there may be specific problems relating to the wearing of spectacles by the user. In terms of solutions, there are various ways in which the workstation can be ergonomically arranged, as discussed in Chapter 4. With regard to the user, it is generally recommended that individuals should be guided by their bodies – fatigue symptoms should be temporary and are to some extent, normal. If it hurts, stop using it. Guidelines exist, for example:

- Take a 10-minute break every hour, with a further longer rest break after 2 hours.
- Frequent short breaks are better than fewer longer ones.
- Locus of control is important and, if possible, should remain with the user, so the individual decides when to take a break, as some people like to achieve task closure.
- When taking breaks, it is preferable to move off-screen, i.e. don't take lunch at the computer.

Control is an important issue. Users like to feel in control and many studies, e.g. Sauter *et al.* (1983), have reported that VDU users feel that they have less control over their work than workers doing similar non-computerised work. A further problem can be boredom (Smith *et al.*, 1980). This, coupled with frequent system breakdowns, long delays in computer response times and unanticipated interruptions can lead to stressful situations (Johansson and Aronsson, 1984).

Sick building syndrome

There have been reports of workers occupying a new building and then suffering from increases in various symptoms of illness, e.g. eye and throat irritations, headaches, dizziness, nausea and skin rashes (Rostron, 1997). These can lead to a general reduction in motivation and work performance, and in absenteeism. Often, the only conclusion that can be reached is that there is a problem with the design of the building itself, and this has become known as 'sick building syndrome'. It has been defined as 'a syndrome of non-specific malaise the onset of which is associated with occupancy of certain modern buildings' (WHO, 1983). It is a fairly recent phenomenon that recognises that working in certain buildings can result in physical illness, as well as affecting the mental health and feelings of wellbeing of their occupants. For example, Baird *et al.* (1994) carried out a study of the University of Stockholm library. They found that 54 per cent of staff using the building reported visual and upper respiratory tract symptoms.

There is little agreement about the primary causes of sick building syndrome (Ryan and Morrow, 1992). Some experts attribute the syndrome to psychological factors (Bauer *et al.*, 1992), while others focus on the physical aspects. For example, one of the causes of sick building syndrome is thought to be poor air quality, which could arise as a result of a closed air recirculation system for climate control (Norback *et al.*, 1990; Skov *et al.*, 1990). Low humidity contributes to a build-up of static electricity; this is exacerbated in the region of the VDU, which attracts dust particles. These contribute specifically to the dry-eye symptoms described in the section above and more generally to feelings of ill-health amongst the workers. Another view put forward is that the presence of various hazardous chemicals used in the manufacturing of soft-furnishings that creates the symptoms described above. A third approach has been to explain sick building syndrome in terms of interactions between job-related factors and personal characteristics (Skov *et al.*, 1989). Skov *et al.* carried-out a questionnaire survey on work-related mucosal irritation, work-related general symptoms, e.g. work functions, job satisfaction, etc., and the building factor, i.e. the indoor climate. Over 3,500 employees participated in the survey and it was found that 'the building factor was strongly associated with the prevalence of work-related mucosal irritation and work-related general symptoms, and the results supported the concept of using the term "sick building syndrome"' (Skov *et al.*, 1989: 294).

Pollutants

In the developed world, people spend most of their time indoors where they can be exposed to a number of chemical hazards. There are estimated to be around 63,000 chemical substances in the world and, of these, about 1,000 are known carcinogens (Bechtel, 1997). One such hazard is radon – a trace element widely found in the ground and suspected of causing cancer. Radon has been shown to be the most prominent pollutant in the indoor environment, with one in five houses in the US having levels above the recommended safe limit (Kerr, 1988). Another substance also found in building materials that has attracted a lot of media attention is asbestos. In the post-war years, buildings were lined with asbestos, which became a serious problem upon removal. Asbestos has been shown to cause meso-thelioma, a type of lung cancer. Lead piping is also a pollutant because the lead dissolves into the drinking water. Although lead pipes carrying water have been banned since the 1980s, more recent concerns have revolved around the lead solder used on pipes and which has been found to seep into the water supply. Radon is also known to pollute the water supplies, with an estimated 40 per cent of public drinking water contaminated by radon (Cothern and Smith, 1987). One of the difficulties of assessing the hazardous effects of pollutants is that it often takes a considerable time to demonstrate any harm.

Stress

Defining occupational stress

The word 'stress' has a number of specific meanings for various groups of people, e.g. a mechanical engineer would view the word differently from a linguist or a psychotherapist. Despite these conflicts, it is probably worth considering the definition of stress being used here within the context of occupational/organisational psychology. Stress would generally be recognised as a physiological or psychological response to demands made on an individual. But because the concept of stress is not concrete, stress is perceived by many individuals as being ill-defined and a particularly problematic topic to study. As an example, Salas *et al.* (1996) cited their experience of being in a meeting on stress and military performance where some participants viewed stress positively, some negatively and some preferred not to discuss it at all! However, the very fact that a meeting was being held on the topic of stress could be construed as evidence that stress exists and is increasing in the workplace.

It is generally recognised that there are a number of occupations that comprise a high-stress environment and demand that the worker performs well because of the risk to human life and property, e.g. the aviation industry, the military, police work, firefighting, diving and medical emergencies. In these occupations, the need to make critical decisions under high stress, e.g. no time and a safety-critical situation, often leads to error. Salas *et al.* (1996) gave the example of American civil airlines striving for a 20-minute turnaround on the ground and the amount of stress that this was putting on operators, as well as increasing the opportunities for human error. The focus here will be on stress in the workplace, i.e. effects on the performance, physical and psychological health of the individual, organisational effects of stress and theories of appraisal and coping.

Physical, psychological and behavioural changes

Hans Selye (1936) is generally recognised as being one of the first people to identify the pattern of physical changes that occur when the body experiences a stressful situation. He defined stress as a non-specific or generalised bodily response (Selye, 1976) and identified distress as a reaction to negative events and eustress (from the word 'euphoria') as a response to positive events. Selye developed the General Adaptation syndrome to describe the process of stress. This comprised three stages: the initial alarm state (where the body prepares for 'fight or flight'), the resistance stage (where the body returns to normal) and, finally, an exhaustion phase (where bodily processes begin to break down). It is now well known that a number of short-term physiological changes occur as a result of stressors, e.g. increased heart rate and blood pressure, laboured breathing and increased respiration, trembling and the release of various hormones. Long-term exposure to stressors is thought to result in conditions such as hypertension, coronary heart disease and stomach ulcers. Evidence for long-term effects comes from studies of the most stressful jobs in the developed world. For example, Evans and Carrere (1991) concluded that driving conditions for bus drivers led to them having higher rates of cardiovascular disease, hypertension, gastrointestinal disorders and absenteeism than other occupations.

Although it is generally agreed that stress can result in a variety of physical illnesses, these can have either an organic or psychosomatic basis. An example of an organic illness would be upper respiratory tract problems that arise after a period of stress. It is thought that prolonged sympathetic nervous system activity tends to suppress the immune system so that, when the stressors cease, the person is not strong enough to fight off flu and similar viruses. In addition to the physical effects, a number of psychosomatic disorders arise when we are subject to stressors (Coleman *et al.*, 1980). Short-term psychological reactions might include tension headaches, problems in sleeping, anxiety and fear (Smither, 1994). These may lead to skin disorders (e.g. eczema, hives), respiratory problems (e.g. bronchial asthma, hyperventilation syndrome), cardiovascular problems (e.g. hypertension) and gastrointestinal disorders. An extreme, longer-term reaction might be job burnout. Burnout is an expression used to describe the feelings of emotional exhaustion and fatigue that a worker might have because of job stress (Lee and Ashforth, 1990). It may also be accompanied by feelings of low self-esteem and inappropriate interpersonal interactions – people suffering from burnout tend to treat people as objects. Burnout can be measured using the Maslach Burnout Inventory (Maslach and Jackson, 1981). Behavioural changes as a result of stressors have not been studied to the same extent as physiological and psychological changes. However,

Muchinsky (1997) highlighted five broad categories of behaviour that result from stressors in the workplace. These were work role (e.g. reduction in job performance, accidents), negative work behaviours (e.g. theft, purposeful damage), job avoidance (e.g. absenteeism), degradation of other life roles (e.g. partner and child abuse) and self-damaging behaviours (e.g. drug and alcohol abuse). Again, it becomes apparent that the work–home interface is transparent and that problems at work manifest themselves in difficulties at home and vice versa.

Effects on performance

Stressors at work come in a variety of forms and attempts have been made to classify them. For example, Lazarus and Cohen (1977) identified three classes of stressors. These are: sudden, powerful events that affect a lot of people (e.g. natural disasters), more localised events affecting fewer people (e.g. family crises) and the daily hassles of everyday life (e.g. traffic jams, poor management at work). Some stressors are predominantly psychological, e.g. work underload and overload, role ambiguity and conflict, while some are physical in nature, e.g. noise, heat and air pollution. Although each stressor has to be considered separately, it does appear that most have comfortable upper and lower limits. Take temporal stressors, for example. Extremely short deadlines have been shown to be stressful, leading to substandard performance. Likewise, too much time to complete a task has been found to lead to boredom (Zakay and Wooler, 1984).

Researchers now agree that a small or moderate amount of stress facilitates performance. However, the extent to which we cope with stress depends very much on the individual, and whereas one worker might thrive on meeting tight deadlines, another could find them extremely stressful. As an example of individual differences, Jenkins *et al.* (1966) found that people who had received promotions had more heart attacks than individuals who had been fired. The amount of stress that individuals feel when not at work is thought to be an important determinant in the levels of stress experienced whilst working (Smither, 1994). This has certainly been demonstrated in the airline industry, where domestic problems have been shown to influence interpersonal relationships in the workplace to the detriment of work performance. Studies of aircraft accidents have indicated that the personal problems of individuals (rather than their personality) may have been a contributory factor in causing some accidents (Alkov *et al.*, 1982, 1985).

Another area that has attracted much research interest is the extent that stressors interact with certain personality dispositions. Friedman and Rosenman (1959, 1974) divided people into two categories: Type A people were alert, ambitious, competitive, impatient, aggressive and achievement driven, and Type B people lived their lives in a less frantic manner. Wright (1988) concluded that Type A people had a high need to achieve and this is what drives them and results in them living life at a more rapid pace. The hypothesis was that people showing Type A behaviour would be more likely than Type B people to develop coronary heart disease problems. Various research studies have given this hypothesis some support. For example, Ganster (1986) concluded that there was enough evidence to suggest that Type A behaviour was a risk factor in heart disease. Spence *et al.* (1987) suggested that the impatience–irritability traits expressed by Type A people may provide an explanation as to the development of coronary heart disease. In terms of an organisation, the management will welcome Type A workers because their behaviour results in high work performance and accomplishment. On the other hand, they may have a tendency to become stressed and develop cardiovascular problems – this is obviously something that the organisation does not want.

The psychosocial aspects of stress are an important consideration in the workplace, given that most workers will spend up to 8 hours a day working in close proximity with people with whom they have not chosen to interact. Cramping and crowding in the workplace can lead to poor performance because workers feel stressed and fail to achieve their best output. Sherrod (1974) found that when people were subject to a crowded place, it reduced stress to have a 'panic button'. Although participants tended not to use the button, its availability helped them cope with the stress of the situation. Further, research has indicated that stress has a detrimental effect on group decision making in that the members lose the team perspective (Driskell and Salas, 1991). In summary, too much stress in the workplace has negative effects. In his review of occupational stress, Holt (1982) stated that work-related stress results in poor work performance, e.g. low productivity, fatigue, job dissatisfaction and job burnout. A recent addition to this list might be WRULDs, as there is currently interest in the role of occupational stress in causing or aggravating work-related musculoskeletal disorders (Carayon *et al.*, 1999).

Theories of appraisal and coping strategies

The theme of individual differences continues when considering the ways in which we appraise stressful situations. People vary in the extent to which they monitor their internal responses to stress; cognitive style and personality are thought to influence the way we appraise stressors and stressful situations. The very act of appraising the situation has been shown to result in the person feeling less stressed (Vinokur *et al.*, 1990). Carver and Scheier (1981) considered the role of private self-consciousness (PSC) in appraising stress. They hypothesised that individuals who have high levels of PSC are more likely to notice that they are becoming stressed and to take remedial actions. In other words, people who are in touch with their feelings will have good PSC and, ultimately, will be less stressed than those who are not in tune with their emotions. This personal characteristic will act as a buffer between the stressors and illness. However, Frone and McFarlin (1989) found the opposite. In their study with blue-collar workers, they concluded that individuals with higher PSC experienced higher stress. As Smither (1994: 473) succinctly explained 'workers will be less stressed if they do not think about stress'. However, there is a large amount of difference between acute temporary stressors, such as layoffs, and chronic long-term stressors, such as overload. Ignoring the stress may be advisable when the stress is temporary but other coping strategies may need to be sought when the stress is longer term, and this may help explain the difference in the research findings.

In contrast, other theories have suggested that individuals fare better if they cope with rather than suppress stress. Workers who have an active coping strategy described themselves as being in better physical and mental health (Parkes, 1990). For example, research has indicated that workers are more likely to suffer from burnout when the mechanisms for coping with stressful situations at work are not present (Jackson *et al.*, 1987; Leiter, 1988). Research has focused on the human service occupations such as teaching, social work and nursing, where it is has been demonstrated that the nature of the work leads to greater incidences of burnout. It reinforces the importance of coping strategies and the need for social support at work.

During the 1980s, stress management programmes gained popularity as a means of addressing and coping with employee stress. Typically, these programmes cover physical exercise, relaxation, meditation, biofeedback and time management techniques, and clear identification of goal setting and means of achievement within the organisation. The benefits of stress management programmes have been demonstrated (Jones *et al.*, 1988). Most programmes aim to help employees develop their own individual strategies for coping with stressors (Murphy, 1986). People who are good at coping have been found to develop strategies that involve considering the stressors from a different perspective (Gilbert and Holahan, 1982). In summary, a combination of cognitive and behaviour modification techniques have found to be beneficial in helping workers cope with stressors and stressful situations.

Case study: health and safety approach to occupational stress – in a large NHS Healthcare Trust (from Vollans, 1999)

In 1988, the Control Of Substances Hazardous to Health (COSHH) Regulations were published (Health and Safety Executive, 1988). These regulations listed six steps to combat the control of hazardous substances: identification of hazards, assessment of risk, implementation of appropriate controls, monitoring of effectiveness, reassessment of risk and review. Cox and Cox (1993) suggested that problem-solving approaches such as the COSHH Regulations could be applied to alleviate psychosocial hazards and stress in the workplace.

Briefly, a control cycle approach to workplace stress would involve:

1. Identification of stress as hazardous to health – this would include an assessment of the nature and levels of stress experienced by employees, and an evaluation of those factors thought to affect the level of stress.
2. Assessment of risk – an indication of those factors most influential on employee perceptions/experience of stress.
3. Implementation of appropriate interventions.
4. Appraisal of effectiveness in reducing stress.
5. Reassessment.
6. Review.

A questionnaire survey was undertaken to carry out the first step in the control cycle, namely, the identification and evaluation of stress as hazardous to health. Eight hundred and forty seven employees (around 20 per cent) of a possible 4,182 returned a stress questionnaire distributed with their pay slips. The short, self-report questionnaire comprised six questions on: symptoms of stress experienced in the last 2 weeks, coping strategies, the degree to which the employee felt supported at work, the cost of stress problems, pressures at work, and whether or not the employee was aware of the staff counselling service. Findings included the following:

- Over 28 per cent of respondents were exhibiting symptoms of stress, with more than 10 per cent very stressed.
- Doctors, NHS managers and nurses were found to be the most stressed.
- Levels of stress and absenteeism were found to correlate significantly.
- Length of service was the only demographic factor found to predict number of stress symptoms.
- Avoidance coping was significantly correlated with symptoms and levels of stress.

The next step will be to carry out a risk assessment to find out those factors that are most influential on employees' perceptions and experience of stress.

Key points

- Occupational hazards associated with computer use are important because large numbers of the working population are now exposed to them on a daily basis.
- Many of the health hazards in the workplace are associated with the introduction and use of new computer technologies. Reasons for this can be considered in terms of the user, the task, and the application.
- Most issues associated with computer use are ill-defined and ill-understood as yet, e.g. RSI disorders, which have no consensual diagnostic criteria.
- To date, there is an inadequate number of well-designed and controlled studies to draw valid conclusions about the causes and effects of computer use.
- Sick building syndrome is a recognised phenomenon but to date there has been little agreement on its causes.
- Radon, asbestos and lead are three pollutants to which many people are exposed on a daily basis.
- Some level of stress is both inevitable and desirable in order to perform well. However, excessive stress can lead to significantly degraded performance and more general ill-health.

7   Safety

If your life is free of failures, you're not taking enough risks.

Anon

How would you like a job where, every time you make a mistake, a big red light goes on and 18,000 people boo?

Jacques Plante (1929–86), Canadian Hockey Player

Each year hundreds of thousands of workers are seriously injured at work and many others are killed or permanently disabled from industrial accidents and incidents in the work environment. Although the number of industrial accidents in the developed world has continued to fall, some would argue that they are still too high and need to be reduced further. For example, in the US, work-related deaths have decreased from an annual rate of 14–15 per 100,000 of the population in the 1930s to 4–5 per 100,000 in the 1980s (National Safety Council, 1991). Interestingly, a larger number of deaths occur each year from non-work accidents. For example, 10,500 deaths occurred as a result of work accidents in 1990. This is in contrast to the 46,300 people who were killed in road accidents and the 21,500 who died in accidents in the home. The number of injuries does not have a similar pattern because there are more home injuries than work-related injuries, with the number of motor vehicle injuries trailing in third place. Like death rates, the 1.8 million people injured at work in 1990 was too high. The costs in terms of human suffering and misery, and to the employer in terms of medical expenses, insurance administration and loss of work, are considerable. Accidents and incidents, the concept of risk, and the role of human error are considered in this chapter in conjunction with regulations and other preventive measures to enhance safety.

Accidents and incidents

Defining accidents

On the 19th July 1989 a serious aircraft accident occurred. United Airlines Flight 232 crashed while attempting to land at Sioux City,

Iowa with 111 of the 296 passengers on board being fatally injured. The aircraft suffered loss of an engine plus total loss of hydraulic pressure that resulted in the crew having no flight controls, i.e. ability to control the aircraft when trying to land.

(National Transportation Safety Board, 1990)

Accidents are frequent occurrences and, wherever there are humans, there will be accidents and incidents (defined as minor accidents). The word 'accident' implies there is something accidental in their occurrence and that they arose as result of happenstance or bad luck. If this stance is taken, it suggests that there is little that we can do to prevent accidents or turn them into mere incidents. One of the first controlled studies to investigate whether accidents were truly accidental was conducted during World War I in an ammunitions factory in the UK (Greenwood *et al.*, 1919). The findings from this study led to the conclusion that accidents were not accidental – they often arose as a result of worker behaviour. Furthermore, some workers were having more accidents than they would have had if chance factors alone were operating. The implications were that the incidence of accidents could be reduced by recognising and 'putting right' hazardous situations. It also laid the foundations for the concept of accident-proneness, which was first suggested by Farmer and Chambers (1939). It is now generally recognised that some individuals have a predisposition to having accidents, and that accident-proneness can be represented as a continuum with accident-prones at one end and non-accident-prones at the other (Porter, 1988; Porter and Corlett, 1989).

Risk perception and behaviour

Closer analyses of accidents at work indicate that some workplaces present more hazards than others. For example, Conroy (1989) identified meat preparation as a high-risk industry. Other industries recognised as having more hazards include agriculture, fishing, mining, construction and transportation. In these workplaces, injuries and death usually result from workers being struck by objects or by falling. The accident itself has been described as 'an unexpected event that interrupts or interferes with the progress of a production activity or process' (Berry and Houston, 1993: 338). It is preceded by what has become termed 'accident behaviour' by the people about to become involved in the accident. Accident behaviour encompasses a number of unsafe acts, such as failure to use personal protective equipment, improper use of equipment, operating at unsafe speeds and inattention to objects in immediate environment. A further, frequently cited human attribute in accident reports is that of excessive risk taking. Risk taking can be viewed as a behavioural characteristic, although some would argue that this is not particularly helpful because it does not take into account the situation or a particular person's subjective assessment of the hazard at that point in time. Depending on the context and the nature of the hazard, we may all have the potential to be risk takers. In one situation, once the possibility of an accident is perceived, one worker may decide to delay action until the last moment in the hope that the hazard will pass, whereas another might take early remedial action to guarantee that an accident will be diverted. When a similar situation arises, the worker who took early action may wait until the last moment, while the other person does the opposite. This is in contrast to risk homeostasis theory put forward by Wilde (1982). This theory suggests that people act in order to maintain a certain level of risk or danger at all times. Wilde's research focused on studying risk perception in vehicle driving. According to the risk homeostasis theory, in times of medium to low risk drivers will tolerate higher levels of danger by driving in a riskier manner. Further, when safety features such as anti-lock braking systems, air bags and seat-belt laws are introduced, people respond by driving faster and taking more risks (Wilde, 1988). Although the research was carried out in the driving domain, it has disturbing implications if people are found to operate in a similar way in the workplace.

Past experience plays a major role in how we respond when carrying out day-to-day activities. Consequently, we have an expectancy of events including accidents and incidents. This expectancy, coupled with the anticipated costs of accidents and incidents, defines the concept of risk. As a general rule, people will underestimate risks in familiar everyday tasks, i.e. the probability that an accident will occur, but overestimate the risk in activities carried out less frequently. Different modes of transport provide a good example of this. In the US the probability of dying in a car accident is 5,000 to 1, compared with 250,000 to 1 in an aircraft (Editorial, 1998). National Transportation Safety Board statistics demonstrate this – 42,860 fatalities from car accidents in the years 1992 and 1993 compared with 79 deaths from the US scheduled airlines in the same period (Orlady and Orlady, 1999). Even if we question the statistics in terms of bias, e.g. differences in the car and airline-travelling populations, the effect is still dramatic. Yet, more people are nervous about flying because of the greater perceived risk of an accident occurring. Presumably, this is partly to do with familiarity, because getting into a car is an everyday activity for a lot of people, unlike flying. Ironically, given the accident statistics, we also know that people take risks when driving a car. Most people have never been in a serious road accident so their subjective risk perception may be set at zero. This may help explain why they choose to display unsafe behaviour when driving, e.g. overtaking at 'blind spots', excessive speeds, driving too close to the car in front, etc. (McKenna, 1988). Further, research has shown that we underestimate the chance of activities with high probabilities happening, i.e. the chance of having a car accident and, conversely, overestimate events with low probabilities such as being in a plane crash (Lichtenstein *et al.*, 1978). As a general rule, we are poor at judging probabilities and especially bad at judging risk. Over-familiarity with the situation, over-confidence in our own skills and general over-optimism will lead us to reduce our appraisal of hazards (Health and Safety Executive, 1999).

In the workplace, attempts are made to design the machinery and environment so that the workers are not exposed to hazards. This may take the form of physical guards and/or personal protection to prevent workers coming to harm when using the machinery. Although there are Health and Safety requirements and obligations on the management, the ultimate responsibility for safe behaviour resides with the worker. At times, workers will choose to ignore these physical guards. A personal, anecdotal example of this is when the author worked on a packaging line in a food production factory during the long university vacations. On many occasions the line would jam and workers would put their hands in amongst the cutting and heat-sealing equipment to clear the blockage. The correct (and safe) procedure was to call an engineer, who would dismantle the line at the point of the problem. However, it was usually much quicker for the workers 'to have a go' than to wait for an engineer, who might take 20 or more minutes to arrive. The pressure on the workers to complete the packing job, combined with the frustration of waiting around for the engineer, plus the fact that the workers on the line had successfully cleared the blockage many times before without adverse effects led them to indulge in unsafe behaviour. In this context, risk taking can be seen as being part of the decision-making process. The 'costs' are typically time, reduced productivity and frustration in not being able to complete the job, as in this example. Individuals have to know that a hazard exists (diagnosis), what remedial actions are available (generation of alternatives) and the consequences of their decision making in terms of safe and other behaviours (evaluation). Researchers have shown that a number of factors affect the evaluation phase. Schacherer (1993) and Young and Laughery (1994) found that the decision to behave in a safe manner was influenced by: (i) seriousness of the hazard and potential for injuries; (ii) novelty and familiarity of the hazard; and (iii) the extent to which exposure was voluntary. A fourth consideration concerns the costs of compliance: for example, the decision to wear safety goggles will include weighing up the benefits (protecting the eyes) against the disadvantages (discomfort, loss of sharp focus, feeling self-conscious). Indeed, a further cost consideration relates to the physical discomfort that arises from wearing protective clothing. This exemplifies the subjective element in risk perception. This is supported by research that has found that the seriousness of the hazard in terms of injury has been found to have a greater influence on an individual's decision making than their perception of the probability of an accident (Young *et al.*, 1992).

A further example of the importance of individual behaviour in the workplace relates to drug and alcohol abuse. There is clear evidence that drugs and alcohol are associated with work accident behaviour, primarily because they alter perceptual and cognitive capabilities (Shain, 1982).

Further, steadiness, co-ordination and motor responses might be affected (Trice and Roman, 1972). In an office this might not be dangerous, but it is certainly dangerous when high-risk behaviour is required, e.g. operating industrial machinery or transport. It is for this reason that most airlines prohibit the crew from drinking any form of alcohol for at least 12 hours before a flight or when being on stand-by (Orlady and Orlady, 1999). It was in order to combat the problems of alcohol in the workplace that the concept of Employee Assistance Programmes (EAPs) was developed. EAPs are referral programmes, i.e. a clinician or counsellor makes an assessment of the situation and, if appropriate, refers the worker elsewhere for help. Although originally developed as interventions against alcohol abuse, the programmes were soon extended to cover drugs and then to other problems such as work-related stress, domestic and personal difficulties that workers may be experiencing (see Philips and Mushinski, 1992, for a review).

Human error

Error and accidents

'Sixty per cent of India's 400 train accidents a year are caused by human error.' This statement was issued in the aftermath of the Gaisal train disaster in eastern Bengal state about 300 miles north of Calcutta on 2nd August 1999. It was one of the country's worst rail accidents, with over 500 people feared dead and about 1,000 injured. The cause was suspected to be a signalling mistake resulting in two overcrowded trains being placed on the same piece of track culminating in a head-on collision.

(Bedi, 1999)

'Human error tops the list of probable causes of the collision, which took place in calm weather, good visibility and between sophisticated ships with radar.' The collision had occurred in the early hours of the 24th August 1999 between the *Norwegian Dream*, a cruise liner heading for Dover, and the *Ever Decent*, a container ship, en route to Tokyo via Zeebrugge, Belgium. The container ship was transporting paint and despite fires breaking out and a tremendous amount of damage to the hulls, there was no loss of life.

(Highfield, 1999)

'Inquiry likely to focus on driver error.' This was the headline on the front of the *Guardian* newspaper following the worst rail accident in the UK for 10 years. On 5th October 1999, a Great Western express train crashed into a Thames commuter train just two miles west of Paddington station, London. It was thought the driver of the Thames train had gone through a red warning signal. Twenty-eight people died and around 150 were taken to hospital, some with serious injuries and requiring intensive care.

(Harper, 1999)

The above excerpts detail three accidents that occurred in less than 3 months. Each was serious, having considerable costs in terms of human suffering and disruption, and immediately after each accident the blame was placed on human error. However, it probably needs to be stated that there are many reasons for placing the blame on the human who was in control of the system. Certainly, in the aircraft industry it is often expedient to cite 'pilot error' as the cause of accidents (Noyes *et al.*, 1996b). There may be economic reasons – in Chapter 5 it was stated that it is easier to 'fix the human than bend the metal', i.e. it is cheaper to provide some extra training for the crew than to retrofit the plane. Human error also suggests that events would be very unlikely to happen again, given that the same people would need to be in an identical situation. Hence, it reinforces the idea that the system is safe because that particular error is unlikely to be repeated. Further, and more importantly, blaming the human for errors that have been made only provides part of the whole picture. Alkov (1977) supported this by suggesting that pilot error should be thought of as a result of precipitating factors rather than a cause of accidents. An accident (or incident) is seldom the result of one 'mistake'. Almost all accidents are multi-causal, resulting from any one of a number of situations including from the design of the workplace, operational procedures, the working environment and the culture of the organisation. This extends to encompass other issues such as the communication between individuals, their training, and the selection and recruitment of personnel. The following case study of the *Herald of Free Enterprise* illustrates this.

> ### Case study: an analysis of an accident – the Herald of Free Enterprise *(adapted from Noyes and Stanton, 1997, and published with permission from the IEE)*
>
> In terms of demonstrating the multi-causal aspects of accidents, it may be useful to consider the *Herald of Free Enterprise* accident that occurred outside Zeebrugge in 1987. Retrospectively, this could be described as an example of 'an accident waiting to happen', i.e. there were a number of resident pathogens already in place before the day when the ferry set sail. As an example, it could be suggested that the precursors of the accident started years before with the design of the 'roll-on/roll-off' ferries themselves. These ferries were designed for fast turnaround times, maximum profit and to load and unload vehicles as quickly as possible: bow doors open, cars drive in, doors

close, ferry departs. Thus, their design was essentially a large hull, which needed only a small amount of water across the deck for the whole structure to turn over. Despite this, the design was accepted by the industry (and the public) and roll-on/roll-off ferries became operational. Admittedly, some concerns were voiced at the time but other designs were rejected primarily on the basis of cost.

A few weeks before the Zeebrugge accident, it was actually suggested to the board of directors that a light should be installed to indicate whether the bow doors were open or closed. This proposal was rejected, again on a cost basis.

The owners had therefore made two fallible board and policy decisions: (i) to accept the roll-on/roll-off design; and (ii) not to fit the warning lights. There were also problems with the management of the ferries: people were working double shifts, the boats were under-manned and seemingly driven by profit-making than by safety. The ferries had built up a culture of job demarcation; it was subsequently found that the person who was supposed to make sure the bow doors were closed was asleep in his bunk when the ferry left harbour, having just finished working a double shift. However, this was not an issue at the time of the accident – the ferries often left harbour with the doors still open. The crew would frequently close them as the ferry was leaving. This saved time and had been done on many occasions without consequence.

On the day in question, the sea was choppy, the bow doors were open and water started to flood in. One deck-hand noticed but took the line that it was not their responsibility, but someone else's – a further example of line management problems. The layers of resident pathogens (i.e. the roll-on/roll-off design), poor safety culture (i.e. the negative reporting system), and poor management procedures resulting in unsafe acts (i.e. leaving port with the doors open) had effectively produced an operation 'riddled with holes'. These combined with local failures, e.g. undermanning, double shifts, ignoring the open doors. In addition, defences were inadequate, e.g. the poor safety culture that had been built-up on the ferries. This has been described in the 'dynamics of accident causation' model, where a number of latent and active failures come together to produce the 'impossible' accident. These failures are indicated by the 'holes' in the model shown in Figure 7.1. Although, it would seem unlikely that a number of events would occur in order to create an accident (demonstrated by the holes lining up in the model) this can happen, as the *Herald of Free Enterprise* accident indicated.

A further point concerns who is blamed for this type of accident. Typically, the people who are prosecuted are the individuals who

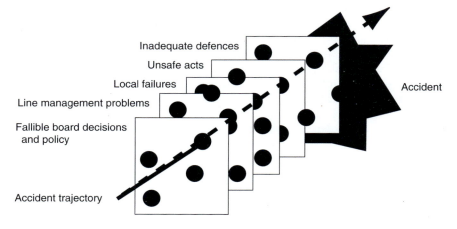

Inadequate defences
Unsafe acts
Local failures
Line management problems
Fallible board decisions and policy

Accident

Accident trajectory

Figure 7.1   'Swiss cheese' accident model (based on the 'Dynamics of Accident Causation' (Reason, 1990))

committed the errors on the day of the disaster. We tend not to look back in time to the people who designed the ferry or instigated the work procedures. The last person to be involved with the system tends to be the one who is blamed; in the *Herald of Free Enterprise* example this was the person who failed to close the bow doors quickly enough. The usual outcome is that these individuals are taken to court, or prevented from having contact with operating the system in the belief that all is safe again. But it is not. The holes are still there, and undoubtedly the errors will be made again.

In conclusion, it can be seen that the *Herald of Free Enterprise* was a catastrophic event arising from the coming-together of several causal chains. Further, the elimination of any one of these chains, represented as layers in the accident model, would have deflected the sequence of events leading to the accident. However, it is always difficult, when considering latent failures, to decide how far back in time to look.

Defining errors

Human error is commonplace and throughout our waking lives we make frequent errors. As an example, Amalberti and Wioland (1997) reported an observation study of civil airline pilots where it was shown that during a flight of 11 hours, the flight deck crew made 162 errors. However, most of these errors were inconsequential and soon forgotten – 157 of the 162 errors were detected and recovered from within 15 seconds. In contrast, some of the errors we make are extremely useful in that recovery from the error allows us to learn from the situation and thus avoid making an error that could lead to disastrous consequences (the so-called 'near-miss' situation). However, some errors are not inconsequential or near-misses but result in negative events. Depending on the circumstances, these are the ones that will result in accidents. There is, however, no obvious quantifiable relationship between errors and accidents, despite one sometimes leading to the other. It is perhaps also worth stating at this point that there is an extreme view that errors do not exist and that they are merely a way of describing human behaviour and normal psychological processes (Senders and Moray, 1991). There are a number of definitions of human error in the literature; that favoured by the author defines error as an out-of-tolerance action where the limits are defined by the particular situation. This seems to sum up the individual nature of errors and the fact that errors are a function of the context in which they occur.

We know that humans make frequent errors – to quote Cicero from 2,000 years ago 'it is the nature of man to err', i.e. to err is human – and we also know that errors generally have negative connotations and that they can lead to accidents. In terms of finding out more about errors, an obvious place to start is to study errors as they occur in natural settings and one of the earliest published studies to do this was carried out by Kollarits (1937). He classified 1,200 errors made by himself and his wife in their daily activities into four types: substitution, omission, repetition and insertion. Subsequently, many individuals have studied errors and attempted a phenomenological classification or taxonomy. One of the simplest methods of classification is simply to refer to errors as 'reversible' or 'irreversible'. Another is to divide errors into 'random', 'systematic' or 'sporadic'; Hawkins (1993) demonstrated this graphically with an example of rifle shots at a target. Random shots pepper the target; in everyday life this type of error would be difficult to predict. Systematic shots would group together to one side of the bull's eye of the target; this would be demonstrated in everyday life as the repeated error that we make in everyday situations. Sporadic shots show both the characteristics of random and systematic shots – they occur across the target (but not with the same degree of randomness as random shots) and have the grouping feature of systematic shots (but again not to the same degree). Further, unlike random and systematic shots, they are closer to the bull's eye. In everyday life, sporadic errors are probably the ones that are most difficult to predict, and therefore, to manage. Hawkins gave three examples relating to landing an aircraft. He stated that a pilot who made a series of landings making a variety of mistakes without any recognisable pattern would be an example of a random error. The pilot who repeatedly makes the same error, e.g. under-shooting the runway, would provide an example of a systematic error and the pilot who normally makes perfect landings but then inexplicably makes an error by under-/over-shooting the runway would be demonstrating a sporadic error.

There are many taxonomies of errors in the literature and four of the more common classifications are given here:

- Classification 1 – 'slips, lapses and mistakes' (Reason and Mycielska, 1982). The categorisation of these failures takes into account planning and intention as well as execution:
    - Execution failures (slips and lapses): actions deviate from the current intention because of execution and/or storage failures. Although the intention is correct for the situation, the task fails to be executed. The example of the commission error given below could be classed as a slip.
    - Planning failures (mistakes): actions that run according to plan but the plans are incorrect for achieving the goal. The task fails to be correctly executed because the intention is incorrect for the situation, e.g. driving deliberately down a one-way street.
- Classification 2 – the generic error-modelling system (GEMS) (Rasmussen, 1986). This is derived from Rasmussen's well-known 'skill–rule–knowledge' classification of human performance from automatic skill-based behaviours (such as riding a bicycle) through to knowledge-based behaviours that require high level cognitive processing.
    - Skill-based slips (and lapses): These usually precede detection of the problem and are mainly associated with monitoring failures. The 'classic' situations that arise when we attempt to reboil a just boiled kettle or attempt to fill a teapot with boiled water when it is already full are examples of skill-based slips. They occur when behaviour is largely skill-based, i.e. automatic.
    - Rule-based mistakes: in any situation there will be rules governing procedures. When these rules are not applied, or are misapplied, this can lead to mistakes. For example, mistakes made when writing that are rule-based grammatical errors.
    - Knowledge-based mistakes: both rule-based and knowledge-based mistakes tend to arise during attempts to find a solution to the problem and are mainly associated with problem-solving failures. Knowledge-based mistakes arise when the individual has to make a serious and conscious effort to solve a problem that may be both unfamiliar and unanticipated (Vicente and Rasmussen, 1992). We know from the decision-making literature that, when solving problems and making decisions, humans are subject to a number of influences, e.g. resource limitations, availability and anchoring heuristics, confirmation bias, overconfidence.
- Classification 3 – (Reason, 1990). Errors of omission and commission are often applied to maintenance tasks – an area that is becoming increasingly important in the safe operation of advanced technologies:

- Errors of omission: the failure to do something, e.g. failing to turn off the power before working on electrical circuitry. These types of errors are particularly prevalent in maintenance tasks.
- Errors of commission: the failure to perform an act correctly, perhaps by inserting extra steps into the process or wrongly carrying out a step. For example, if a computer user editing a document is presented with the onscreen message 'Hit "enter" to begin printing' and they press the 'enter' key and accidentally start the printing process before the editing is finished.

- Classification 4 – (Norman, 1981; Wickens, 1984). The five examples given here all relate to tasks involving human–machine interaction. It should also be noted that there are other types of error in this classification; hence, these examples should not be taken as being a complete list of possible errors.
  - Mode errors: these errors occur when an action is performed in an inappropriate operating mode, e.g. text in capital letters may be generated unintentionally by hitting the 'caps lock' key in error.
  - Capture errors: these are errors where the action is correct but performed in a situation that is not correct, e.g. typing some words frequently may eventually trigger an automatic response so that similar words are typed instead of the frequent word.
  - Misperception errors: these errors arise because perceptual cues are misused, resulting in a wrong decision and a wrong action, e.g. misreading text and omitting words when typing.
  - Sequence errors: these arise from performing an action (or a step in an action) out of the expected order, e.g. the operator on the check-out till ringing up the total before entering all the relevant information.
  - Timing errors: these arise from performing an action either too quickly or too slowly, e.g. some aspects of keyboard/computer operation.

It can be seen that implicit in the definition of human error is the fact that the action or decision was not intended, i.e. we do not try to make errors. When we do deliberately 'break the rules' and intentionally make an error, these are referred to as violations. Violations are defined as 'any deliberate deviations from rules, procedures, instructions and regulations' (Health and Safety Executive, 1999: 16). Within the context of the workplace, violation errors are important because of their implications for compromising safety. The Health and Safety Executive (1999) divided violations into three categories: routine, situational and exceptional. Routine violations occur when workers have broken the rule to such an extent that it becomes the normal way of working. This may be to save time and energy or due to the fact workers believe the rules to be too restrictive or that they no longer apply. New workers may not even realise violations are occurring. The resultant enquiry into the Clapham rail crash found that routine violations of maintenance practices had been made (Human Factors in Reliability Group, 1995). Situational violations occur when workers break the rules because of particular pressures arising from a specific job, e.g. the right equipment may not be available and workers may be forced to improvise. The Health and Safety Executive (1999) gave the example of a steel worker who was killed when he fell 20 metres. Although harnesses were available, there was no facility for fixing them. Further, there were no other safeguards present. In contrast, exceptional violations are rare. They occur when workers have good intentions but make risky decisions. For example, the operators in the Chernobyl nuclear power plant continued to carry out preplanned tests when they should have taken action to attend to a situation that was rapidly becoming safety critical.

Managing human error

Since World War II, machines and equipment have become more complex in nearly every industry. It could be argued that greater use of advanced technologies coupled with increased automation has implications in terms of the types and consequences of errors that will be made. This is in contrast to the 1930s where a worker making a mistake might have to discard a piece of work or merely waste some time. Consider the three transport examples given at the start of this section. In each of these cases, human error in the operation of the systems is alleged to have led to devastating consequences. Similarly, Reason (1990) documents the role of human error in the King's Cross underground fire, the Chernobyl nuclear disaster and the Bhopal tragedy. Consequently, it is important that the role of human error is understood and addressed in the workplace. Further, it could also be argued that many of the advances in human–machine system design are the result of the investigation of systematic errors that have occurred. The airline industry might provide one example of this. In the last couple of decades there has been a documented increase in the number of airline accidents and near misses (Boeing Commercial Airplane Group, 1996). Although this increase could be explained in terms of a greater volume of air traffic, aircraft accidents and incidents are usually well documented and we have learned much about human error from this source. For example, the incident at the Texaco Refinery at Milford Haven on 24 July 1994 was thoroughly investigated by the UK Health and Safety Executive and fourteen recommendations were produced that have been acted upon (Health and Safety Executive, 1997).

One commonly held view is that errors arise as a result of a mismatch between the characteristics of the human and the design of the task (Rasmussen, 1987). Frequent errors arising from this mismatch are likely to be considered design errors, while occasional errors may be due to system variability (e.g. component failures) or the human (i.e. human errors). In terms of accounting for the source of errors, it is generally thought that the characteristics of the human, e.g. levels of experience and possessing the appropriate skills, are not as influential as factors that arise from the design of the workplace, environment and organisation. However as indicated in Chapter 3, when considering human–machine interaction and systems design, it is not only the cognitive attributes of the human that need to be considered. All human work is physical in nature, at least to some degree. A physical task can require only the slightest muscular activity, e.g. pressing a key on a keyboard, or it can involve the whole body, as in lifting and carrying boxes. These actions, which can be physically great or small, contribute to the operator being able to execute his/her decisions. In this context, the human–machine interface and its contribution to human error needs to be considered in terms of both cognitive and physical attributes. Growing awareness of the need to get the design of the interface right has resulted in the concept of the 'system design-induced error' (Wiener, 1987). Note that one of the recommendations in the Texaco Refinery incident mentioned that 'operators were not provided with information systems configured to help them identify the root cause of [such] problems' (Health and Safety Executive, 1997: 35). It is now beginning to be recognised that placing the blame on human error is only part of the story because these errors might arise from faults and shortcomings in the design of the human–machine interface. This shift of emphasis has occurred relatively recently.

When considering the management of human error in the workplace, there are basically two approaches that can be taken: (i) the personnel approach; and (ii) the design approach.

The personnel approach is to select and train only those workers suited to the operation of the machines and equipment needed to perform the job, and to develop training programmes to teach workers to carry out the job safely with a minimum number of errors. Education and training comprise a vital aspect in promoting safe worker behaviour in the workplace. One way of achieving this is through introducing a goal-setting and feedback programme – the aims, very simply, being to promote safe behaviours in the workplace and reduce unsafe behaviours. The programme may focus on unsafe behaviours that have previously been identified in the organisation, perhaps by analysing accident and incident records. Further, the techniques of behaviour sampling, modelling and modification could be used. For example, a checklist of safe behaviours might be developed. Workers are then observed in order to see the extent to which they employ safe and unsafe practices. Feedback is given both to the individual and the group and, as a result, performance goals are set. These might include use of protective equipment, adherence to warnings and safer working methods in terms of lifting and bending. One of the advantages of the training approach to safety is that it provides an opportunity for the workers to be confronted with their own behaviours in the workplace. It also allows them to become actively involved in health and safety issues. The Health and Safety Executive report following the Texaco Refinery incident (Health and Safety Executive, 1997: 36) exemplifies the importance of training programmes:

> Recommendation 5
> The training of staff should include:
> (a) assessment of their knowledge and competence for their actual operational roles under high stress conditions;
> (b) guidance on when to initiate controlled or emergency shutdowns and how to manage unplanned events including working effectively under the stress of an incident.

The design approach involves designing equipment, procedures and environments that reduce the likelihood of errors or the consequences of errors when they do occur. This is particularly true in safety-critical situations such as those experienced in avionics, the process control industries and medicine, where the outcome could be seriously disadvantaged by human error. These applications share many common characteristics, e.g. the personnel are highly qualified and extensively trained, often carrying out complex and risky procedures in high information load and time pressured situations.

In conclusion, we are still some way from having a real, in-depth understanding of human error, and even the development of a precise definition continues to prove to be a difficult and elusive goal. There currently exists no single theory or model for predicting the occurrence of human errors, and which would provide an initial step towards understanding more about the causes, and the prevention of errors. Furthermore, errors are caused not only by changes in performance with respect to the norm, but also by changes in the criteria of judgements. A relatively recent approach has been to use machine learning in accident research where an algorithm creates decision trees to distinguish the characteristics of accidents resulting in injury or damage only (Clarke *et al.*, 1998). As errors can arise because of a person's judgement in a specific situation, they cannot be defined objectively by considering the performance of humans or equipment in isolation. Rasmussen *et al.* (1987) supported this by stating that the wide range of human errors represented the immense variety of our environment rather than psychological processes and mechanisms *per se*. The complexities of human behaviour make studying human error a challenging task with many difficult theoretical and methodological problems. Consequently, when designing training programmes, procedures and systems, we need to capitalise on our current understanding of human error and make use of contextually relevant information.

Regulations

Historical perspective

In 1867, Massachusetts was the first state in the US to pass a law relating to safety and the design of industrial machinery. At this time, there were many textile mills in Massachusetts and workers and management were becoming concerned about the large number of accidents and injuries that were occurring. Consequently, a factory inspection law was passed in 1867, followed a year later by a law relating to the installation of guards around dangerous machinery (Hunter, 1992). Other states soon followed. Laws were also being passed in the UK with the Factory Acts. These were introduced in the nineteenth century 'to ameliorate the worst excesses of the Victorian industries – long hours, appalling working conditions, and the exploitation of child labour' (Bridger, 1995: 469). For example, the 1833 Factory Act banned children under the age of nine from working, as well as stating the maximum number of hours that children could work, i.e. no more than 69 hours a week for 13–18 years olds with a maximum of 12 hours in a day. The 1844 Factory Act stated that children had to receive 3 hours of schooling a day and also included women in the maximum of 12 hours a day of work. The 12 hours was soon reduced to 10 for women and young persons by the 1847 Ten Hours Act. Interestingly, no laws were passed during the whole of the nineteenth century to limit the working hours of men because it was considered that this would interfere with their freedom to negotiate over hours and wages. Over a century later, legislation is now commonplace in regulating conditions in the workplace and organisations are legally bound to comply with regulations to ensure the safety of the worker.

A further milestone was the formation of the International Labour Organisation (ILO) in 1919 as part of the treaty of Versailles following World War I. The constitution of the ILO states that all humans, irrespective of their race, creed or sex, have the right to pursue both their material wellbeing and their spiritual development in conditions of freedom, dignity, economic security and equal opportunity. One of the key features of the ILO structure was the concept of tripartism – all decision making is based on representation from three groups of people from government, employers and employees.

In the UK, regulations are decided by a Regulatory Committee. This is in contrast to standards. A standard is a voluntary set of guidelines that may or may not be adopted as legal policy. However, because they have been developed for the general good, adherence to the standard generally follows. In the US, many standards are set by voluntary, non-governmental bodies (Anshel, 1998). Consequently, they do not establish governmental policy or law and are therefore not enforceable or binding. Examples of this type of legislation are the European Community (EC) directives. The International

Standards Organisation (ISO) is one of the major influences in the development of standards. It was established in 1946 by the national standards associations of twenty-five countries, and its work is carried out by 164 technical committees. Many ergonomists sit on these committees and it needs to be noted that the development of standards is a lengthy and slow process (Stewart, 1998). Further, the standards developed by ISO and others are usually related to products and systems; they do not test standards. This needs to be done by the appropriate bodies.

Ergonomics (Human Factors) are gradually being included in health and safety regulations, standards and directives. However, the relative recency of doing this means that many developments are currently ongoing and the situation has yet to stabilise. A further point concerns the fact that most countries have their own legislation, and that described here will relate primarily to Europe and the US and specifically to the UK, where appropriate. Further, it should be noted that although legal and regulatory constraints are important in determining behaviour, the individual may feel very tightly constrained by fears of litigation. The result is 'fail-safe' behaviour, where risky choices are discarded in favour of conservative outcomes that will be in the best interest of the decision maker (Moray, 1994). In the medical setting, this may mean that fear of litigation results in options being taken that 'cover' the medical professional(s) in case things do not turn out well rather than being in the best interests of the patient. A further disadvantage of regulations is that they promote rigid behaviour as people follow a 'checklist' approach, and as a result, are not well-equipped to cope with unforeseen events.

Occupational Safety and Health Act (1970)

In the US, the federal Occupational Safety and Health Administration (OSHA) Act was passed in 1970. The Act begins by stating:

> . . . to ensure safe and healthful working conditions for working men and women; by authorising enforcement of the standards developed under the Act; by assisting and encouraging the States in their efforts to assure safe and healthful working conditions; by providing for research, information, education, and training in the field of occupational safety and health; and for other purposes.

It continues by stating thirteen ways in which these goals will be achieved. These relate to the recognition of hazards, the responsibilities of the employers and the employees, training programmes and reporting procedures, the establishment of causal connections in occupational diseases and the development of standards. Keeping abreast of standards remains a problem. The administrators of OSHA were allowed to make use of the large body of existing standards because a considerable effort had been invested in developing these. They had been developed via a variety of sources, e.g. the American National Standards Institute (ANSI), the National Fire Protection Association (NFPA), the American Society of Mechanical Engineers (ASME), the American Society of Agricultural Engineers (ASAE), the American Society for Testing and Materials (ASTM) and the Underwriters Laboratories (UL). These provided some of the primary sources for the preparation of the regulations (Hunter, 1992). The difficulty is that some of the original regulations are still in use as they have not been updated or modernised. But, because they are national law, they have to be respected. For example, in 1992 OSHA inspectors carried out over 42,000 inspections and imposed over 116 million dollars-worth of fines (National Safety Council, 1993). In an attempt to overcome this problem, annual revisions to the regulations are published. In addition, about half the American states have their own health and safety laws, and some of these may differ significantly from the federal regulations. OSHA exemplifies some of the problems that surround the development and application of regulations, and indeed, has been the centre of much controversy and discussion.

For further information on the OSHA Act, see the Internet site: http://www.osha.gov/

Americans with Disabilities Act (ADA) (1990)

The Americans with Disabilities Act (ADA) became law on 26 July 1990. It encompasses a number of different aspects intended to make American society more suited to individuals with disabilities. A person is disabled if they meet one of the following criteria:

- Impairment – the person is substantially impaired with regard to a major life activity.
- History – the person has a history of such an impairment.
- Attitude – the person is regarded as having an impairment.

ADA is in five parts, with named titles. These are as follows:

- Title I. Employment
    Organisations must provide appropriate accommodation for disabled workers, e.g. this may require modification of the workspace and/or equipment, and the design of jobs. Further, all aspects of the selection, recruitment and training procedures must protect the rights of individuals with disabilities.
- Title II. Public Services
    All public services, including transportation and those run by local government, must be available for individuals with disability. Services that are open for individuals without disability cannot be denied to people with disability.

- Title III. Public Accommodation

  All public accommodation, including restaurants, hotels, shops and other retail outlets, should be made accessible to disabled individuals. This may mean modification in the case of existing accommodation; accessibility is a requirement for all newly constructed buildings.
- Title IV. Telecommunications

  All telecommunication companies offering telephone services to the general public must have appropriate systems for those individuals who are deaf.
- Title V. Miscellaneous

  The final, fifth title concerns the rights of disabled individuals under ADA and prohibits coercing, threatening or retaliating behaviour against this group or their helpers.

In essence, ADA exists to prevent discrimination against disabled individuals in the workplace. Its British equivalent is the Disability Discrimination Act.

Disability Discrimination Act (1995)

The aim of this act is to end the discrimination that many disabled workers experience in the workplace. It gives disabled people new rights in the areas of employment, access to goods, facilities and services, and the buying and renting of land or property. In addition, it requires schools, colleges and universities to provide information for disabled people, as well as allowing the British Government to set minimum standards so that disabled people can use public transport easily. The definition of disability is quite broad and covers anyone 'who has a physical or mental impairment which has an effect on his or her ability to carry out normal day-to-day activities' (Section 2.9 of the Act). Physical or mental impairment includes sensory and hidden impairments such as mental health problems, learning disabilities, diabetes, epilepsy and similar conditions. Disability statements are published every 3 years by individual institutions and provide information on relevant institutional policies (e.g. applications and admissions) and services (e.g. counselling and welfare). In addition, the act set up the National Disability Council (in Northern Ireland, the Northern Ireland Disability Council) to advise the Government on discrimination against disabled people.

There are three stages to the timing of the duties on service providers.

- Stage 1

  Since 2 December 1996, it has been unlawful to treat disabled people less favourably than those without disability; service providers must not discriminate against a disabled person.

- Stage 2
    Since 1 October 1999, service providers have to make 'reasonable adjustments' for disabled people.
- Stage 3
    From 2004, service providers will have to make 'reasonable adjustments' to the physical features of premises.

For further information on the Code of Practice and information about the Act, see Internet site: http://www.dfee.gov.uk/

Display screen equipment

Since the introduction of the PC in the late 1970s, there has been an increase in the number of reports of office-based, work-related injuries. The response of governments and legislative bodies has been to draft statutes for safe working environments. In the UK, these take the form of British Standards (BS), EC/EU (European Union) Directives and International Standard Organisation (ISO) guidance. The work of the ISO is important for two main reasons. First, there is an increasing move towards manufacturers who are international; therefore, it is in the best interests of countries to adopt international standards. Second, the European Standardisation Organisation (CEN) has chosen to adopt a strategy of using ISO standards.

Human Factors and ergonomics have been incorporated into the laws of the EC. For example, on 27 May 1990, the Commission adopted a directive on 'the minimum safety and health requirements for work with display screen equipment'. This became law in Europe 2 years later, in 1992 (Health and Safety Executive, 1992a). Individuals who do not adhere to the issues in this directive leave themselves open to litigation that could prove very costly and inconvenient. Many view this directive as long overdue given the problems associated with the use of visual display equipment. The document comprises a series of ten articles in three sections.

- Section 1: General Provisions
    Article 1: Subject
    Article 2: Definitions
- Section 2: Employer's Obligations
    Article 3: Analysis of workstations
    Article 4: Workstations put into service for the first time
    Article 5: Workstations already put into service
    Article 6: Information for, and training of, workers
    Article 7: Daily work routine
    Article 8: Worker consultation and participation
    Article 9: Protection of workers' eyes and eyesight
- Section 3: Miscellaneous Provisions
    Article 10: Adaptations to the annex

As an example, EC90/270 states that 'employers shall be obliged to perform an analysis of (computer) workstations in order to evaluate the safety and health conditions to which they give rise for their workers, particularly as regards possible risks to eyesight, physical problems and problems of mental stress' (EC 90/270, Section II.3.1). At the same time, a directive on manual handling was published (Health and Safety Executive, 1992b).

Summary

The list of standards relating to the workplace is endless and only a flavour of them can be given here. There are EU standards relating to the 'Supply of Machinery (Safety) Regulations'. From 1 January 1996, machinery must comply with these regulations and meet health and safety requirements under forty-five headings. Ergonomic principles must be utilised to ensure that 'hazards, workloads, discomforts, fatigue and psychological stresses' are minimal (see Corlett and Clark, 1995). For example, ISO TC SC4 Ergonomics of Human System Interaction, and BSI PSM/39/2 User System Interfaces, both deal with ergonomic issues. There are numerous references relating to the visual environment (see the section on technical standards in Anshel, 1998, where the fifteen standards relating to vision and eye wear are given). Megaw (1992: 292) concluded that there was 'no lack of recommendations, codes of practice, guidelines and standards on lighting conditions'. With reference to computer technology, there are standards relating to hardware and the environment, office furniture and workstations, software ergonomics and the user interface. The display screen equipment directive has had a major impact on organisations in the UK because it requires them to check that they comply with EC recommendations. The following case study illustrates an ergonomic audit carried out to do this.

Case study: ergonomic audit – ergonomic audit of VDUs and manufacturing workstations (from Noyes et al., 1994)

To demonstrate compliance with EC recommendations, British organisations are required to carry out ergonomic audits of their workstations. The study reported here is an ergonomic survey of VDUs and production line workstations at a large manufacturing site on the outskirts of Bristol. The emphasis here is on the tools used in the audit rather than reporting the specific findings of the survey.

To audit effectively within a limited timescale, a wide range of measurement tools was used together with informal discussions with the workforce. Tools used, included the following:

1. Workstation assessment checklist – this comprised five sections on the nature of the job, posture and furniture adjustability, visual factors, general safety and environmental considerations. The aim was to locate areas in the workplace where reforms could be made to improve the physiological and psychological wellbeing of the workers.
2. Musculoskeletal problems – a self-report tool was used to collect data on the frequency and type of musculoskeletal problems. Individuals were required to complete a version of the Nordic questionnaire addressing any postural discomfort or musculoskeletal problems that they were currently experiencing.
3. Physical measurements – this tool involved measuring the height of the working seat and desk and observing the posture, i.e. seated eye height, elbow height and wrist height, adopted by employees in a naturalistic setting.
4. Environmental conditions – measurements of noise and lighting levels were taken in a variety of locations within two large open-plan buildings housing over 800 workers.
5. Subjective discomfort ratings – a specifically designed checklist was used to collect discomfort ratings. Employees rated the level of subjective discomfort experienced in various body parts over the course of a working day. It was intended that this tool would give an indication of the possible development of problems over time.
6. *Ad hoc* posture analysis – workers' postures were sampled at random for a period of about 5 minutes. The tool used was based on a combination of the Renault (Kragt, 1992) and OWAS (developed by the Finnish Institute of Occupational Health (1992), in conjunction with the company Ovako Oy) checklists. In addition, a number of 'spot checks' were made and photographs of individuals working at their VDUs were taken in order to demonstrate postural problems such as shoulder depression, wrist extensions and abduction, and elbow deviations.

Several conclusions were drawn about the use of the measurement tools. It was found to be advantageous to have several of these to look at possible problems from a number of angles, e.g. interviews, checklists, self-report questionnaires. Data collected also covered a range of quantitative and qualitative data. It was felt that this variety helped ensure a comprehensive and detailed audit. Finally, a number of pointers emerged that might be useful for individuals carrying out similar surveys.

Some tips for ergonomic audits:

1. Be prepared to spend considerable time with individuals pro-
    viding advice and guidance – we found that a number of workers
    needed specific help and information on how to set up their
    workstations.
2. Try to pilot the tools onsite before the actual audit – this will help
    to identify redundant questions.
3. Find out before the visit if any related studies have been con-
    ducted and whether any aspects of the environment have already
    been checked by professionals – in our survey, we learned that
    the humidity had been the topic of investigation by the air-
    conditioning engineers.
4. At the start of the visit, check the availability of participants –
    our onsite time management would have been better if we had
    screened individuals initially for availability at a later time.
5. Allow some time for debriefing – although not part of the audit,
    individuals in the organisation like to have a debriefing session.

Design of healthy and safe systems of work

The responsibility for healthy and safe systems lies with both the organisation and the individual. There is much the organisation can do in terms
of the identification of hazards and the assessment and management of risk.
Haslegrave and Corlett (1995) stated that these evaluations take place at
two levels: (i) the organisation needs to know where the hazards and risks
are in the workplace; and (ii) jobs need to be analysed to assess the
demands of working on the individual. With reference to the hazards, the
first need is for them to be identified. Essentially, hazards arise because of a
mismatch between the worker and their environment, and carrying out an
assessment or ergonomic audit of the match between people and their
workplace will allow the hazards to be recognised. An example of a technique that will allow this is the Loads and Causes Survey (Åberg, 1981).
The loads include those aspects that may be contributing to hazards, e.g.
dust, information load, monotony, while the cause factors relate to features
of the situation, e.g. the buildings, tools, work schedule. Each load factor is
given a weighting so that the loads can be calculated for each cause factor.
This survey is often used in the initial stages of identifying hazards, and the
loads and causes are compiled in conjunction with the workforce.

At the level of jobs, job analysis methods can be used to identify risks.
Job analysis is a frequently used technique that can be considered as a form
of observational research where observations are used in conjunction with
interviews and questionnaires. In addition, some more specific tools can be

used, such as task analysis, critical incidents and standard questionnaires, e.g. the Position Analysis Questionnaire (PAQ) devised by McCormick *et al.* (1972). This questionnaire can be used to locate stressors and comprises 194 statements that describe the human attributes needed to perform the job. These are broken down into six categories: information input, mental processes, work output, relationships with other people, job context and other job requirements. The PAQ is recognised as having contributed much to our understanding of jobs. It is worker-oriented as opposed to job-oriented and thus has the advantage of being applicable across a broad range of jobs. This is in contrast to job-oriented procedures that often have to be modified for each job (McCormick, 1976).

Task analysis is a technique that was developed by the US Department of Labor (1972) to find out the duties that made up various jobs. Interviews and questionnaires are used systematically to find out about the composition of different jobs and the frequency, importance and time spent on various tasks. Since the 1970s, task analysis has been used in a number of different situations and is one of the techniques favoured by Human Factors specialists and ergonomists. The wide range of uses and applications of task analysis are listed in Kirwan and Ainsworth's (1992) book on the topic. These include interface/system design and evaluation, job design, personnel selection and training issues, and human reliability analysis. A number of task analysis techniques are available. One of the simplest and most well known is Hierarchical Task Analysis (HTA) developed by Annett and Duncan (1967) and the topic of a book by Shepherd (2000). In an HTA, tasks are broken down according to the actions needed for successful completion. Baber and Stanton (1994) used this technique in their research on the identification of human errors in everyday tasks such as boiling a kettle. Other forms of task analysis include sequential task analysis (Drury, 1983), tabular format decision task analysis (Pew *et al.*, 1987) and cognitive task analysis (Diaper, 1989). For a full review, see Kirwan and Ainsworth (1992), who list forty-one techniques in an appendix. More recently, task analysis has been used as part of Human Reliability Assessments (HRAs; see Bowler *et al.*, 1999). An HRA is a generic methodology for identifying, quantifying and reducing human errors. In Kirwan's (1994) framework for HRA, task analysis comprises the first step once the problem has been defined. Although it could be argued that task analysis and HRA are relatively recent developments and are still evolving and undergoing modification, it is likely they will soon become an accepted component of risk assessments carried out by organisations.

Critical Incidents Technique was first used by the military in the 1940s (Flanagan, 1954). Individuals are asked to describe specific incidents that are vital for the success or failure of the job. They may do this by keeping a log or diary of critical incidents as they occur. These critical incidents are then grouped by aspects of performance, e.g. leadership qualities. Essentially, the critical incidents describe the behaviours that are needed for good or poor job performance. In the original technique, the end product is a list of behaviours. More recent techniques attempt to quantify the various behaviours by providing them with scores. Three examples of refinements of the original critical incident technique include the Behavioural Anchoring Rating Scales (BARS; Smith and Kendall, 1963), the Mixed Standard Rating Scale (MSRS; Blanz and Ghiselli, 1972) and the Behavioural–Observation Scale (BOS; Latham and Wexley, 1977).

The psychosocial characteristics of the workplace are important when considering health and safety aspects. Jobs and the working environment may be well designed but workers' reactions to the demands of the job may result in behaviours that increase the risk of injury and harm. Although it is unrealistic (and undesirable) to control workers to the point where they do not have 'free choice', there are various ways in which the organisation can help their employees. Reber *et al.* (1984) asked employees to develop a list of safe and unsafe behaviours at work. Using this checklist as a basis, they were then trained to improve their safety performance. It was found over a period of time that this training resulted in a 54 per cent reduction of lost time through injuries. Similar findings were found by McAfee and Winn (1989) in their review of twenty-four studies – incentives and/or feedback were successful in improving safety and/or reducing accidents in every case. One area that is a safety concern in the workplace is that of risk-taking behaviour. However, risk taking is a product of the organisational culture, the situation and the individual worker and other reasons. A participative approach where workers take part in the decision making is likely to prove beneficial. In the 1980s, a group of French ergonomists reported a series of studies where they had provided workers with training in order to analyse their own work problems (Boel *et al.*, 1985; Montreuil and Laville, 1986). Training and awareness programmes followed by cascaded training, where initial training is passed on to other workers can raise the profile of health and safety aspects and appropriate remedial actions. The Health and Safety Executive (1999: 26) recommended that employee involvement and participation is 'an important tool in the reduction of both stress levels and safety risks'. However, they did warn that a participative approach can raise the expectation levels of the workers to the point where they may be unrealistic. Further, the approach may appear to undermine the role of the managers who are used to making the decisions. However, in recent years, employee participation has grown significantly in the UK and the US, with up to half of all large manufacturing companies running participation programmes (Langan-Fox *et al.*, 1998).

In conclusion, the behaviour of the workers is only one factor affecting safety in the organisation. It is important that the organisation has an effective health and safety management system and develops a culture where health and safety are foremost in the workers' minds. An organisational culture is important, as demonstrated by the *Herald of Free Enterprise* accident, where shortcomings were found in the safety culture of those working on the cross-channel ferries. The Health and Safety Executive (1999: 45) list some key aspects of an effective safety culture:

- Good ways of informing and consulting the workforce.
- Recognition of the fact that everyone has a role to play.
- Commitment by top management to involving the workforce.
- Co-operation between employees.
- Open, two-way communications.
- High quality of training.

Communication is important, and the Confidential Human Factors Incident Reporting Programme (CHIRP) that exists in the British avionics industry is one such example. This scheme is a confidential, non-punitive incident-reporting system similar to the first Aviation Safety Reporting System (ASRS) devised in the US (Reynard *et al.*, 1986). Crews are encouraged to report their errors under the guarantee that there will be no come-back on them. Many countries now operate these schemes and they provide a wealth of information about pilot behaviours.

Murphy (1988) summarised three levels of intervention in such incident-reporting schemes: (i) primary or organisational stressor reduction; (ii) secondary or stress management training; and (iii) tertiary or employee assistance programmes. The benefits from such programmes are well documented: Cox *et al.* (1981) followed 1,125 employees for 3 months before and 6 months after the introduction of a fitness programme. General attitudes of the employees towards their employment improved, as did their fitness levels as measured by a gain in oxygen uptake and loss of body fat. Safe behaviours can be facilitated through education and training programmes, employee assistance programmes and workplace counselling, and the active promotion of health issues in the workplace. These can prevent injury in the workplace by teaching workers to recognise hazards and symptoms arising from stress, poor working postures and repetitive tasks. The Health and Safety Executive (1988) recommended a control cycle approach for managing physical hazards in the workplace and, more recently, it has been suggested this approach could be extended to control causes of stress at source (Lancaster, 1998). The case study on pages 134–135 outlined how the first step in the control cycle could be carried out. In addition, the application of ergonomics in the design of human–machine interactions, the workplace and the environment plus well-designed jobs and work schedules will also contribute to health and safety.

Key points

- The view that accidents are 'accidental' is outmoded – accidents and incidents are the results of human behaviour.

- Risk homeostasis theory suggests that people act to maintain a certain level of risk or danger at all times. This has important implications for design because, by making systems safer, we may be inviting people to behave in a riskier manner.
- Employee Assistance Programmes have been developed to help workers sort out their personal problems because it is now recognised that difficulties outside of the workplace can compromise an individual's safety at work.
- The blame for accidents is often placed on human error.
- Very few accidents arise as a direct result of an error made by one individual. Research has indicated that accidents are multi-causal, arising from aspects of the situation that may go back many years in time (the so-called 'resident pathogens').
- Many error classifications and taxonomies exist.
- It is probably fair to conclude that we are still some way from having an in-depth understanding of human error.
- There are two main approaches to managing human error in the workplace – these include focusing on either the personnel or the system design of human–machine interactions.
- Since the mid-nineteenth century an increasing number of regulations have been introduced to improve safety in the workplace.
- Regulations are in a constant state of flux.
- Responsibility for health and safety lies both with the individual and with the organisation.

Epilogue

He who makes no mistakes never makes anything.

English Proverb

Ergonomics is all about design and evaluation; about ensuring that the Man-made world meets our requirements in terms of being designed for us. When stated in this way, it seems so blindingly obvious that one is tempted to question whether we need to have ergonomics/Human Factors at all. The statement 'informed common sense' is sometimes used by engineers to describe ergonomics. And yes, it is an appropriate statement – but with one proviso – it can only be said after the event. When a product or system has been designed and is operational, it is at that point that, retrospectively, we are able to say that the design needs obvious modifications – the 'isn't that obvious' syndrome.

In general, humans find it difficult to predict the difficulties that will occur when humans actually begin to use and maintain a device. There are likely to be many reasons for this:

- The designers are seldom the end-users – they design from the position of focusing on, say, the engineering of the product, and the user-needs and requirements are seen as secondary to this. Fortunately, the days when the industrial designer used to design everything is an archaic model; the contemporary model is to have a team of experts who contribute throughout the design lifecycle.
- The goal is often to produce a workable product as quickly and as efficiently as possible, and perhaps the psychologists are not viewed as core to the production process and, thus, are seen as expendable.
- To be cynical, perhaps the extra expense of incorporating human factors into the design process is not seen as necessary, especially if they are viewed as an 'extra'. The aim in business is to sell as many products as possible and once a product (e.g. a software package) has been sold, this goal has been achieved.

These arguments collapse, of course, when we consider safety-critical situations where health and safety issues are paramount and Human Factors/ergonomics has a high profile.

We know that industries using advanced and complex technologies have had a profound effect on the development of the Human Factors/ergonomics discipline, what then have we learned from industries such as avionics, process control, nuclear power and the military? Rouse and Boff (1997) summarised the cost/benefits of a number of military systems. These included considerable cost savings from: (i) reducing 134 tools to six in the maintenance of an engine; (ii) decreasing the number of human-related errors in weapon design; (iii) a decrease in the number of personnel needed to operate an airborne system when it was redesigned; and (iv) a reduction in the amount of compensation and medical expenses. Benefits eschewed included a reduction in injuries as a result of a vehicle rollover system, while increased training resulted in a decrease in the number of traffic violations in one study. For further information, see Rouse and Cacioppo (1989) and Booher and Rouse (1990). These studies demonstrate that there are a number of cost/benefits to be gained from the incorporation of Human Factors in military systems. Of course, a further difficulty is that a number of benefits are impossible to quantify, e.g. increased job satisfaction or worker well-being, or injuries that have been avoided, or a reduced turnover of personnel. It is impossible to measure these in the monetary terms of a cost-to-benefit ratio. These 'hidden' benefits of Human Factors probably help explain why the application of ergonomics often seems to end up as a 'sticking plaster' approach. People design systems and then, when other people begin to use them, they find that, in fact, they are not designed well and Human Factors personnel are brought in, late in the day, to try to rectify the situation. Several of the case studies provided by the Health and Safety Executive (1999) demonstrate this point. Examples are given of a number of manufacturing companies who were finding operators were making errors as a result of poor interface design. Evaluation of the interactions led to identification and correction of the errors and this immediately led to an increase in productivity and efficiency, and improved worker satisfaction as measured by absenteeism rates.

Every year, ergonomists add to the number of evaluation methods that already exist; some are specific to Human Factors, e.g. heuristic evaluations, and some are mainstream to psychology, e.g. indirect methods such as questionnaires and interviews (Stanton and Young, 1999). Many methods are specifically devised to improve the design of the human–machine interface (input/output, software/hardware) as well as the workplace, the environment and the functioning of the organisation. However, a word of caution is needed here. It is seldom enough just to design for one part of the system or from one perspective. Take, for example, Volvo cars. The safety image portrayed by these cars is an important element of their design. If the designers had focused on the parts rather than the whole, this dimension could have been neglected. A further example might come from the work on usability. In the past, this has tended to focus on the quality of the design of the product or system. It is suggested that attention needs to shift from the design of the system to consideration of the quality of users' interactions with the product or system. The strongly supported 'scientific method' may not be the most appropriate paradigm by which to do this. How, then, do we assess the quality of the users' experience? Do we need to develop and refine techniques that provide us with richer, contextual, ethnographic data?

A common output from evaluation work is the generation of guidelines but, at a recent design workshop attended by the author, guidelines were viewed as often a waste of time because people do not use them. Certainly, Forsythe *et al.* (1998) would support this. They found that for an inter-active website only fifty-seven of 141 guidelines were actually being endorsed by the eleven practising Human Factors professionals who were asked to assess their usefulness. Thus, it seems that one of the challenges for Human Factors is the communication of knowledge amongst the design team and others. How do we ensure the transfer of information from one knowledge base to another? Do we need tools to synthesise the knowledge that we already have?

Looking to the future, it is likely that design and evaluation will become an even more important component of the development of products and systems. One of the ironies of complex systems and increased automation is a need for more carefully designed human–machine interactions. This is counterintuitive, in that it would be envisaged that by having the system take more control there would be less need to spend time working on the human element. We have a lot of knowledge and understanding relating to designs today but the real skills will be needed for the innovative, quality designs of tomorrow that will allow for change and evolution. As we enter the twenty-first century, this must pose one of the greatest challenges for Human Factors/ergonomics.

But, as George Orwell said in 1954 'who controls the past, controls the future . . .'

References

Abbott, K., Slotte, S. and Stimson, D. (1996). *The interfaces between flightcrews and modern flight deck systems*. Report of the Federal Aviation Administration Human Factors Team. Washington, DC: Department of Transportation.

Åberg, U. (1981). Techniques in redesigning routine work. In E.N. Corlett and J. Richardson (eds) *Stress, work design and productivity*, pp. 157–163. Chichester, UK: Wiley.

Abernethy, C.N. and Hodes, D.G. (1987). Ergonomically determined pointing device (mouse) design. *Behaviour and Information Technology*, 6, 311–314.

Adams, J.S. (1965). Inequity in social exchange. In L. Berkowitz (ed.) *Advances in experimental social psychology*, vol. 2. New York: Academic Press.

Åhsberg, E., Gamberale, F. and Gustafsson, K. (2000). Perceived fatigue after mental work: An experimental evaluation of a fatigue inventory. *Ergonomics*, 43(2), 252–268.

Alkov, R.A. (1977). Life changes and pilot error accidents. In *Proceedings of Human Factors Symposium*. Herndon, VA: Air Line Pilots Association.

Alkov, R.A., Borowsky, M.S. and Gaynor, J.A. (1982). Stress, coping and the US Navy aircrew factor mishap. *Aviation, Space, and Environmental Medicine*, 53, 1112–1115.

Alkov, R.A., Gaynor, J.A. and Borowsky, M.S. (1985). Pilot error as a symptom of inadequate stress coping. *Aviation, Space, and Environmental Medicine*, 56, 244–247.

Allgeier, A.R. and Byrne, D. (1973). Attraction towards the opposite sex as a determinant of physical proximity. *Journal of Social Psychology*, 90, 213–219.

Amalberti, R. and Wioland, L. (1997). Human error in aviation. In H.M. Soekkha (ed.) *Proceedings of International Aviation Safety Conference '97*, pp. 91–108. Rotterdam, Netherlands: VSP BV.

Anderson, C. (1993). The rocky road to a data highway. *Science*, 260, 1064–1065.

Andre, A.D. and Wickens, C.D. (1995). When users want what's *not* best for them. *Ergonomics in Design*, October, 10–13.

Annett, J. and Duncan, K.D. (1967). Task analysis and training design. *Occupational Psychology*, 41, 211–221.

Anshel, J. (1998). *Visual ergonomics in the workplace*. London: Taylor & Francis.

Arbuckle, P.D., Abbott, K., Abbott, T. and Schutte, P. (1998). Future flight decks. In *Proceedings of 21st Congress of International Council of the Aeronautical Sciences*, Paper No. 98–1.9.3. Melbourne, Australia.

Argyle, M. (1975). *Bodily communication*. London: Methuen.

Arksey, H. (1998). *RSI and the experts: The construction of medical knowledge.* London: Taylor & Francis.

Ashmos, D.P. and Huber, G.P. (1987). The system paradigm in organization theory: Correcting the record and suggesting the future. *Academy of Management Review*, 12, 607–621.

ASHRAE (1985). *American Society of Heating, Refrigerating, and Air-conditioning Engineers (ASHRAE) handbook.* New York: ASHRAE.

Åstrand, P.O. and Rodahl, L. (1986). *Textbook of work physiology*, 3rd edn. New York: McGraw-Hill.

Ayoub, M.M. (1973). Work place design and posture. *Human Factors*, 15(3), 265–268.

Baber, C. (1991). *Speech technology in control room systems: A human factors perspective.* Chichester, UK: Ellis Horwood.

Baber, C. and Noyes, J.M. (eds) (1993). *Interactive speech technology: Human factors issues in the application of speech input/output to computers.* London: Taylor & Francis.

Baber, C. and Noyes, J.M. (1996). Speech recognition in adverse environments. *Human Factors*, 38, 142–155.

Baber, C. and Stanton, N.A. (1994). Task analysis for error identification: A methodology for designing error-tolerant consumer products. *Ergonomics*, 37, 1923–1941.

Baddeley, A.D. (1992). Working memory. *Science*, 255(5044), 556–559.

Badler, N.I., Barsky, B.A. and Zelter, D. (eds) (1990). *Making them move: Mechanics, control, and animation of articulated figures.* Palo Alto, CA: Morgan-Kaufmann.

Bainbridge, L. (1983). Ironies of automation. *Automatica*, 19, 755–779.

Baird, J., Berglund, B. and Esfandabad, H. (1994). Longitudinal assessment of sensory reactions in eyes and upper airways of staff in a sick building. *Environment International*, 20, 141–160.

Bammer, G. and Martin, B. (1988). The arguments about RSI: An examination. *Community Health Studies*, 12, 348–358.

Barnes, R.M. (1940). *Motion and time study*, 2nd edn. New York: Wiley.

Bartlett, F.C. (1943). Fatigue following highly skilled work. In *Proceedings of the Royal Society*, B. 131, 247–257.

Barton, J. (1994). Choosing to work at night: A moderating influence on individual tolerance to shiftwork. *Journal of Applied Psychology*, 79, 449–454.

Barton, J., Folkard, S., Smith, L.R., Spelton, E.R. and Tattersall, P.A. (1990). *Standard shiftwork index manual.* Sheffield, UK: MRC/ESRC Social and Applied Psychology Unit.

Bartram, D. (1986). The development of a new keyboard for outward sorting foreign mail. *IMechE*, 57–64. In *Proceedings of Institutes of Mechanical Engineers International Conference on Postal Engineering* (pp. 57–64). London: IMechE.

Bauer, R.M., Greve, K.W., Besch, E.L. and Schramke, C.J. (1992). The role of psychological factors in the report of building related symptoms in sick building syndrome. *Journal of Consulting and Clinical Psychology*, 60(2), 213–219.

Bechtel, R.B. (1997). *Environment and behavior: An introduction.* Thousand Oaks, CA: Sage.

Bedi, R. (1999). Reports on Gaisal train crash. *Daily Telegraph*, 3 August 1999, p. 4.

Beldie, L.P., Pastoor, S. and Schwarz, E. (1983). Fixed versus variable letter width for televised text. *Human Factors*, 25, 273–277.

Bell, P.A., Loomis, R.J. and Cervone, J.C (1982). Effects of heat, social facilitation, sex differences, and task difficulty on reaction time. *Human Factors*, 24, 19–24.

Bendix, T. and Hagberg, M. (1984). Trunk posture and load on the trapezius muscle while sitting at sloping desks. *Ergonomics*, 27, 873–882.

Berg, M. (1989). Facial skin complaints and work at visual display units: Epidemiological, clinical and histopathological studies. *Acta Dermato-Venereologica*, 150, 1–40.

Berners-Lee, T., Cailliau, R., Luotonen, A., Nielsen, H.F. and Secret, A. (1994). The World Wide Web. *Communications of the ACM*, 37(8), 76–82.

Berry, L.M. and Houston, J.P. (1993). *Psychology at work: An introduction to industrial and organisational psychology*. Madison, WI: Brown & Benchmark.

Billings, C.E. (1997). *Aviation automation: The search for a human-centred approach*. Mahwah, NJ: LEA.

Birmingham, H.P. and Taylor, F.V. (1954). *A human engineering approach to the design of man-operated continuous control systems* (report No. 433). Washington DC: US Naval Laboratory.

Blanz, F. and Ghiselli, E.E. (1972). The mixed standard scale: A new rating system. *Personnel Psychology*, 25, 185–199.

Blum, M.L. and Naylor, J.C. (1968). *Industrial psychology: Its theoretical and social foundations*. New York: Harper & Row.

Boeing Commercial Airplane Group (1996). *Statistical summary of commercial jet accidents: Worldwide operations – 1959–1996*. Seattle, WA: Boeing Commercial Airplane Group.

Boel, M., Daniellou, F., Desmores, E. and Teiger, C. (1985). Real work analysis and workers' involvement. In *Proceedings of the 9th Congress of the International Ergonomics Association*, pp. 235–237. Bournemouth, UK: IEA.

Bonney, R.A. (1995). Human response to vibration: Principles and methods. In J.R. Wilson and E.N. Corlett (eds) *Evaluation of human work: A practical ergonomics methodology*, 2nd edn, pp. 541–556. London: Taylor & Francis.

Booher, H.R. and Rouse, W.B. (1990). MANPRINT as the competitive edge. In H.R. Booher (ed.) *MANPRINT: An approach to systems integration*. New York: Van Nostrand Reinhold.

Borg, G.A.V. (1985). *An introduction to Borg's RPE-Scale*. Ithaca, NY: Movement Publications.

Boulding, K. (1956). General systems theory – the skeleton of science. *Management Science*, 2, 197–208.

Bowcott, O. (1990). Computers 'safe' in pregnancy. *The Guardian*, 9 May 1990.

Bowler, Y., Cullen, L. and Hutchinson, E. (1999). Enhancing the safety of future systems. In *Proceedings of People In Control Conference*. Publication No. 463, pp. 179–183. London: IEE.

Boyce, P.R. and Simons, R.H. (1977). Hue discrimination and light sources. *Lighting Research and Technology*, 9, 125–136.

Bramel, D. and Friend, R. (1981). Hawthorne, the myth of the docile worker and class bias in psychology. *American Psychologist*, 36, 867–878.

Breaugh, J.A. (1983). The 12-hour work day: Differing employee reactions. *Personnel Psychology*, 36, 277–288.

Bridger, R.S. (1995). *Introduction to ergonomics*. New York: McGraw-Hill.

Bridger, R.S., Sparto, P. and Marras, W.S. (1995). The ergonomics of digging and the evaluation of a novel design of spade. In S.A. Robertson (ed.) *Contemporary ergonomics*, pp. 391–396. London: Taylor & Francis.

Bristow, G. (1986). *Electronic speech recognition*. London: Collins.

BS 5959 (1980). *Specifications for key numbering system and layout charts for keyboards on office machines*. London: British Standards Institute.

Broadbent, D.E. (1958). *Perception and communications*. New York: Pergamon.

Broadbent, D.E. (1979). Human performance and noise. In C.S. Harris (ed.) *Handbook of noise control*, pp. 2066–2085. New York: McGraw-Hill.

Brookes, M.J. (1972). Office landscape: Does it work? *Applied Ergonomics*, 3(4), 224–236.

Brookes, M.J. and Kaplan, A. (1972). The office environment: Space planning and affective behavior. *Human Factors*, 14, 373–392.

Brown, C.M. (1999). *Human–computer interface design guidelines*. Exeter, UK: Intellect Books.

Bunnell, D.E. and Horvath, S.M. (1989). Interactive effects of heat, physical work and CO exposure on metabolism and cognitive task performance. *Aviation, Space and Environmental Medicine*, 60, 428–432.

Burns, N.R., Nettelbeck, T., White, M. and Willson, J. (1999). Effects of car window tinting on visual performance: A comparison of elderly and young drivers. *Ergonomics*, 42(3), 428–443.

Cain, W.S., Leaderer, B.P., Cannon, L., Tosun, T. and Ismail, H. (1987). Odorization of inert gas for occupational safety: Psychophysical considerations. *American Industrial Hygiene Journal*, 48, 47–55.

Cakir, A., Hart, D.J. and Stewart, T.F.M. (1980). *Visual display terminals*. Chichester, UK: Wiley.

Campion, M.A. and McClelland, C.L. (1991). Interdisciplinary examination of the costs and benefits of enlarged jobs: A job design quasi-experiment. *Journal of Applied Psychology*, 76, 186–198.

Cannon-Bowers, J.A., Salas, E. and Converse, S. (1993). Shared mental models in expert team decision making. In J. Castellan Jr (ed.) *Individual and group decision making*, pp. 221–246. Hillsdale, NJ: LEA.

Caple, D.C. and Betts, N.J. (1991). RSI – Its rise and fall in Telecom Australia 1981–1990. In *Proceedings of the 11th Congress of the International Ergonomics Association*, pp. 1037–1039. London: Taylor & Francis.

Carayon, P., Smith, M.J. and Haims, M.C. (1999). Work organization, job stress, and work-related musculoskeletal disorders. *Human Factors*, 41, 644–663.

Card, S.K., English, W.K. and Burr, B.J. (1978). Evaluation of mouse, rate-controlled isometric joystick, step keys, and task keys for text selection on a CRT. *Ergonomics*, 21(8), 601–613.

Carey, T. (1982). User differences in interface design. *Computer*, 18, 14–20.

Carver, C.S. and Scheier, M.F. (1981). *Attention and self-regulation: A control theory approach to human behaviour*. New York: Springer-Verlag.

Casali, J.G. and Park, M.Y. (1990). Attenuation performance of four hearing protectors under dynamic movement and different user fitting conditions. *Human Factors*, 32, 9–25.

Case, K. and Porter, J.M. (1980). SAMMIE: A computer aided ergonomics design system. *Engineering*, 220, 21–25.

Cassidy, T. (1997). *Environmental psychology: Behaviour and experience in context.* Hove, UK: Psychology Press.

Chapanis, A. (1965). On the allocation of functions between men and machines. *Occupational Psychology*, 39, 1–11.

Chapanis, A. (1990). The International Ergonomics Association: Its first 30 years. *Ergonomics*, 33(3), 275–282.

Chapanis, A. (1999). *The Chapanis chronicles: 50 years of human factors research, education, and design.* Santa Barbara, CA: Aegean Publishing Company.

Chapanis, A. and Lindenbaum, L.E. (1959). A reaction time study of four control-display linkages. *Human Factors*, 1(4), 1–7.

Chapanis, A., Garner, W. and Morgan, C. (1949). *Applied experimental psychology: Human factors in engineering design.* New York: Wiley.

Christensen, J.M. (1976). Ergonomics: Where have we been and where are we going: II. *Ergonomics*, 19(3), 287–300.

Christensen, J.M. and Talbot, J.M. (1986). Psychological aspects of space flight. *Aviation, Space, and Environmental Medicine*, 57, 203–212.

Christie, A.W. and Fisher, A.J. (1966). The effect of glare from street lighting lanterns on the vision of drivers of different ages. *Transactions of the Illuminating Engineering Society (London)*, 31, 93–108.

CIBS (1984). *Code for interior lighting.* London: Chartered Institution of Building Services.

Clarke, D.D., Forsyth, R. and Wright, R. (1998). Machine learning in road accident research: Decision trees describing road accidents during cross-flow turns. *Ergonomics*, 41(7), 1060–1079.

Cochrane, P., Payne, R. and MacDonald, B. (1997). From Kirk to Picard – A vision of mobility. *Personal Technologies*, 1, 6–10.

Coleman, J.C., Butcher, J.N. and Carson, R.C. (1980). *Abnormal psychology and modern life*, 6th edn. Glenview, IL: Scott, Foresman.

Collins, M.J., Brown, B. and Bowman, K.J. (1991). Task variables and visual discomfort associated with the use of VDTs. *Optometry and Visual Science*, 68(1), 27–33.

Conrad, R. and Hull, A.J. (1968). The preferred layout for numeral data-entry keysets. *Ergonomics*, 11, 165–173.

Conroy, C. (1989). Work-related injuries in the meatpacking industry. *Journal of Safety Research*, 20, 47–53.

Coppola, A. (1984). Artificial intelligence applications to maintenance. In *Artificial intelligence in maintenance*, pp. 23–44. Brooks AFB, TX: Air Force Human Resources Laboratory.

Corlett, E.N. and Bishop, R.P. (1976). A technique for accessing postural discomfort. *Ergonomics*, 19, 175–182.

Corlett, E.N. and Clark, T.S. (1995). *The ergonomics of workspaces and machines: A design manual*, 2nd edn. London: Taylor & Francis.

Cothern, C. and Smith, J. (1987). *Environmental radon.* New York: Plenum.

Courtney, A.J. (1986). Chinese population stereotypes: Color associations. *Human Factors*, 28, 97–99.

Cox, E.A. (1984). Radiation emissions from visual display units. In B.G. Pearce (ed.) *Health hazards of VDTs?* pp. 25–37. Chichester, UK: Wiley.

Cox, R., Shepherd, J. and Corey, P. (1981). Influence of an employee fitness programme upon fitness, productivity and absenteeism. *Ergonomics*, 24, 795–806.

Cox, T. and Cox, S. (1993). Psychosocial and organisational hazards at work: Control and monitoring. In *European Occupational Health Series No. 5.* Copenhagen: World Health Organisation (Europe).

Dain, S.J., McCarthy, A.K. and Chan-Ling, T. (1988). Symptoms in VDU operators. *American Journal of Optometry and Physiological Optics*, 6, 162–167.

Damon, A., Stroudt, H.W. and McFarland, R.A. (1966). *The human body in equipment design.* Cambridge, MA: Harvard University Press.

Davies, D.R. and Parasuraman, R. (1982). *The psychology of vigilance.* London: Academic Press.

Davis, G.F. and Powell, W.W. (1992). Organization–environment relations. In M.D. Dunnette and L.M. Hough (eds) *Handbook of industrial and organizational psychology*, vol. 3, pp. 315–375. Palo Alto, CA: Consulting Psychologists Press.

Degani, A., Asfour, S.S., Waly, S.M. and Koshy, J.G. (1993). A comparative study of two shovel designs. *Applied Ergonomics*, 24, 306–312.

Deininger, R.L. (1960). Human factors engineering studies of the design and use of pushbutton telephone sets. *The Bell System Technical Journal*, 39, 995–1012.

Dempster, W.T. (1955). *Space requirements of the seated operator: Geometrical, kinematic and mechanical aspects of the body with special reference to the limbs* (WADC Technical Report 55–159). Ohio: Wright Patterson Air Force Base.

Diaper, D. (1989). *Task analysis for human–computer interaction.* Chichester, UK: Ellis Horwood.

Dickinson, C.E., Campion, K., Foster, A.F., Newman, S.J., O'Rourke, A.M.T. and Thomas, P.G. (1992). Questionnaire development: An examination of the Nordic musculoskeletal questionnaire. *Applied Ergonomics*, 23, 197–201.

Donnelly, D.M., Noyes, J.M. and Johnson, D.M. (1998). Development of an integrated decision making model for avionics application. In M. Hanson (ed.) *Contemporary ergonomics*, pp. 424–428. London: Taylor & Francis.

Dreyfus, H.L. and Dreyfus, S.E. (1986). *Minds over machines.* New York: Macmillan.

Driskell, J.E. and Salas, E. (1991). Group decision making under stress. *Journal of Applied Psychology*, 76, 473–478.

Drucker, P.F. (1954). *The practice of management.* New York: Harper & Row.

Drury, C.G. (1983). Task analysis methods in industry. *Applied Ergonomics*, 14, 19–28.

Duchon, J.C., Wagner, J. and Keran, C.M. (1989). Forward versus backward shift rotation. In *Proceedings of the 33rd Annual Meeting of the Human Factors Society*, pp. 806–810. Santa Monica, CA: Human Factors Society.

Duchon, J.C., Keran, C.M. and Smith, T.J. (1994). Extended workdays in an underground mine: A work performance analysis. *Human Factors*, 36, 258–268.

Dunham, R.B., Pierce, J.L. and Castaneda, M.B. (1987). Alternative work schedules: Two field quasi-experiments. *Personnel Psychology*, 40, 215–242.

Dutra, A.R.A. (1997). Evaluation of comfort for a study room based on anthropometric data. In *Proceedings of 13th Triennial Congress of the International Ergonomics Association, Tampere, Finland*, vol. 2, pp. 287–289. International Ergonomics Association IEA.

Eason, K.D. (1984). Job design and VDU operation. In B.G. Pearce (ed.) *Health hazards of VDTs?* pp. 217–229. Chichester, UK: Wiley.

Edholm, O.G. and Murrell, K.F.H. (1973). *The Ergonomics Society: A history*

1949–1970. (London: Ergonomics Research Society), Winchester, UK: Warren & Sons, Ltd.

Editorial (1957). Ergonomics Research Society. *Ergonomics*, 1, 1–3.

Editorial (1993). What is in a name? *The Ergonomist*, 275, 1 and 4.

Editorial (1998). World report: Record lottery creates frenzy. *The Globe and Mail International News*, 29 July 1998, p. A13.

Editorial (2000). Purely editorial. *Theoretical Issues in Ergonomics Science*, 1(1), 1–2.

Edwards, A.D.N. (1991). *Speech synthesis: Technology for disabled people.* London: Chapman.

Edwards, E. (1972). Man and machine: Systems for safety. In *Proceedings of the BALPA Technical Symposium 'Outlook on Safety'*, pp. 21–36. London: BALPA (British Air Line Pilot Association).

Edwards, E. and Edwards, M. (1990). *The aircraft cabin: Managing the Human Factors.* Aldershot, UK: Gower.

Edwards, W. (1954). The theory of decision making. *Psychological Bulletin*, 51, 380–417.

Edworthy, J. and Adams, A. (1996). *Warnings design: A research prospective.* London: Taylor & Francis.

Eilam, Z. (1989). Human engineering the one-handed keyboard. *Applied Ergonomics*, 20, 225–229.

Ellis, H.D. (1982). The effects of cold on the performance of serial choice reaction time and various discrete tasks. *Human Factors*, 24, 589–598.

Enander, A. (1984). Performance and sensory aspects of work in cold conditions: A review. *Ergonomics*, 27(4), 365–378.

Ernszt, R.P. and O'Connor, P.J. (1988). *Report on accident countermeasures focussing on elderly drivers.* South Australia: Road Safety Division.

Evans, C. (1983). *The mighty micro: The impact of the computer revolution.* London: Victor Gollancz.

Evans, G.W. and Carrere, S. (1991). Traffic congestion, perceived control, and psychophysiological stress among urban bus drivers. *Journal of Applied Psychology*, 76, 658–663.

Fanger, P.O., Breum, N.O. and Jerking, E. (1977). Can colour influence man's thermal comfort? *Ergonomics*, 20, 11–18.

Farmer, E.W. (1992). Ionization. In A.P. Smith and D.M. Jones (eds) *Handbook of human performance: Volume I – The physical environment*, pp. 237–260. London: Academic Press.

Farmer, E. and Chambers, E.G. (1939). *A study of accident proneness amongst motor drivers.* Industrial Health Research Board Report No. 84. London: Industrial Health Research Board.

Fayol, H. (1949). *General and industrial management.* London: Pitman & Sons.

Feuer, D. (1985). Training at Three Mile Island: Six years later. *Training*, 22, 26–40.

Finnish Institute of Occupational Health. (1992). *OWAS, a method for the evaluation of postural load during work.* Publications Office, Topeliuksenkatu 41 aA, SF 00250 Helsinki, Finland.

Fitts, P.M. (1951). Engineering psychology and equipment design. In S.S. Stevens (ed.) *Handbook of experimental psychology.* New York: Wiley.

Fitts, P.M. (1954). The information capacity of the human motor system in controlling amplitude of movement. *Journal of Experimental Psychology*, 47, 381–391.

Fitts, P.M. and Jones, R.E. (1947). Psychological aspects of instrument display. 1: Analysis of 270 'pilot error' experiences in reading and interpreting aircraft instruments. Aeromedical Laboratory Report AMRL-TSEAA-694-12A. Reprinted in H.W. Sinaiko (ed.) (1961). *Selected papers on the design and use of control systems*. New York: Dover.

Fitts, P.M. and Seeger, C.M. (1953). S–R compatibility: Spatial characteristics of stimulus and response codes. *Journal of Experimental Psychology*, 46, 199–210.

Flach, J.M. (1989). An ecological alternative to egg-sucking. *Human Factors Society Bulletin*, 32, 4–6.

Flanagan, J.C. (1954). The critical incident technique. *Psychological Bulletin*, 51, 327–358.

Flinn, M.W. (1966). *The origins of the industrial revolution*. London: Longmans.

Foley, J.D. (1987). Interfaces for advanced computing. *Scientific American*, Special Issue on Advanced Computing.

Foley, J.D., Wallace, V.L. and Chan, P. (1984). The human factors of computer graphics interaction techniques. *IEEE Computer Graphics & Applications*, 4(11), 13–48.

Folkard, S. (1987). Irregular and abnormal hours of work. *Ergonomics*, 30, Special Issue.

Forsythe, C., Grose, E. and Ratner, J. (eds) (1998). *Human factors and web development*. Mahwah, NJ: LEA.

Frankish, C.R. (1999). Pen-based computing. In J.M. Noyes and M.J. Cook (eds) *Interface technology: The leading edge*, pp. 59–72. Baldock, UK: Research Studies Press.

Fried, Y. and Ferris, G.R. (1987). The validity of the job characteristics model: A review and meta-analysis. *Personnel Psychology*, 40, 287–322.

Friedman, M. and Rosenman, R.H. (1959). Association of specific overt behavior pattern with blood and cardiovascular findings. *Journal of the American Medical Association*, 169, 1286–1296.

Friedman, M. and Rosenman, R.H. (1974). *Type A behavior and your heart*. New York: Knopf.

Frievalds, A. (1986). The ergonomics of shovelling and shovel design – a review of the literature. *Ergonomics*, 29, 3–18.

Frone, M.R. and McFarlin, D.B. (1989). Chronic occupational stressor, self-focused attention, and well-being: Testing a cybernetic model of stress. *Journal of Applied Psychology*, 74, 876–883.

Frost, P.J. and Jamal, M. (1979). Shift work, attitudes and reported behaviors: Some association between individual characteristics and hours of work and leisure. *Journal of Applied Psychology*, 64, 77–81.

Fukui, S. (1983). Psychopathology of psychiatric patients in terms of personal space: A comparative study of schizophrenic, depressive and neurotic patients. *Kyushu Neuropsychiatry*, 29, 181–204.

Gannon, M.J., Norland, D.L. and Robeson, F.E. (1983). Shift work has complex effects on lifestyles and work habits. *Personnel Administrator*, 28, 93–97.

Ganster, D.C. (1986). Type A behavior and occupational stress. *Journal of Organizational Behavior Management*, 8(2), 61–84.

Gardiner, M.M. and Christie, B. (1987). *Applying cognitive psychology to interface design.* Chichester, UK: Wiley.

Gasaway, D. (1984). 1984 NIOSH compendium hearing protector attenuation. *National Safety News*, November Issue, 26–34.

Gavin, H. (1998). *The essence of cognitive psychology.* Hemel Hempstead, UK: Prentice Hall.

Gawron, V. (1982). Performance effects of noise intensity, psychological set, and task type and complexity. *Human Factors*, 24, 225–243.

Gibson, J. (1979). *The ecological approach to visual perception.* Boston, MA: Houghton Mifflin.

Gifford, R. (1987). *Environmental psychology: Principles and practice.* Boston, MA: Allyn & Bacon.

Gilbert, L.A. and Holahan, C.K. (1982). Conflicts between student/professional, parental, and self-development roles: A comparison of high and low effective copers. *Human Relations*, 35, 635–648.

Gilbreth, F.B. and Gilbreth, L.M. (1921). *First steps in finding the one best way to do work.* Paper presented at the Annual Meeting of the American Society of Mechanical Engineers, New York.

Gillespie, R. (1991). *Manufacturing knowledge: A history of the Hawthorne experiments.* Cambridge: University Press.

Goodstein, L.P. (1981). Discriminative display support for process operators. In J. Rasmussen and W.B. Rouse (eds) *Human detection and diagnosis of system failures*, pp. 433–449. New York: Plenum.

Gorayska, A. and Mey, J.L. (eds) (1996). *Cognitive technology: In search of a humane interface.* New York: Elsevier.

Grandjean, E. (1968). Fatigue: Its physiological and psychological significance. *Ergonomics*, 11, 427–436.

Grandjean, E. (1981). *Fitting the task to the man.* London: Taylor & Francis.

Grandjean, E. (1984). Summary. In B.G. Pearce (ed.) *Health hazards of VDTs?* pp. 61–74. Chichester, UK: Wiley.

Grandjean, E. (1987). *Ergonomics in computerised offices.* London: Taylor & Francis.

Grandjean, E. (1988). *Fitting the task to the man*, 4th edn. London: Taylor & Francis.

Grandjean, E., Boni, A. and Krestzschmer, H. (1969). The development of a rest chair profile for healthy and notalgic people. *Ergonomics*, 12(2), 307–315.

Greene, B.G., Logan, J.S. and Pisoni, D.B. (1986). Perception of synthetic speech produced automatically by rule: Intelligibility of eight text to speech systems. *Behavior, Research Methods, Instruments and Computers*, 18, 100–107.

Greenwood, M., Woods, H.M. and Yule, G.U. (1919). A report on the incidence of industrial accidents upon individuals with special reference to multiple accidents. Industrial Fatigue Research Board, Report No. 4. In W. Haddon, E.A. Suchmann and D. Flein (eds) (1964) *Accident research.* New York: Harper.

Gregory, R.L. (1972, June 23). Seeing as thinking. *Times Literary Supplement*, 707–708.

Greiner, T.M. and Gordon, C.C. (1990). *An assessment of long-term changes in anthropometric dimensions: Secular trends of US Army males* (Natick/TR-91/006). Natick, MA: US Army Natick Research, Development and Engineering Center.

Grether, W.F. (1949). Instrument reading 1. The design of long-scale indicators for speed and accuracy of quantitative readings. *Journal of Applied Psychology*, 33, 363–372.

Grether, W.F., Harris, C.S., Mohr, G.C., Nixon, C.W., Ohlbaum, M., Sommer, H.C., Thaler, V.H. and Veghte, J.H. (1971). Effects of combined heat, noise and vibration stress on human performance and physiological functions. *Aerospace Medicine*, 42, 1092–1097.

Grieco, A. (1986). Sitting posture: An old problem and a new one. *Ergonomics*, 29, 345–362.

Grieve, D. and Pheasant, S. (1982). Biomechanics. In W.T. Singleton (ed.) *The body at work*. Cambridge, UK: Cambridge University Press.

Griffin, M.J. (1982). *The effects of vibration on health*. Memorandum 632. University of Southampton: Institute for Sound and Vibration Research.

Griffin, M.J. (1990). *Handbook of human vibration*. San Diego, CA: Academic Press.

Griffin, M.J. (1992). Vibration. In A.P. Smith and D.M. Jones (eds) *Handbook of human performance: Volume I – The physical environment*, pp. 55–78. London: Academic Press.

Griffin, M.J., Parsons, K. and Whitham, E. (1982). Vibration and comfort. IV. Application of experimental results. *Ergonomics*, 25, 721–739.

Hackman, J.R. and Oldham, G.R. (1976). Motivation through the design of work: Test of a theory. *Organizational Behavior and Human Performance*, 16, 250–279.

Hackos, J.T. (1994). *Managing your documentation projects*. New York: Wiley.

Hackos, J.T. and Redish, J.C. (1998). *User and task analysis for interface design*. New York: Wiley.

Haigh, R. (1993). The ageing process: A challenge for design. *Applied Ergonomics*, 24(1), 9–14.

Hall, E.T. (1959). *The silent language*. New York: Doubleday.

Hall, E.T. (1966). *The hidden dimension*. Garden City, NY: Doubleday.

Hall, E.T. (1976). The anthropology of space: An organising model. In H.M. Proshansky, W.H. Ittleson and L.G. Rivlin (eds) *Environmental psychology*, 2nd edn. New York: Holt, Rinehart & Winston.

Hancock, P.A. (1981). The limitation of human performance in extreme heat conditions. In *Proceedings of the Human Factors Society*, pp. 74–78. Santa Monica, CA: Human Factors Society.

Hancock, P.A. and Warm, J.S. (1989). A dynamic model of stress and sustained attention. *Human Factors*, 31, 519–537.

Harper, K. (1999). Inquiry to focus on driver error. *The Guardian*, 6 October 1999, p. 1.

Hart, S.G. and Staveland, L.E. (1988). Development of NASA-TLX (Task Load Index): Results of experimental and theoretical research. In P.A. Hancock and N. Meshkati (eds) *Human mental workload*, pp. 139–183. Amsterdam: North Holland.

Hartley, J. (1998). Return to sender: Why written communications fail. *The Psychologist*, vol. 11, No. 10. 477–480.

Haslam, D.R. (1985). Sustained operations and military performance. *Behavior Research Methods, Instruments and Computers*, 17, 9–95.

Haslegrave, C.M. (1995). Auditory environment and noise assessment. In J.R. Wilson and E.N. Corlett (eds) *Evaluation of human work: A practical ergonomics methodology*, 2nd edn., pp. 506–540. London: Taylor & Francis.

Haslegrave, C.M. and Corlett, E.N. (1995). Evaluating work conditions and risk of injury – techniques for field surveys. In J.R. Wilson and E.N. Corlett (eds) *Evaluation of human work: A practical ergonomics methodology*, 2nd edn., pp. 892–920. London: Taylor & Francis.

Hastings, S., Woods, V., Haslam, R.A. and Buckle, P. (2000). Health risks from mice and other non-keyboard input devices. In P.T. McCabe, M.A. Hanson and S.A. Robertson (eds) *Contemporary ergonomics*, pp. 312–316. London: Taylor & Francis.

Hawkins, F.H. (1984). Human factors education in European air transport operation. In *Breakdown in human adaptation to stress: Towards a multi-disciplinary approach*, vol. 1 (for the Commission of the European Communities). The Hague: Martinus Nijhoff.

Hawkins, F.H. (1993). *Human factors in flight*, 2nd edn. Aldershot, UK: Ashgate.

Health and Safety Executive (1988). *Control of substances hazardous to health regulations*. London: HMSO.

Health and Safety Executive (1990). *Work related upper limb disorders: A guide to prevention*. London: HMSO.

Health and Safety Executive (1992a). *Display screen equipment work: Guidance on regulations*. London: HMSO.

Health and Safety Executive (1992b). *Manual handling: Guidance on regulations*. London: HMSO.

Health and Safety Executive (1997). *The explosion and fires at the Texaco Refinery, Milford Haven, 24 July 1994*. Norwich: HSE Books.

Health and Safety Executive (1999). *Reducing error and influencing behaviour*. Norwich: HSE Books.

Helander, M. (1995). *A guide to the ergonomics of manufacturing*. London: Taylor & Francis.

Hendy, K.C., Liao, J. and Milgram, P. (1997). Combining time and intensity effects in assessing operator information-processing load. *Human Factors*, 39, 30–47.

Henneberg, M. (1992). Continuing human evolution: Bodies, brains and the role of variability. *Transactions of the Royal South African Society*, Part 1, 159–182.

Herbert, C. (2000). Challenges of neurorehabilitation. *The Psychologist*, 13(1), 24–26.

Herzberg, F. (1966). *Work and the nature of man*. Cleveland, OH: World.

Hewes, G.W. (1957). The anthropology of posture. *Scientific American*, 196, 122–132.

Highfield, R. (1999). Investigators will focus on human error as likeliest cause. *Daily Telegraph*, 25 August 1999, p. 4.

Hill, S. (1995). *A practical introduction to the human–computer interface*. London: DP Publications.

Hobday, S.W. (1996). The Maltron keyboards. In *Proceedings of IEE Colloquium 'Interfaces – The Leading Edge'*, Digest No. 96/126, 8/1–8/10. London: IEE.

Hoc, J-M. (2000). From human–machine interaction to human–machine cooperation. *Ergonomics*, 43(7), 833–843.

Hocking, B. (1987). Epidemiological aspects of 'Repetition Strain Injury' in Telecom Australia. *The Medical Journal of Australia*, 147 (September Issue), 218–222.

Hoekstra, P.N. (1999). Centre-dependent spatial density functions of 3D surface anthropometry data. In M.A. Hanson, E.J. Lovesey and S.A. Robertson (eds) *Contemporary ergonomics*, pp. 396–400. London: Taylor & Francis.

Hollnagel, E. (1999). Control versus dependence: Striking the balance in function allocation. *CSERIAC Gateway*, IX(4), 12–13.

Holt, R.R. (1982). Occupational stress. In L. Goldberger and S. Breznitz (eds) *Handbook of stress: Theoretical and clinical aspects*. New York: Free Press.

Hone, K.S., Graham, R., Maguire, M.C., Baber, C. and Johnson, G.I. (1998). Speech technology for automatic teller machines: An investigation of user attitude and performance. *Ergonomics*, 41(7), 962–981.

Hopkinson, R.G., Waldram, J.M. and Stevens, W.R. (1941). Brightness and contrast in illuminating engineering. *Transactions of the Illuminating Engineering Society (London)*, 6, 37–47.

Horne, J.A., Anderson, N.R. and Wilkinson, R.T. (1983). Effects of sleep deprivation on signal detection measures of vigilance: Implications for sleep function. *Sleep*, 6, 347–358.

Horvath, S.M. and Drechsler-Parks, D.M. (1992). Air pollution and behaviour. In A.P. Smith and D.M. Jones (eds) *Handbook of human performance: Volume I – The physical environment*, pp. 131–148. London: Academic Press.

Howarth, P.A. (1995). Assessment of the visual environment. In J.R. Wilson and E.N. Corlett (eds) *Evaluation of human work: A practical ergonomics methodology*, 2nd edn., pp. 445–482. London: Taylor & Francis.

Hsu, S-H. and Peng, Y. (1993). Control/display relationship of the four-burner stove: A reexamination. *Human Factors*, 35, 745–749.

Hsu, S-H. and Wu, S-P. (1991). An investigation for determining the optimum length of chopsticks. *Applied Ergonomics*, 22(6), 395–400.

Huey, M.B. and Wickens, C.D. (eds) (1993). *Workload transition: Implications for individual and team performance*. Washington, DC: National Academy Press.

Hughes, P.C. and McNelis, J.F. (1978). Lighting, productivity, and the working environment. *Lighting, Research and Application*, 8, 32–40.

Human Factors in Reliability Group (1995). *Improving compliance with safety procedures: Reducing industrial violations*. Norwich: HSE Books.

Hundert, A. and Greenfield, N. (1969). Physical space and organizational behavior: A study of an office landscape. In *Proceedings of the 77th Annual American Psychological Association*, 4, 601–602.

Hunt, R. and Shelley, J. (1988). *Computer and common sense*, 4th edn. Hemel Hempstead, UK: Prentice Hall.

Hunter, T.A. (1992). *Engineering design for safety*. New York: McGraw-Hill.

Huse, E.F. and Cummings, T.G. (1985). *Organizational development and change*, 3rd edn. St Paul, MN: West.

Hutchinson, T.E., White, K.P., Martin, W.N., Reichert, K.C. and Frey, L.A. (1989). Human–computer interaction using eye-gaze input. *IEEE Transactions on Systems, Man, & Cybernetics*, 19(6), 1527–1534.

Huws, U. (1993). *Teleworking in Britain. A report to the Employment Department*. Employment Department Research Series No. 18.

IES (1984). *IES Lighting handbook: Reference volume*. New York: Illuminating Engineering Society of North America.

IES (1987). *IES Lighting handbook: Application volume*. New York: Illuminating Engineering Society of North America.

IRS (1999). The state of telework. *Employment Trends*, 673, 11.

ISO 1999 (1990). *Acoustics – Determination of occupational noise exposure and estimation of noise-induced hearing impairment*. Geneva: International Standards Organisation.

ISO 4169 (1979). *Office machines – keyboards – keynumbering system and layout charts*. Geneva: International Standards Organisation.

ISO 5349 (1986). *Guidelines for the measurement and assessment of human exposure to hand transmitted vibration*. Geneva: International Standards Organisation.

ISO 9241 (1991). *Ergonomic requirements for office work with visual display terminals, Part 4: Keyboard requirements*. Geneva: International Standards Organisation.

ISO 9241 (1997). *Guidance on usability*. (Final Draft 9241, Part 11, 24 pp.). Geneva: International Standards Organisation.

ISO DIS 11399 (1993). *Ergonomics of the thermal environment: Principles and application of international standards*. Geneva: International Standards Organisation.

Istance, H.O. (1997). Eye-based interaction for users with special needs. *Interfaces*, 35, 9–12.

Jackson, A. and Monnington, S. (1999). Safety critical dimensions in go-kart design. In M.A. Hanson, E.J. Lovesey and S.A. Robertson (eds) *Contemporary ergonomics*, pp. 163–167. London: Taylor & Francis.

Jackson, S.E., Turner, J.A. and Brief, A.P. (1987). Correlates of burnout among public service lawyers. *Journal of Occupational Behaviour*, 8, 339–349.

Jaschinski-Krusza, W. (1991). Eyestrain in VDU users: Viewing distance and the resting position of ocular muscles. *Human Factors*, 33(1), 69–83.

Jenkins, C.D., Rosenman, R. and Friedman, M. (1966). Components of the coronary-prone behavior pattern: Their relation to silent myocardial infarction and blood lipids. *Journal of Chronic Diseases*, 19, 599–609.

Jenkins, J.A. (1991). *Alternative input methods*. (Report for ISE 5614). Blacksburg, VA: Virginia Tech (VPI & SU).

Johansson, G. and Aronsson, G. (1984). Stress reactions in computerised administrative work. *Journal of Occupational Behaviour*, 5, 159–181.

Johnson-Laird, P.N. (1983). *Mental models*. Cambridge, UK: Cambridge University Press.

Jones, A. (ed.) (1996). *Chambers Dictionary of Quotations*. Edinburgh: Chambers Harrap.

Jones, D.M. and Chapman, A.J. (eds) (1984). *Noise and society*. Chichester, UK: Wiley.

Jones, D.M. and Davies, D.R. (1984). Individual and group differences in the response to noise. In D.M. Jones and A.J. Chapman (eds) *Noise and society*, pp. 125–153. Chichester, UK: Wiley.

Jones, J.W., Barge, B.N., Steffy, B.D., Fay, L.M., Kunz, L.K. and Wuebker, L.J. (1988). Stress and medical malpractice: Organizational risk assessment and intervention. *Journal of Applied Psychology*, 73, 727–735.

Jordan, N. (1963). Allocation of functions between man and machine in automated systems. *Journal of Applied Psychology*, 47, 161–165.

Jordan, P.W. (1998). *An introduction to usability*. London: Taylor & Francis.

Jordan, P.W., Thomas, B., Weerdmeester, B.A. and McClelland, I.L. (eds) (1996). *Usability evaluation in industry*. London: Taylor & Francis.

Juergens, H.W., Aune, I.A. and Pieper, U. (1990). *International data on anthropometry* (Occupational Safety and Health Series No. 65). Geneva: International Labour Office.

Kahneman, D., Slovic, P. and Tversky, A. (eds) (1982). *Judgements under uncertainty: Heuristics and biases.* Cambridge, UK: Cambridge University Press.

Kakar, S. (1970). *Frederick Taylor: A study in personality and motivation.* Cambridge, MA: MIT Press.

Kanki, B.G. (1996). Stress and aircrew performance: A team-level perspective. In J.E. Driskell and E. Salas (eds) *Stress and human performance*, pp. 127–162. Mahwah, NJ: LEA.

Karwowski, W. (1991). Complexity, fuzziness, and ergonomic incompatibility issues in the control of dynamic work environments. *Ergonomics*, 34, 671–686.

Karwowski, W., Genaidy, A. and Asfour, S. (eds) (1990). *Computer-aided ergonomics.* London: Taylor & Francis.

Kast, F.E. and Rosenzweig, J.E. (1972). General systems theory: Applications for organization and management. *Academy of Management Journal*, 15, 444–465.

Katzell, R.A., Bienstock, P. and Faerstein, P.H. (1977). *A guide to worker productivity experiments in the United States, 1971–1975.* New York: University Press.

Kaufman, J.E. and Haynes, H. (eds) (1981). *IES Lighting handbook: Application volume.* New York: Illuminating Engineering Society of North America.

Keisler, S. and Finholt, T. (1988). The mystery of RSI. *American Psychologist*, 43, 1004–1015.

Keller, E. (ed.) (1994). *Fundamentals of speech synthesis and speech recognition: Basic concepts, state of the art and future challenges.* Chichester, UK: Wiley.

Kemeny, J. (1979). *The need for change: The legacy of TMI.* Report of the President's Commission on the Accident at Three Mile Island. New York: Pergamon.

Kemp, M.S., Noyes, J.M. and Mills, S. (1995). Usability of menu- versus icon-based software in automatic test equipment (ATE) control. In *Proceedings of IEE Colloquium 'Man–Machine Interfaces for Instrumentation'*, Digest 95/175. London: IEE.

Kemsley, W.F.F. (1950). Weight and height of a population in 1943. *Annals of Eugenics*, 15, 161–183.

Kennedy, K.W. (1964). *Reach capability of the USAF population: Phase 1, the outer boundaries of grasping reach envelopes for the shirt sleeved, seated operator.* (Report AMRL-TDR-64-59.) Ohio: Wright Patterson Air Force Base.

Kerr, R. (1988). Indoor radon: The deadliest pollutant. *Science*, 240, 606–608.

Keys, E. (1993). Typography, color, and information structure. *Technical Communication*, 40, 638–654.

Kilbom, A. (1995). Measurement and assessment of dynamic work. In J.R. Wilson and E.N. Corlett (eds) *Evaluation of human work: A practical ergonomics methodology*, 2nd edn., pp. 640–661. London: Taylor & Francis.

Kirakowski, J. (2000). *Usability evaluation by questionnaire.* London: Taylor & Francis.

Kirwan, B. (1994). *A guide to practical human reliability assessment.* London: Taylor & Francis.

Kirwan, B. and Ainsworth, L.K. (eds) (1992). *A guide to task analysis.* London: Taylor & Francis.

Klein, G. (1993). A recognition-primed decision model of rapid decision making. In

G. Klein, J. Orasanu, R. Calderwood and C. Szambok (eds) *Decision making in action: Models and methods*. Norwood, NJ: Ablex.

Knauth, P. and Kiesswetter, E. (1987). A change from weekly to quicker shift rotations: A field study of discontinuous three-shift workers. *Ergonomics*, 30, 1311–1321.

Knave, B.G. (1983). The visual display unit. In *Ergonomic principles in office automation*. Stockholm: Ericsson International.

Knight, G. and Noyes, J.M. (1999). Children's behaviour and the design of school furniture. *Ergonomics*, 42(5), 747–760.

Knutsson, A., Åkerstedt, T., Jonsson, B.G. and Orth-Gorner, K. (1986). Increased risk of ischaemic heart disease in shift workers. *The Lancet*, 12, Vol. 2, 89–92.

Kogi, K. (1991). Job content and working time: The scope for joint change. *Ergonomics*, 34, 757–773.

Kollarits, J. (1937). Beobachtungen über Dyspraxien (Fehlhandlungen). *Archives für die Gesamte Psychologie*, 99, 305–399.

Konz, S. (1990). *Work design: Industrial ergonomics*. Worthington, OH: Publishing Horizons.

Koradecka, D. (2000). *Wojciech Jastrzebowski – An Outline of Ergonomics, or The Science of Work based upon the truths drawn from the Science of Nature, 1857*. Poland: Central Institute for Labour Protection.

Kraft, J.A. (1958). A follow-up survey of human factors research in aircraft, missiles and supporting industries. *Human Factors*, 1, 23–25.

Kragt, H. (1992). *Enhancing industrial performance*. London: Taylor & Francis.

Kramer, A. (1991). Physiological metrics of mental workload: A review of recent progress. In D. Damos (ed.) *Multiple task performance*, pp. 279–328. London: Taylor & Francis.

Kroemer, K.H.E. (1989). Engineering anthropometry. *Ergonomics*, 32, 767–784.

Kroemer, K.H.E. (1992). Performance on a prototype keyboard with ternary chorded keys. *Applied Ergonomics*, 23, 83–90.

Kroemer, K.H.E., Kroemer, H. and Kroemer-Elbert, K. (1994). *Ergonomics: How to design for ease and efficiency*. Englewood Cliffs, NJ: Prentice-Hall.

Kryter, K.D. (1970). *The effects of noise on man*. London: Academic Press.

Kryter, K.D. (1985). *The effects of noise on man*, 2nd edn. London: Academic Press.

Kukkonen-Harjula, K. and Rauramaa, R. (1984). Oxygen consumption of lumberjacks in logging with a power saw. *Ergonomics*, 27, 59–65.

Kumar, S. (1999). *Biomechanics in ergonomics*. London: Taylor & Francis.

Kuorinka, I. and Viikari-Juntura, E. (1982). Prevalence of neck and upper limb disorders (NLD) and work load in different occupational groups. Problems in classification and diagnosis. *Journal of Human Ergology*, 11, 65–72.

Kuorinka, I., Jonsson, B., Kilbom, A., Vinterberg, H., Biering-Sorensen, F., Andersson, G. and Jorgensen, K. (1987). Standardized Nordic questionnaires for the analysis of musculoskeletal symptoms. *Applied Ergonomics*, 18, 233–237.

Kwallek, N. and Lewis, C.M. (1990). Effects of environmental colour on males and females: A red or white or green office. *Applied Ergonomics*, 21, 275–278.

Lam, S-T. and Greenstein, J.S. (1984). The effects of input medium and task allocation strategy on the performance of a human computer system. In *Proceedings of 1st IFIP Conference on HCI, Interact '84*, pp. 458–463. Amsterdam: IFIP, North-Holland.

Lamb, K.R. and Brodie, D.A. (1991). Leisure time physical activity as an estimator of physical fitness: A validation study. *Journal of Clinical Epidemiology*, 44, 41–52.

Lancaster, R.J. (1998). A risk assessment and control cycle approach to managing workplace stress. In M.A. Hansen (ed.) *Contemporary ergonomics*, pp. 167–171. London: Taylor & Francis.

Langan-Fox, J., Code, S. and Edlund, G. (1998). Team organisational mental models: An integrative framework for research. In M.A. Hansen (ed.) *Contemporary ergonomics*, pp. 186–190. London: Taylor & Francis.

Large, P. (1980). *The micro revolution*. London: Fontana.

Latack, J.C. and Foster, L.W. (1985). Implementation of compressed work schedules: Participation and job redesign as critical factors for employee acceptance. *Personnel Psychology*, 38, 75–93.

Latham, G.P. and Wexley, K.N. (1977). Behavioral observation scales for performance appraisal purposes. *Personnel Psychology*, 30, 255–268.

Läubli, Th., Hünting, W. and Grandjean, E. (1981). Postural and visual loads of VDT workplaces. II Lighting conditions and visual impairment. *Ergonomics*, 24, 933–944.

Lawler, E.E. (1969). Job design and employee motivation. *Personnel Psychology*, 22, 426–435.

Lazarus, R.S. and Cohen, J.B. (1977). Environmental stress. In I. Altman and J.F. Wohlwill (eds) *Human behaviour and environment*, vol. 1. New York: Plenum.

Leatherwood, J., Dempsey, T. and Clevenson, S. (1980). A design tool for estimating passenger ride discomfort within complex ride environments. *Human Factors*, 22, 291–312.

Lee, J.D. and Moray, N. (1992). Trust, control strategies and allocation of function in human–machine systems. *Ergonomics*, 35, 1243–1270.

Lee, J.D. and Moray, N. (1994). Trust, self confidence and operators' adaptation to automation. *International Journal of Human–Computer Studies*, 40, 153–184.

Lee, R.T. and Ashforth, B.E. (1990). On the meaning of Maslach's three dimensions of burnout. *Journal of Applied Psychology*, 75, 743–747.

Leggatt, A. and Noyes, J.M. (1996). Workload under complex task conditions. In S.A. Robertson (ed.) *Contemporary ergonomics*, pp. 281–286. London: Taylor & Francis.

Leibowitz, H.W. (1996). The symbiosis between basic and applied research. *American Psychologist*, 51, 366–370.

Leiter, M.P. (1988). Burnout as a function of communication patterns: A study of a multidisciplinary mental health team. *Group & Organization Studies*, 13, 111–128.

Lerner, E.J. (1983). The automated cockpit. *IEEE Spectrum*, 20, 57–62.

Lewis, M.J., Esterman, A.J. and Dorsch, M.M. (1982). A survey of the health consequences to females of operating visual display units. *Community Health Studies*, 6(2), 130–134.

Liao, M.-H. and Drury, C.G. (2000). Posture, discomfort and performance in a VDT task. *Ergonomics*, 43(3), 345–359.

Lichtenstein, S., Slovic, P., Fischhoff, B., Layman, M. and Combs, B. (1978). Judged frequency of lethal events. *Journal of Experimental Psychology: Human Learning and Memory*, 4, 551–578.

Lidén, C. and Wahlberg, J.E. (1985). Work at video display terminals: An epidemiological health investigation of office employees. *Scandinavian Journal of Work, Environment and Health*, 11, 489–493.

Liebman, M. (1970). The effects of sex and race norms on personal space. *Environmental Behaviour*, 2, 208–246.

Lightner, N.J., Bose, I. and Salvendy, G. (1996). What is wrong with the World Wide Web?: A diagnosis of some problems and prescription of some remedies. *Ergonomics*, 39, 995–1004.

Linton, S.J., Hellsing, A.-L., Halme, T. and Akerstedt, K. (1994). The effects of ergonomically designed school furniture on pupils' attitudes, symptoms and behaviour. *Applied Ergonomics*, 25, 299–304.

Lloyd, E.L. (1986). *Hypothermia and cold stress*. London: Croom Helm.

Lovesey, E.J. (1998). Are we getting larger? In P.A. Scott, R.S. Bridger and J. Charteris (eds) *Proceedings of Global Ergonomics Conference* (Cape Town, South Africa), pp. 337–343. Oxford: Elsevier.

Luberto, F., Gobba, F. and Brogha, A. (1989). Temporary myopia and subjective symptoms in video display terminal operators. *Medicina del Lavoro*, 80(2), 155–163.

Lukiesh, M. and Holladay, L.L. (1925). Glare and visibility. *Transactions of the Illuminating Engineering Society*, 20, 221–252.

Luthans, F. and Kreitner, R. (1985). *Organizational behavior modification*, 2nd edn. New York: Scott, Foresman.

Lutz, M.C. and Chapanis, A. (1955). Expected locations of digits and letters on 10-button keysets. *Journal of Applied Psychology*, *39*, 314–317.

Lynch, C. (1997). Searching the Internet. *Scientific American*, 276(3), 52–56.

McAfee, R.B. and Winn, A.R. (1989). The use of incentives/feedback to enhance workplace safety: A critique of the literature. *Journal of Safety Research*, 20, 7–19.

Macaulay, L. (1995). *Human–computer interaction for software designers*. London: International Thomson Computer Press.

McClelland, J. (1981). Retrieving general and specific knowledge from stored knowledge of specifics. In *Proceedings of the 3rd Annual Conference of the Cognitive Science Society*, pp. 170–172. Mahwah, NJ: LEA.

McCormick, E.J. (1976). Job and task analysis. In M.D. Dunnette (ed.) *Handbook of industrial and organizational psychology*. Chicago, IL: Rand McNally.

McCormick, E.J., Jeanneret, P.R. and Mecham, R.C. (1972). A study of job characteristics and job dimensions as based on the Position Analysis Questionnaire (PAQ). *Journal of Applied Psychology*, 56, 347–368.

McDonald, A.D., McDonald, J.C., Armstrong, B., Cherry, N., Nolin, A.D. and Robert, D. (1988). Work with visual display units in pregnancy. *British Journal of Indirect Medicine*, 45, 509–515.

McEvoy, G.M. and Cascio, W.F. (1985). Strategies for reducing employee turnover: A meta-analysis. *Journal of Applied Psychology*, 70, 342–353.

Mackay, C. (1987). The alleged reproductive hazards of VDUs. *Work and Stress*, 1(1), 49–57.

McKenna, F.P. (1988). What role should the concept of risk play in theories of accident involvement? *Ergonomics*, 31, 469–484.

MacKenzie, I.S. (1992). Movement time prediction in human–computer interfaces. In *Proceedings of Graphics Interface '92*, pp. 140–150. San Francisco, CA: Morgan Kaufmann.

McKie, R. (1999). How to grow chips on a speck of dust. *The Observer*, 25 July 1999, p. 23.

Mackworth, N.H. (1948). The breakdown of vigilance during prolonged visual search. *Quarterly Journal of Experimental Psychology*, 1, 5–61.

Mackworth, N.H. (1950). *Researches of the measurement of human performance.* (Medical Research Council Special Report No. 268). London: HMSO. (Reprinted in H.W. Sinako (ed.) (1961). *Selected papers on Human Factors in the design and use of control systems*, pp. 174–331. New York: Dover.)

Mackworth, N.H. (1953). Finger numbness in very cold winds. *Journal of Applied Physiology*, 5, 533–543.

Maddix, F. (1990). *Human–computer interaction: Theory and practice.* Chichester, UK: Ellis Horwood.

Malone, T.B., Kirkpatrick, M., Mallory, K., Eike, D., Johnson, J.H. and Walker, R.W. (1980). *Human factors evaluation of control room design and operator performance at Three Mile Island–2.* Report prepared for the Nuclear Regulatory Commission by the Essex Corporation, Fairfax, VA.

Mandal, A.C. (1982). The correct height of school furniture. *Human Factors*, 24, 257–269.

Mandal, A.C. (1993). Evaluation of working position of school children. *Talkback Magazine*, January Issue, National Back Pain Association, UK.

Marans, R. and Spreckelmeyer, K. (1982). Measuring overall architectural quality: A component of the building environment. *Environment & Behavior*, 14, 652–670.

Marr, D. (1982). *Vision: A computational investigation into the human representation and processing of visual information.* San Francisco, CA: Freeman.

Marras, W.S., Fathallah, F.A., Miller, R.J., Davis, S.W. and Mirka, G.A. (1992). Accuracy of a three-dimensional motion monitor for recording trunk motion characteristics. *International Journal of Industrial Ergonomics*, 9, 75–87.

Marras, W.S., Lavender, S.A., Leurgans, S.E., Fathallah, F.A., Ferguson, S.A., Allread, W.G. and Rajulu, S.L. (1995). Biomechanical risk factors for occupationally related low back disorders. *Ergonomics*, 38, 377–410.

Marriott, I.A. and Stuchly, M.A. (1986). Health aspects of work with visual display terminals. *Journal of Occupational Medicine*, 28, 833–848.

Martin, T.B. (1976). Practical applications of voice input to machines. *Proceedings of the IEE*, 64, 487–501.

Maslach, A.H. and Jackson, S.E. (1981). The measurement of experienced burnout. *Journal of Occupational Behavior*, 2, 99–113.

Maslow, A. (1954). *Motivation and personality.* New York: Van Nostrand Rheinhold.

May, J.L., Lomas, S.M. and Gale, A.G. (1999). Self measurement of body measurements: The reliability of anthropometric measurements. In M.A. Hanson, E.J. Lovesey and S.A. Robertson (eds) *Contemporary ergonomics*, pp. 391–395. London: Taylor & Francis.

Meese, G.B., Kok, R., Lewis, M.I. and Wyon, D.P. (1984). A laboratory study of the effects of moderate thermal stress on the performance of factory workers. *Ergonomics*, 27, 19–43.

Megaw, E. (1992). The visual environment. In A.P. Smith and D.M. Jones (eds) *Handbook of human performance: Volume I – The physical environment*, pp. 261–296. London: Academic Press.

Melamed, S., Ben-Avi, I., Luz, J. and Green, M. (1995). Objective and subjective work monitoring: Effects on job satisfaction, psychological distress, and absenteeism in blue-collar workers. *Journal of Applied Psychology*, 80, 29–42.

Miller, J.C. (1996). Fit for duty? *Ergonomics in Design*, 4 April 1996, 11–17.

Miller, J.C. (1999). A conceptual framework for the estimation of worker fatigue. *CSERIAC Gateway*, X(2), 1–3.

Mintzberg, H. (1979). *The structuring of organization*. Englewood Cliffs, NJ: Prentice-Hall.

Mirvis, P.H. (1990). Organizational development: Part II – A revolutionary perspective. In W.A. Pasmore and R.W. Woodman (eds) *Research in organisational change and development*, vol. 4, pp. 1–66. Greenwich, CT: JAI.

Molenbroek, J.F.M. (1994). *Made to measure*. Delft, Netherlands: University Press.

Monk, A.F., Wright, P.C., Haber, J. and Davenport, L. (1993). *Improving your human–computer interface: A practical technique*. London: Prentice-Hall.

Monk, T.M. and Folkard, S. (1992). *Making shift work tolerable*. London: Taylor & Francis.

Montreuil, S. and Laville, A. (1986). Cooperation between ergonomists and workers in the study of posture in order to modify work conditions. In E.N. Corlett, J.R. Wilson and I. Manenica (eds) *The ergonomics of working postures*, pp. 293–304. London: Taylor & Francis.

Moray, N. (1994). Error reduction as a systems problem. In M.S. Bogner (ed.) *Human error in medicine*, pp. 67–91. Hillsdale, NJ: LEA.

Moray, N. (1999a). Personal communication at the People In Control Conference, Bath, UK, 21–23 June 1999.

Moray, N. (1999b). Human operators and automation. In *Proceedings of People In Control Conference*. Publication No. 463 (8 pp.). London: IEE.

Muchinsky, P.M. (1997). *Psychology applied to work: An introduction to industrial and organizational psychology*, 5th edn. Pacific Grove, CA: Brooks/Cole.

Muir, B.M. (1989). Operators' trust in and percentage of time spent using the automatic controllers in a supervisory process control task. Unpublished doctoral thesis, University of Toronto, Canada.

Muir, B.M. (1994). Trust in automation. Part I: Theoretical issues in the study of trust and human intervention in automated systems. *Ergonomics*, 37(11), 1905–1923.

Muir, B.M. and Moray, N. (1996). Trust in automation. Part II: Experimental studies of trust and human intervention in a process control simulation. *Ergonomics*, 39(3), 429–461.

Mullaly, J. and Grigg, L. (1988). RSI: Integrating the major theories. *Australian Journal of Psychology*, 40, 19–33.

Murphy, L.R. (1986). A review of organizational stress management research: Methodological considerations. *Journal of Organizational Behavior Management*, 8, 215–227.

Murphy, L.R. (1988). Workplace interventions for stress reduction and prevention. In C.L. Cooper and R. Payne (eds) *Causes, coping and consequences of stress at work*. Chichester, UK: Wiley.

Muter, P., Latremouille, S.A., Treurniet, W.C. and Beam, P. (1982). Extended reading of continuous text on television screens. *Human Factors*, 24, 501–508.

Narayanan, V.K. and Nath, R. (1982). Hierarchical level and the impact of flextime. *Industrial Relations*, 21, 216–230.

NASA (1978). *Anthropometric source book*. NASA Defence Publication No. 1024, US Washington, DC: National Aeronautics and Space Administration.

National Research Council Committee on Vision. (1983). *Video displays, work and vision*. Washington, DC: National Academy Press.

National Safety Council. (1991). *Accident facts, 1991 edition*. Chicago, IL: National Safety Council.

National Safety Council. (1993). OSHA update. *Safety and Health Magazine*, 10 May 1993.

National Transportation Safety Board. (1988). *Aircraft accident report: Northwest Airlines, Inc. McDonnell Douglas DC-9-82 N312RC, Detroit Metropolitan Wayne County Airport, Romulus, Michigan, 16 August 1987*. (Report No. NTSB-AAR-88-05) Washington DC: National Transportation Safety Board.

National Transportation Safety Board (1990). *Aircraft accident report: United Airlines DC-10-10 engine explosion and landing at Sioux City, Iowa*. (Report No. NTSB-AAR-90-06). Washington, DC: National Transportation Safety Board.

Neisser, U. (1976). *Cognition and reality*. San Francisco, CA: Freeman.

Nelson, D. (1980). *Frederick W. Taylor and the rise of scientific management*. Milwaukee, WI: University of Wisconsin Press.

Nemecek, J. and Grandjean, E. (1973). Noise in landscaped offices. *Applied Ergonomics*, 4, 19–22.

Network Wizards (1999). Growth of the Internet. *The Guardian*, 29 April 1999.

Nevola, V.R. (1998). *Drinking for optimal performance during military operations in the heat: A guide for commanders*. Farnborough, UK: DERA (Defence Evaluation and Research Agency).

Newell, A.F. (1984). Speech – the natural modality for man–machine interaction. In *Proceedings of 1st IFIP (International Federation of Information Processing) Conference on HCI, Interact '84*. Amsterdam: IFIP, North-Holland.

Nickerson, R.S. (1997). Reflections on a long history and promising future. *Cognitive Technology*, 2(1), 6–20.

Nielsen, C.V., Brandt, L., Helsborg, L., Waldstrom, B. and Nielsen, L.T. (1989). *The effect of VDT work on the course of pregnancy*. Internal report, Department of Social Medicine, University of Aarhus, Aarhus.

Nielsen, J. (1993). *Usability engineering*. London: Academic Press.

Nielsen, J. (1994). Heuristic evaluation. In J. Nielsen and R.L. Mack (eds) *Usability inspection methods*. New York: Wiley.

NIOSH (1981). Work practices guide for the design of manual handling. Cincinnati, OH: National Institute for Occupational Safety and Health.

Norback, D., Michel, I. and Widstrom, J. (1990). Indoor air quality and personal factors related to the sick building syndrome. *Scandinavian Journal of Work, Environment and Health*, 16, 121–128.

Nordqvist, T., Ohlsson, K. and Nilsson, L. (1986). Fatigue and reading text on videotex. *Human Factors*, 28, 353–363.

Norman, D.A. (1981). Categorization of action slips. *Psychological Review*, 88, 1–15.

Norman, D.A. (1988). *The psychology of everyday things*. New York: Basic Books.

Norman, D.A. and Draper, S. (1986). *User-centred systems design: New perspectives on human–computer interaction*. Hillsdale, NJ: LEA.

Noyes, J.M. (1983a). The QWERTY keyboard: A review. *International Journal of Man–Machine Studies*, 18, 265–281.

Noyes, J.M. (1983b). Chord keyboards. *Applied Ergonomics*, 14, 55–59.

Noyes, J.M. (1993). Speech technology in the future. In C. Baber and J.M. Noyes (eds) *Interactive speech technology: Human factors issues in the application of speech input/output to computers*, pp. 189–208. London: Taylor & Francis.

Noyes, J.M. (1998). QWERTY – the immortal keyboard. *Computing & Control Engineering Journal*, 9, 117–122.

Noyes, J.M. (in press). Talking and working – how natural is human-machine interaction? *International Journal of Human-Computer Studies.*

Noyes, J.M. and Baber, C. (1999). *User-centred aspects of system design.* London: Springer.

Noyes, J.M. and Cook, M.J. (eds) (1999). *Interface technology: The leading edge.* Baldock, UK: Research Studies Press.

Noyes, J.M. and Mills, S. (1998). *Display design for human–computer interaction.* Cheltenham, UK: Cheltenham & Gloucester CHE.

Noyes, J.M. and Stanton, N.A. (1997). Engineering psychology: Contribution to system safety. *Computing & Control Engineering Journal*, 8(3), 107–112.

Noyes, J.M. and Starr, A.F. (2000). Civil aircraft warning systems: Future directions in information management and presentation. *International Journal of Aviation Psychology*, 10(2), 169–188.

Noyes, J.M. and Thomas, P.J. (1995). Information overload: An overview. In *Proceedings of IEE Colloquium 'Information overload'*, Digest 95/223. London: IEE.

Noyes, J.M., Haigh, R. and Starr, A.F. (1989). Automatic speech recognition for disabled people. *Applied Ergonomics*, 20, 293–298.

Noyes, J.M., Baber, C. and Steel, A. (1994). Ergonomic survey of VDTs and manufacturing workstations. In I. Hamilton (ed.) *Proceedings of Ergonomics and Health & Safety Conference 'The Record of Achievement'*. Loughborough, UK: Ergonomics Society.

Noyes, J.M., Starr, A.F. and Frankish, C.R. (1996a). User involvement in the early stages of the development of an aircraft warning system. *Behaviour & Information Technology*, 15(2), 67–75.

Noyes, J.M., Starr, A.F. and Rankin, J.A. (1996b) Human error in aviation: Designing warning systems from a user perspective. In *Proceedings of IEE Colloquium 'Control Rooms, Cockpits and Command Centres'*, Digest 96/033, 3/1–3/3.

Noyes, J.M., Leggatt, A.P. and Irwin, H.J. (1997). Altimeter design in avionics: Analogue versus digital? In D. Harris (ed.) *Proceedings of 1st International Conference on Engineering Psychology & Cognitive Ergonomics*, pp. 39–45. Aldershot, UK: Ashgate.

Nurminen, T. and Kurppa, K. (1988). Office employment, work with video display terminals and course of pregnancy. *Scandinavian Journal of Work, Environment and Health*, 14, 293–298.

Oborne, D.J. (1995). *Ergonomics at work*, 3rd edn. Chichester, UK: Wiley.

Oborne, D.J., Heath, T. and Boarer, P. (1981). Variation in human response to whole-body vibration. *Ergonomics*, 24, 301–313.

Oldham, G.R. and Fried, Y. (1987). Employee reactions to workspace characteristics. *Journal of Applied Psychology*, 72, 75–80.

Orasanu, J. and Backer, P. (1996). Stress and military performance. In J. Driskell and E. Salas (eds) *Stress and human performance*. Mahwah, NJ: LEA.

Orlady, H.W. and Orlady, L.M. (1999). *Human factors in multi-crew flight operations*. Aldershot, UK: Ashgate.

Osborne, D.W. and Ellingstad, V.S. (1987). Using sensor lines to show control–display linkages on a four-burner stove. In *Proceedings of 31st Annual Meeting of the Human Factors Society*, pp. 581–584. Santa Monica, CA: Human Factors Society.

Palinkas, L.A., Petterson, J.S., Russell, J. and Downs, M.A. (1993). Community patterns of psychiatric disorders after the Exxon Valdez oil spill. *American Journal of Psychiatry*, 150(10), 1517–1523.

Parasuraman, R. and Riley, V. (1997). Humans and automation: Use, misuse, disuse, abuse. *Human Factors*, 39(2), 230–253.

Parkes, K.R. (1990). Coping, negative affectivity, and the work environment: Additive and interactive predictors of mental health. *Journal of Applied Psychology*, 75, 399–409.

Parsons, H.M. (1974). What happened at Hawthorne? *Science*, 183, 922–932.

Parsons, H.M. (1990). Assembly ergonomics in the Hawthorne studies. In *Proceedings of the International Ergonomics Association Conference on Human Factors in Design for Manufacturing and Process Planning*, pp. 299–305. Buffalo, NY: Helander, Dept. of IE, SUNYAB.

Parsons, K.C. (1995). Ergonomics assessment of thermal environments. In J.R. Wilson and E.N. Corlett (eds) *Evaluation of human work: A practical ergonomics methodology*, 2nd edn., pp. 483–505. London: Taylor & Francis.

Pastoor, S., Schwarz, E. and Beldie, I.P. (1983). The relative suitability of four dot matrix sizes for text presentation on color television screens. *Human Factors*, 25, 265–272.

Patterson, M.L. and Sechrest, L.B. (1970). Interpersonal distance and impression formation. *Journal of Personality*, 38, 161–166.

Payne, D.E. (1967). Readability of typewritten material: Proportional vs. standard spacing. *Journal of Typographic Research*, 1(2), April issue.

Payne, S.J. (1995). Naïve judgments of stimulus–response compatibility. *Human Factors*, 37, 495–506.

Pearce, B.G. (1984). Health hazards in perspective. In B.G. Pearce (ed.) *Health hazards of VDTs?* pp. 5–12. Chichester, UK: Wiley.

Pearce, B.G. (1995). 'RSI' and the media. *Occupational Health Review*, 57, 14–18.

Pearce, B.G. (1998). An ergonomist's perspective on claims for WRULDS. In A.I. McDonald and A. Georges *Tort Law Library*. London: Sweet & Maxwell Ltd.

Pearson, G. and Weiser, M. (1986). Of moles and men: The design of foot controls for workstations. In *Proceedings of CHI '86 'Human Factors in Computing Systems'*, pp. 333–339. New York: ACM (Association for Computing Machinery).

Pearson, I. (1999). *Our view of the future: The future of information technology*. Article on BT (British Telecom) Innovation & Technology Website: http// innovate.bt.com/viewpoints/pearson/it.html

Pejtersen, A.M. and Rasmussen, J. (1997). Effectiveness testing of complex systems. In G. Salvendy (ed.) *Handbook of human factors and ergonomics*, 2nd edn., pp. 1514–1542. New York: Wiley.

Perrow, C. (1981). Normal accident at Three Mile Island. *Society*, 18(5), 17–26.

Perrow, C. (1984). *Normal accidents: Living with high-risk technologies*. New York: Basic Books.

Peters, T.J. and Waterman, R.H. Jr. (1982). *In search of excellence*. New York: Warner Books.

Petersen, P.J., Banks, W.W. and Gertman, D.J. (1981). Performance-based evaluation of graphic displays from nuclear power plant control rooms. In *Proceedings of Conference on Human Factors in Computer Systems*. New York: ACM (Association for Computing Machinery).

Petherbridge, P. and Hopkinson, R.G. (1950). Discomfort glare and the lighting of buildings. *Transactions of the Illuminating Engineering Society (London)*, 15, 39–79.

Pew, R.W., Miller, D.C. and Feehrer, C.G. (1987). *Evaluation of proposed control room improvements through analysis of critical operator decisions*. Palo Alto, CA: Electrical Power Research Institute.

Pheasant, S.T. (1986). *Bodyspace*. London: Taylor & Francis.

Pheasant, S.T. (1992). Does RSI exist? Balance of opinion. *Occupational Medicine*, 42, 167–168.

Pheasant, S.T. (1997). *Body space: Anthropometry, ergonomics and the design of work*, 2nd edn. London: Taylor & Francis.

Philips, S.B. and Mushinski, M.H. (1992). Configuring an employee assistance program to fit the corporation's structure: One company's design. In J.C. Quick, L.R. Murphy and J.J. Hurrell (eds) *Stress and well-being at work: Assessments and interventions for occupational mental health*, pp. 317–328. Washington, DC: American Psychological Association.

Phillips, J. (1979). An exploration of perception of body boundary, personal space and body size in elderly persons. *Perceptual & Motor Skills*, 48, 299–308.

Pickering, T. (1987). 'RSI': Putting the epidemic to rest. *The Medical Journal of Australia*, 147 (September issue), 213–218.

Porkorny, J., Smith, V.C., Verriest, G. and Pinckers, A.J.L. (1979). *Congenital and acquired color vision defects*. New York: Grune & Stratton.

Porter, C.S. (1988). Accident proneness: A review of the concept. *International Reviews of Ergonomics*, 2, 177–206.

Porter, C.S. and Corlett, E.N. (1989). Performance differences of individuals classified by questionnaire as accident prone or non-accident prone. *Ergonomics*, 32, 317–333.

Porter, J.M., Freer, M., Case, K. and Bonney, M.C. (1995). Computer aided ergonomics and workspace design. In J.R. Wilson and E.N. Corlett (eds) *Evaluation of human work: A practical ergonomics methodology*, 2nd edn., pp. 574–620. London: Taylor & Francis.

Porter, J.M., Case, K. and Freer, M. (1998). Computer-aided-design and human models. In W. Karwowski and W. Marras (eds) *Handbook of industrial ergonomics*. Boca Raton, FL: CRC Press.

Potasova, A. and Arochova, O. (1994). Effects of toxic agents in the environment on mental functions in children: Some methodological approaches and findings. *Ceskoslovensha Psychologie*, 38(2), 131–142.

Poulton, E.C. (1978). Increased vigilance with vertical vibration at 5 Hz: An alerting mechanism. *Applied Ergonomics*, 9, 73–76.

Price, H.E. (1985). The allocation of functions in systems. *Human Factors*, 27(1), 33–45.

Pugh, D.S. (1966). Modern organization theory: A psychological and sociological study. *Psychological Bulletin*, 66, 235–251.

Purdham, J. (1980). *A review of the literature on health hazards of video display terminals*. Hamilton, Canada: Canadian Centre for Occupational Health and Safety.

Putz-Anderson, V. (1988). *Cumulative trauma disorders: A manual for musculoskeletal diseases of the upper limbs*. London: Taylor & Francis.

Quinter, J.L. and Elvey, R.L. (1993). Understanding 'RSI': A review of the role of peripheral neural pain and hyperalgesia. *Journal of Manual and Manipulative Therapy*, 1, 99–105.

Rabbitt, P. (1993). When do old people find displays difficult? In *Proceedings of IEE Colloquium 'Special Needs and the Interface'*, Digest No. 93/005. London: IEE.

Radl, G.W. (1980). Experimental investigations for optimal presentation-mode and colours of symbols on the CRT screen. In E. Grandjean and E. Vigliani (eds) *Ergonomic aspects of visual display terminals*. London: Taylor & Francis.

Ramazzini, B. (1713). *The diseases of workers* (translated by W. Wright, 1940). Chicago, IL: University of Chicago Press.

Rasmussen, J. (1986). *Information processing and human–machine interaction*. Amsterdam: North-Holland.

Rasmussen, J. (1987). The definition of human error and a taxonomy for technical system design. In J. Rasmussen, K. Duncan and J. Leplat (eds) *New technology and human error*. Chichester, UK: Wiley.

Rasmussen, J. (1993). Deciding and doing: Decision making in natural contexts. In G. Klein, J. Orasanu, R. Calderwood and C. Zsambok (eds) *Decision making in action: Models and methods*. Norwood, NJ: Ablex.

Rasmussen, J., Duncan, K. and Leplat, J. (1987). *New technology and human error*. Chichester, UK: Wiley.

Rasmussen, J., Pejtersen, A. and Goodstein, L. (1995). *Cognitive engineering: Concepts and applications*. New York: Wiley.

Ray, R.D. and Ray, W.D. (1979). An analysis of domestic cooker control design. *Ergonomics*, 22, 1243–1248.

Rayson, M.P., Pynn, H., Rothwell, A. and Nevill, A. (2000). The development of physical selection procedures for the British Army. Phase 3: Validation. In P.T. McCabe, M.A. Hanson and S.A. Robertson (eds) *Contemporary ergonomics*, pp. 140–144. London: Taylor & Francis.

Reason, J.T. (1990). *Human error*. Cambridge, UK: Cambridge University Press.

Reason, J.T. and Mycielska, K. (1982). *Absent minded: The psychology of mental lapses and everyday errors*. Englewood Cliffs, NJ: Prentice Hall.

Reber, R.A., Wallin, J.A. and Chhokar, J.S. (1984). Reducing industrial accidents: A behavioral experiment. *Industrial Relations*, 23, 119–125.

Redlin, U. and Mrosovsky, N. (1997). Exercise and human rhythms: What we know and what we need to know. *Chronobiology International*, 14, 221–229.

Reeves, E.M., Mills, S. and Noyes, J.M. (1996). Sounds like HELP: The use of voice for procedural instructions in GUI HELP. In *Proceedings of OzCHI'96, 6th Australian Conference on Computer–Human Interaction*, pp. 108–114. Los Alamitos, CA: IEEE Computer Society Press.

Reid, G.B. and Nygren, T.E. (1988). The subjective assessment workload technique: A scaling procedure for measuring mental workload. In P.A. Hancock and N. Meshkati (eds) *Human mental workload*, pp. 185–218. Amsterdam: North-Holland.

Reilly, T. (1991). Assessment of some aspects of physical fitness. *Applied Ergonomics*, 22, 291–294.

Reilly, T., Waterhouse, J. and Atkinson, G. (1997). Ageing, rhythms of physical performance and adjustment to changes in the sleep-activity cycle. *Occupational and Environmental Medicine*, 54, 812–816.

Reilly, T., Coldwells, A., Atkinson, G. and Waterhouse, J. (1998). The effects of age and habitual physical activity on the adjustment to nocturnal shiftwork. In M.A. Hansen (ed.) *Contemporary ergonomics*, pp. 208–212. London: Taylor & Francis.

Reinecke, S.M., Hazard, R.G., Coleman, K. and Pope, M.H. (1992). A continuous passive lumbar motion device to relieve back pain in prolonged sitting. In S. Kumar (ed.) *Advances in industrial ergonomics and safety IV*. London: Taylor & Francis.

Reynard, W.D., Billings, C.E., Cheaney, E.S. and Hardy, R. (1986). The development of the NASA Aviation Safety Reporting System. (NASA Reference Publication 1114). Moffett Field, CA: NASA–Ames Research Center.

Richardson, R.M.M., Telson, R.U., Koch, C.G. and Chrysler, S.T. (1987). Evaluations of conventional, serial, and chord keyboard options for mail encoding. In *Proceedings of 31st Annual Meeting of the Human Factors Society*, pp. 911–915. Santa Monica, CA: Human Factors Society.

Riddle, H.F.V. and Taylor, W. (1982). Vibration-induced white finger among chain sawyers nine years after the introduction of anti-vibration measures. In A.S. Brammer and W. Taylor (eds) *Vibration effects on the hand and arm in industry*, pp. 169–172. New York: Wiley.

Rioux, M. and Bruckart, T. (1995). Data collection. In K.M. Robinette, M.W. Vannier, M. Rioux and P.R.M. Jones (eds) *3-D surface anthropometry: Review of technology*. Draft report, AGARD (Advisory Group for Aerospace Research and Development) Proceedings. Neuilly-sur-Seine, France: AGARD.

Rodger, A. and Cavanagh, P. (1962). Training occupational psychologists. *Occupational Psychology*, 36, 82–88.

Rodgers, S.H. (1997). Work physiology – fatigue and recovery. In G. Salvendy (ed.) *Handbook of human factors and ergonomics*, 2nd edn., pp. 268–297. New York: Wiley.

Roethlisberger, F.J. and Dickson, W.J. (1939). *Management and the worker*. Cambridge, MA: Harvard University Press.

Rogers, A.S., Spencer, M.B., Stone, B.M. and Nicholson, A.N. (1989). The influence of a 1-hr nap on performance overnight. *Ergonomics*, 32, 1193–1205.

Rogers, Y. (1989). Icons at the interface: Their usefulness. *Interacting With Computers*, 1, 105–117.

Rohles, F.H. Jr. (1974). The modal comfort envelope and its use in current standards. *Human Factors*, 64(3), 314–323.

Rosa, R.R. and Colligan, M.J. (1988). Long workdays versus restdays: Assessing fatigue and alertness with a portable performance battery. *Human Factors*, 30, 305–317.

Rostron, J. (1997). *Sick building syndrome: Concepts, issues and practice*. London: Taylor & Francis.

Roth, J.T., Ayoub, M.M. and Halcomb, C.G. (1977). Seating, console and workplace design: Seated operator reach profiles. In *Proceedings of the Human Factors 21st Annual Meeting*, pp. 83–87. Santa Monica, CA: Human Factors Society.

Rouse, W.B. and Boff, K.R. (1997). Assessing cost/benefits of human factors. In G.

Salvendy (ed.) *Handbook of human factors and ergonomics*, 2nd edn., pp. 1617–1633. New York: Wiley.

Rouse, W.B. and Cacioppo, G.M. (1989). *Prospects for modeling the impact of human resource investments on economic return.* Washington, DC: Department of the Army, Office of the Deputy Chief of Staff for Personnel.

Rubin, J. (1994). *Handbook of usability testing: How to plan, design and conduct effective tests.* New York: Wiley.

Rubinstein, T. and Mason, A.F. (1979). The accident that shouldn't have happened: An analysis of Three Mile Island. *IEEE Spectrum*, November issue, 33–57.

Ryan, C.M. and Morrow, L.A. (1992). Dysfunctional buildings or dysfunctional people: An examination of the sick building syndrome and allied disorders. *Journal of Consulting and Clinical Psychology*, 80(2), 220–224.

Ryan, T.A. and Smith, P.C. (1954). *Principles of industrial psychology.* New York: Ronald Press.

Rycroft, R.J.G. and Calnan, C.D. (1984). Facial rashes among visual display unit (VDU) operators. In B.G. Pearce (ed.) *Health hazards of VDTs?* pp. 13–15. Chichester, UK: Wiley.

Salas, E., Driskell, J.E. and Hughes, S. (1996). Introduction: The study of stress and human performance. In J.E. Driskell and E. Salas (eds) *Stress and human performance*, pp. 1–45. Mahwah, NJ: LEA.

Sanders, M.S. and McCormick, E.J. (1987). *Human factors in engineering and design*, 6th edn. New York: McGraw-Hill.

Sanderson, P.M. (1989). The human planning and scheduling role in advanced manufacturing systems: An emerging human factors role. *Human Factors*, 31(6), 635–666.

Sandover, J. and Champion, D.F. (1984). Some effects of a combined noise and vibration environment on a mental arithmetic task. *Journal of Sound and Vibration*, 95, 102–212.

Sasse, M.A. (1997). Eliciting and describing users' models of computer systems. Unpublished doctoral thesis, University of Birmingham, UK.

Sauter, S.L., Gottlieb, M.S., Jones, K.C., Dodson, V.N. and Rohrer, K.M. (1983). Job and health implications of VDT use: Initial results of the Wisconsin–NIOSH study. *Communications of the ACM*, 26, 284–294.

Sauter, S.L., Schleifer, L.M. and Knutson, S.J. (1991). Work posture, workstation design and musculoskeletal discomfort in a VDT data entry task. *Human Factors*, 33, 151–167.

Schacherer, C. (1993). Toward a general theory of risk perception. In *Proceedings of the 37th Annual Meeting of the Human Factors and Ergonomics Society*, pp. 984–988. Santa Monica, CA: Human Factors and Ergonomics Society.

Scholz, R.W. (1983). *Decision making under uncertainty.* Amsterdam: North-Holland.

Scott, W.G., Mitchell, T.R. and Birnbaum, P.H. (1981). *Organization theory: A structural and behavioural analysis.* Homewood, IL: Richard D. Irwin.

Seidel, H., Meister, A., Metz, A-M., Rothe, R., Ullsperger, P., Blüthner, R., Bräuer, D., Menzel, G. and Sroka, Ch. (1988). Effects of exposure to whole-body vibration and noise on the TTS, performance, postural sway, and auditory evoked brain potentials. In O. Manninen (ed.) *Recent advances in researches on the combined effects of environmental factors.* International Society of Complex Environmental Studies.

Selye, H. (1936). A syndrome produced by various nocuous agents. *Nature*, 138, 32.

Selye, H. (1976). *The stress of life*, 2nd edn. New York: McGraw-Hill.

Sen, R.N. (1984). Application of ergonomics to industrially developing countries. *Ergonomics*, 27, 1021–1032.

Senders, J.W. and Moray, N.P. (1991). *Human error: Cause, prediction and reduction*. Hillsdale, NJ: LEA.

Severy, L.J., Forsyth, D.R. and Wagner, P.J. (1979). A multi-method assessment of personal space development in female and male, black and white children. *Journal of Nonverbal Behaviour*, 4, 68–86.

Shackel, B. (1997). Human–computer interaction – Whence and whither? *Journal of the American Society for Information Science*, 48(11), 970–986.

Shackel, B., Chidsey, K.D. and Shipley, P. (1969). The assessment of chair comfort. *Ergonomics*, 12, 169–306.

Shain, M. (1982). Alcohol, drugs and safety: An updated perspective on problems and their management in the workplace. *Accident Analysis and Prevention*, 14, 239–246.

Sharp, M.A., Harman, E., Vogel, J.A., Knapik, J.J. and Legg, S.J. (1988). Maximal aerobic capacity for repetitive lifting: Comparison with three standard exercise testing modes. *European Journal of Applied Physiology*, 57, 753–760.

Sheedy, J.E. (1992). Vision problems at video display terminals: A survey of optometrists. *Journal of American Optometric Association*, 63, 687–692.

Shein, F., Hamann, G., Brownlow, N., Treviranus, J., Milner, M. and Parnes, P. (1991). WIVIK: A visual keyboard for Windows 3.0. In *Proceedings of 14th Annual Conference of the Rehabilitation Engineering Society of North America*, pp. 160–162. Arlington, VA: RESNA.

Shepherd, A. (2000). *Hierarchial task analysis*. London: Taylor & Francis.

Sheridan, J.E. (1992). Organizational culture and employee retention. *Academy of Management Journal*, 35, 1036–1056.

Sheridan, T.B. (1997). Supervisory control. In G. Salvendy (ed.) *Handbook of human factors and ergonomics*, 2nd edn., pp. 1295–1327. New York: Wiley.

Sherman, B. (1985). *The new revolution: The impact of computers on society*. Chichester, UK: Wiley.

Sherrod, D.R. (1974). Crowding, perceived control and behavioral after-effects. *Journal of Applied Social Psychology*, 4, 171–186.

Sherwood, N. and Griffin, M.J. (1992). Evidence of impaired learning during whole body vibration. *Journal of Sound and Vibration*, 152, 219–225.

Shinar, D. and Acton, M.B. (1978). Control-display relationships on the four-burner range: Population stereotypes versus standards. *Human Factors*, 20, 13–17.

Shneiderman, B. (1991). Touch screens now offer compelling uses. *IEEE Software*, 8(2), 93–94, 107.

Shneiderman, B. (1998). *Designing the user interface: Strategies for effective human–computer interaction*, 3rd edn. Reading, MA: Addison-Wesley.

Shute, S.J. and Starr, S.J. (1984). Effects of adjustable furniture on VDT users. *Human Factors*, 2, 157–170.

Singh, J., Peng, C.M., Kim, M.K. and Org, C.N. (1995). An anthropometric study of Singapore candidate aviators. *Ergonomics*, 38, 651–658.

Singleton, W.T. (1974). *Man–machine systems*. London: Penguin.

Singleton, W.T. (1989). *The mind at work: Psychological ergonomics.* Cambridge, UK: Cambridge University Press.

Sinha, S.P. and Sinha, S.P. (1991). Personal space and density as factors in task performance and feeling of crowding. *Journal of Social Psychology*, 131, 831–837.

Skov, P., Valbjørn, O. and Pedersen, B.V. (1989). Influence of personal characteristics, job-related factors and psychosocial factors on the sick building syndrome. *Scandinavian Journal of Work, Environment and Health*, 15, 288–295.

Skov, P., Valbjørn, O., Pedersen, B.V. and Gravensen, S. (1990). The influence of indoor climate on the sick building syndrome in an office environment. *Scandinavian Journal of Work, Environment and Health*, 16, 363–371.

Smetena, J., Bridgeman, D. and Bridgeman, B. (1978). A field study of interpersonal distance in early childhood. *Personality & Social Psychology Bulletin*, 4, 309–313.

Smith, A. (1997). *Human–computer factors: A study of users and information systems.* London: McGraw-Hill.

Smith, M.J. (1987). Mental and physical strain at VDU workstations. *Ergonomics*, 6, 243–255.

Smith, A.P. and Jones, D.M. (1992). Noise and performance. In A.P. Smith and D.M. Jones (eds) *Handbook of human performance: Volume I – The physical environment*, pp. 1–28. London: Academic Press.

Smith, P.B. and Bond, M.H. (1993). *Social psychology across cultures: Analysis and perspectives.* London: Harvester/Wheatsheaf.

Smith, P.C. and Kendall, L.M. (1963). Retranslation of expectations: An approach to the construction of unambiguous anchors for rating scales. *Journal of Applied Psychology*, 47, 149–155.

Smith, S.L. and Mosier, J.N. (1986). Design guidelines for user-system interface software. Report MTR-9420, Mitre Corporation, Bedford, MA.

Smith, S.W. and Rea, M.S. (1976). Performance of complex tasks under different levels of illumination. Part 1: Needle probe task. *Journal of the Illuminating Engineering Society*, 6, 235–242.

Smith, S.W. and Rea, M.S. (1978). Proofreading under different levels of illumination. *Journal of the Illuminating Engineering Society*, 8, 47–52.

Smith, S.W. and Rea, M.S. (1979). Relationships between office task performance and ratings of feelings and task evaluations under different light sources and levels. In *Proceedings of 19th Session of the CIE*, pp. 207–211. Kyoto, Japan.

Smith, S.W. and Rea, M.S. (1982). Performance of a reading task under different levels of illumination. *Journal of the Illuminating Engineering Society*, 12, 29–33.

Smith, M.J., Stammerjohn, L.W., Cohen, G.F. and Lalich, N.R. (1980). Job stress in video display operations. In E. Grandjean and E. Vigliani (eds) *Ergonomics aspects of visual display terminals.* London: Taylor & Francis.

Smither, R.D. (1994). *The psychology of work and human performance*, 2nd edn. New York: HarperCollins.

Smithies, C.P.K. (1994). The handwritten signature in pen computing. In *Proceedings of the IEE Colloquium 'Handwriting and Pen-based Input'*, Digest 94/065. London: IEE.

Snyder, H.L. (1984). Lighting characteristics, legibility and visual comfort at VDTs. In E. Grandjean (ed.) *Ergonomics and health in modern offices.* London: Taylor & Francis.

Snyder, H.L. (1988). Image quality. In M. Helander (ed.) *Handbook of human–computer interaction*, pp. 437–474. Amsterdam: Elsevier.

Sommer, R. (1969). *Personal space*. Englewood Cliffs, NJ: Prentice-Hall.

Spector, P.E. (1992). A consideration of the validity and meaning of self-report measures of job conditions. In C.L. Cooper and I.T. Robertson (eds) *International review of industrial and organisational psychology*, pp. 123–151. London: Wiley.

Spence, J.T., Helmreich, R.L. and Pred, R.S. (1987). Impatience versus achievement strivings in the Type A pattern: Differential effects on students' health and academic achievement. *Journal of Applied Psychology*, 72, 522–528.

Srivastava, P. and Mandal, M. (1990). Proximal spacing to facial affect expressions in schizophrenics. *Comprehensive Psychiatry*, 31, 119–124.

Stammerjohn, L.W., Smith, M.J. and Cohen, B.G.F. (1981). Evaluation of workstation design factors in VDT operations. *Human Factors*, 23, 401–412.

Stanney, K.M., Maxey, J. and Salvendy, G. (1997). Socially centred design. In G. Salvendy (ed.) *Handbook of human factors and ergonomics*, 2nd edn., pp. 637–656. New York: Wiley.

Stanton, N.A. and Young, M.S. (1999). *A guide to methodology in ergonomics*. London: Taylor & Francis.

Sternberg, R.J. (1999). *Cognitive psychology*, 2nd edn. Fort Worth, TX: Harcourt Brace.

Stewart, T.F.M. (1998). Ergonomics standards – the good, the bad and the ugly. In M.A. Hansen (ed.) *Contemporary ergonomics*, pp. 3–7. London: Taylor & Francis.

Stewart, T.F.M. and Miles, P.D. (1977). Improvements in or relating to keyboards. Patent Specification 1,492,538 (23 November 1977).

Stirling, M. and Parsons, K.C. (1999). The effect of hydration state of exposure to extreme heat by trainee firefighters. In M. A. Hansen, E.J. Lovesey and S.A. Robertson (eds) *Contemporary ergonomics*, pp. 380–384. London: Taylor & Francis.

Storr-Paulsen, A. and Aagaard-Hansen, J. (1994). The working positions of school children. *Applied Ergonomics*, 25, 63–64.

Straub, H.R. and Granaas, M.M. (1993). Task-specific preference for numeric keypads. *Applied Ergonomics*, 24, 289–290.

Sutcliffe, A. (1988). *Human–computer interface design*. London: Macmillan.

Swanbeck, G. and Bleeker, T. (1989). Skin problems from visual display units. *Acta Dermato-Venereologica*, 69, 46–51.

Tapagaporn, S. and Saito, S. (1990). How polarity and lighting conditions affect the pupil size of VDT operators. *Ergonomics*, 33, 201–208.

Tattersall, A.J. (1992). Visual display units. In A.P. Smith and D.M. Jones (eds) *Handbook of human performance: Volume I – The physical environment*, pp. 297–324. London: Academic Press.

Taylor, F.W. (1903). Shop management. *Transactions of the American Society of Mechanical Engineers*, 24, 1337–1481.

Taylor, F.W. (1907). *On the art of cutting metals*. New York: American Society of Mechanical Engineers.

Taylor, F.W. (1911). *The principles of scientific management* (reprinted in 1967). New York: Norton.

Taylor, F.W. (1947). Scientific management: Comprising shop management, the principles of scientific management and testimony before the special house committee. New York: Harper & Row.

Tepas, D.I. (1985). Flexitime, compressed work weeks and other alternative work schedules. In S. Folkard and T.H. Monk (eds) *Hours of work*, pp. 147–164. Chichester, UK: Wiley.

Thomas, H.A. (1969). *Automation for management*. London: Gower Press.

Thompson, C. (1999). An investigation of the usability of retail web sites: Do mental models matter? Unpublished undergraduate thesis, Department of Experimental Psychology, University of Bristol, UK.

Tichauer, E.R. (1973). *The biomechanical basis of ergonomics*. New York: Wiley.

Tjønn, H.H. (1984). Report of facial rashes among VDU operators in Norway. In B.G. Pearce (ed.) *Health hazards of VDTs?* pp. 17–23. Chichester, UK: Wiley.

Tom, G., Poole, M.F., Galla, J. and Berrier, J. (1981). The influence of negative ions on human performance and mood. *Human Factors*, 23(5), 633–636.

Totterdell, P., Spelten, E., Smith, L., Barton, J. and Folkard, S. (1995). Recovering from work shifts: How long does it take? *Journal of Applied Psychology*, 80, 43–57.

Travis, D. (1991). *Effective colour displays: Theory and practice*. London: Academic Press.

Tregenza, P. and Loe, D. (1998). *The design of lighting*. London: Taylor & Francis.

Trenner, L. and Bawa, J. (1998). *The politics of usability*. London: Springer.

Tribukait, B., Cekan, E. and Paulsson, L.E. (1986). Effects of pulsed magnetic fields on embryonic development in mice. In B. Knave and P.-G. Wideback (eds) *Work with Display Units 86: Selected papers from the International Scientific Conference on Work with Display Units*, pp. 129–134. Amsterdam: North-Holland.

Trice, H.M. and Roman, P.M. (1972). *Spirits and demons at work: Alcohol and other drugs on the job*. New York: New York School of Industrial and Labor Relations, Cornell University.

Trist, E.L., Higgin, G.W., Murray, H. and Pollock, A.B. (1963). *Organisation choice*. London: Tavistock.

Tsang, P. and Wilson, G. (1997). Mental workload. In G. Salvendy (ed.) *Handbook of human factors and ergonomics*, 2nd edn., pp. 417–449. New York: Wiley.

Tsubota, K. and Nakamori, K. (1993). Dry eyes and video display terminals. *New England Journal of Medicine*, 328, 8.

Tversky, A. and Kahneman, D. (1974). Judgement under uncertainty: Heuristics and biases. *Science*, 185, 1124–1131.

Udo, H., Tanida, H., Otani, T., Yokata, Y., Udo, A., Omoto, Y., Tuboya, A. and Yokoi, Y. (1991). Visual load of working with visual display terminal – introduction of VDT to newspaper editing and visual effect. *Journal of Human Ergonomics*, 20(2), 109–121.

UK Government Survey (1998). Labour market trends. October Publication, Vol. 106. No. 10, p. 496. Norwich, UK: The Stationery Office.

Urban, J.M., Weaver, J.L., Bowers, C.A. and Rhodenizer, L. (1996). Effects of workload and structure on team process and performance: Implications for complex team decision making. *Human Factors*, 38(2), 300–310.

US Department of Labor (1972). *Handbook for analyzing jobs*. Washington, DC: US Government Printing Office.

USNRC (1980). *Three Mile Island: A report to the commissioners and to the public (The Rogovin Report)*. USNRC Report Nureg/CR-1250–V. Washington, DC: USNRC.

Veijalainen, M. (2000). Listen to your body talking. *Work Health Safety*, Helsinki, Finland: Finnish Institute of Occupational Health, p. 25.

Veitch, R. and Arkkelin, D. (1995). *Environmental psychology: An interdisciplinary perspective*. Englewood Cliffs, NJ: Prentice-Hall.

Vicente, K.J. and Harwood, K. (1990). A few implications of an ecological approach to Human Factors. *Human Factors Society Bulletin*, 33, 1–4.

Vicente, K.J. and Rasmussen, J. (1992). Ecological interface design: Theoretical foundations. *IEEE Transactions on Systems, Man and Cybernetics*, 22(4), 589–606.

Vicente, K.J., Moray, N., Lee, J.D., Rasmussen, J., Jones, B.G., Brock, R. and Djemil, T. (1996). Evaluation of a Rankine cycle display for nuclear power plant monitoring and diagnosis. *Human Factors*, 38(3), 506–521.

Vinokur, A.D., Threatt, B.A., Vinokur-Caplan, D. and Satariano, W.A. (1990). The process of recovering from breast cancer in younger and older patients. *Cancer*, 65, 1242–1254.

Violante, F. and Kilbom, A. (2000). *Occupational ergonomics: Work related musculoskeletal disorders*. London: Taylor & Francis.

Vollans, D. (1999). A health and safety approach to occupational stress in a large NHS healthcare trust. Unpublished master's thesis, Department of Experimental Psychology, University of Bristol, UK.

Vroom, V.H. (1964). *Work and motivation*. New York: Wiley.

Wachtel, P.L. (1967). Conceptions of broad and narrow attention. *Psychological Bulletin*, 68, 417–419.

Wallace, M. and Buckle, P. (1987). Ergonomic aspects of neck and upper limb disorders. *International Reviews of Ergonomics*, 1, 173–200.

Warm, J.S., Dember, W.N. and Hancock, P.A. (1996). Vigilance and workload in automated systems. In R. Parasuraman and M. Mouloua (eds) *Automation and human performance: Theory and applications*, pp. 183–199. Mahwah, NJ: LEA.

Waterman, L. (1999). Isocynates exposure – new control guidance. *Hazardous Substances*, 10(11), pp. 1–12.

Waterworth, J. and Thomas, C.M. (1985). Why is synthetic speech harder to remember than natural speech? In *Proceedings of CHI '85 'Human Factors in Computing Systems'*. New York: ACM Press.

Watson, O.M. (1970). *Proxemic behavior: A cross-cultural study*. The Hague, Netherlands: Mouton.

Watten, R.G. and Lie, I. (1992). Time factors in VDT-induced myopia and visual fatigue: An experimental study. *Journal of Human Ergonomics*, 21(1), 13–20.

Weber, M. (1947). *The theory of social and economic organization*. Glencoe, IL: Free Press.

Wedderburn, A.A. (1978). Some suggestions for increasing the usefulness of psychological and sociological studies of shiftwork. *Ergonomics*, 21, 827–833.

Welford, A.T. (1976a). Ergonomics: Where have we been and where are we going: 1. *Ergonomics*, 19, 275–286.

Welford, A.T. (1976b). *Skilled performance*. Glenview, IL: Scott, Foresman.

Weston, H.C. and Taylor, A.K. (1926). *The relation between illumination and efficiency in fine work (typesetting by hand)*. London: HMSO.

Whittaker, J. (1994). *Whittakers' Almanac 1995*, 127th edn. London: J. Whittaker & Sons, Ltd.

WHO (1983). Indoor air pollutants: Exposure and health effects. *World Health Organisation, Euro Reports and Studies*, 78, 23–26.

Wickens, C.D. (1984). *Engineering psychology and human performance*. Columbus OH: Merrill.

Wickens, C.D. (1992). *Engineering psychology and human performance*, 2nd edn. New York: HarperCollins.

Wickens, C.D., Gordon, S.E. and Liu, Y. (1998). *An introduction to human factors engineering*. New York: Longman.

Wiener, E.L. (1977). Controlled flight into terrain accidents: System-induced errors. *Human Factors*, 19, 171–181.

Wiener, E.L. (1987). Management of human error by design. In *Proceedings of the 1st Conference on Human Error Avoidance Techniques*, Paper 872505, pp. 7–11. Warrendale, PA: SAE International.

Wierwille, W.W. and Eggemeier, F.T. (1993). Recommendations for mental workload measurement in a test and evaluation environment. *Human Factors*, 35(2), 263–281.

Wierwille, W.W., Rahimi, M. and Casali, J. (1985). Evaluation of 16 measures of mental workload using a simulated flight task emphasizing mediational activity. *Human Factors*, 27, 489–502.

Wiklund, M.E. (1994). *Usability in practice: How companies develop user-friendly products*. London: Academic Press.

Wilde, G.J.S. (1982). The theory of risk homeostasis: Implications for safety and health. *Risk Analysis*, 2, 209–225.

Wilde, G.J.S. (1988). Risk homeostasis theory and traffic accidents: Propositions, deductions and discussion of dissension in recent reactions. *Ergonomics*, 31(4), 441–468.

Wilkins, A.L. and Dyer, W.G. Jr. (1988). Toward culturally sensitive theories of culture change. *Academy of Management Review*, 13, 522–533.

Wilkinson, R.T., Allison, S., Feeney, M. and Kaminska, Z. (1989).Alertness of night nurses: Two shift systems compared. *Ergonomics*, 32, 281–292.

Wogalter, M.S., Hancock, P.A. and Dempsey, P.G. (1998). On the description and definition of human factors/ergonomics. In *Proceedings of the 42nd Annual Meeting of the Human Factors and Ergonomics Society*, pp. 671–674. Santa Monica, CA: Human Factors and Ergonomics Society.

Wolinsky, J. (1982). Beat the clock. *APA Monitor*, 13(12), Washington, DC: APA (American Psychological Society).

Woods, D., Wise, J. and Hanes, L. (1981). An evaluation of nuclear power plant safety parameter display systems. In R.C. Sugarman (ed.) *Proceedings of 25th Annual Meeting of the Human Factors Society*, pp. 110–114. Santa Monica, CA: Human Factors Society.

Woodson, W. (1981). *Human factors design handbook*. New York: McGraw-Hill.

Woodward, J. (1965). *Industrial organisation: Theory and practice*. Oxford, UK: Oxford University Press.

Wright, L. (1988). The type A behavior pattern and coronary heart disease: Quest for the active ingredients and the elusive mechanisms. *American Psychologist*, 43, 2–14.

Wright, P.H. (1997). A technologist's overview of the development of cognitive technology. *Cognitive Technology*, 2(1), 60–68.

Wulfeck, J.W. and Zeitlin, L.R. (1962). Human capabilities and limitations. In R.M.

Gagne (ed.) *Psychological principles in system development.* New York: Holt, Rinehart & Winston.

Xiao, Y., Hunter, W.A., MacKenzie, C.F. and Jefferies, N.J. (1996). Task complexity in emergency medical care and its implications for team coordination. *Human Factors*, 38(4), 636–645.

Yates, J. (1990). *Judgement and decision making.* Upper Saddle River, NJ: Prentice-Hall.

Yeh, Y.Y. and Wickens, C.D. (1988). Dissociation of performance and subjective measures of workload. *Human Factors*, 30, 111–120.

Youle, A. (1990). *The thermal environment* (Technical Guide No. 8, British Occupational Hygiene Association). Leeds, UK: Science Reviews Ltd., and H & H Scientific Consultants, Ltd.

Young, S.L. and Laughery, K.R. (1994). Components of perceived risk: A reconciliation of previous findings. In *Proceedings of the 38th Annual Meeting of the Human Factors and Ergonomics Society*, pp. 888–892. Santa Monica, CA: Human Factors and Ergonomics Society.

Young, S.L., Wogalter, M.S. and Brelsford, J.W. (1992). Relative contribution of likelihood and severity of injury to risk perceptions. In *Proceedings of the 36th Annual Meeting of the Human Factors Society*, pp. 1014–1018. Santa Monica, CA: Human Factors Society.

Zakay, D. and Wooler, S. (1984). Time pressure, training, and decision effectiveness. *Ergonomics*, 27, 273–284.

Zalesnik, A. (1966). *Human dilemmas of leadership.* New York: Harper.

Zaret, M.M. (1984). Cataracts and visual display units. In B.G. Pearce (ed.) *Health hazards of VDTs?* pp. 47–59. Chichester, UK: Wiley.

Zecevic, A., Miller, D.I. and Harburn, K. (2000). An evaluation of the ergonomics of three computer keyboards. *Ergonomics*, 43(1), 55–72.

Zedeck, S., Jackson, S.E. and Summers, E. (1983). Shift work schedules and their relationship to health, adaptation, satisfaction, and turnover intention. *Academy of Management Journal*, 26, 297–310.

Zeitlin, L. (1969). *A comparison of employee attitudes toward the conventional office and the landscaped office.* New York: Port Authority.

Zhai, S., Milgram, P. and Buxton, W. (1996). The influence of muscle groups on performance of multiple degree-of-freedom input. In *Proceedings of CHI '96 'Human Factors in Computing Systems'*, pp. 308–315. New York: ACM.

Zsambok, C.E. (1997). Naturalistic decision making: Where are we now? In C.E. Zsambok and G. Klein (eds) *Naturalistic decision making*, pp. 3–16. Mahwah, NJ: LEA.

Zuboff, S. (1988). *In the age of the smart machine: The future of work and power.* New York: Basic Books.

Annex: The British Psychological Society Occupational Psychology syllabus, year 2000

Section 1. Human–machine interaction

Basic ideas

1. Overview of Human Factors. The importance of anthropometric, physiological and psychological constraints on the operation of equipment for industrial, domestic and other settings. Information flow, information processing and decision making in humans and machines. User-friendliness in the design of equipment. The human–machine system and the human–machine relationship.

Display design

2. Simple numeric indicators ('dials'), text, tables, graphs, VDUs. Analytic approaches to the design of complex information displays.

Control design

3. Simple physical controls ('knobs'), keyboards, stimulus–response compatibility, pointing, selecting and Fitt's Law.

Learning and performance of interactive procedures

4. Task-based approaches; consistency and learnability. Understandability and mental models: the importance of hidden machine states in process control learning and fault finding; the acquisition and use of mental models, signposted by aids to fault finding.

Human error

5. The role of human error in breakdown of complex systems and in the everyday use of everyday artefacts. Psychological accounts of human error.

Approaches to user-centred design

6. 'Cognitive engineering' approaches, user participation, usability testing. Iterative design and evaluation. Task analysis, functional allocation, mental workload, concept measurement, stressors and human information processing.

Section 2. Design of environments and work: health and safety

Legal context

1. Legal requirements for the provision of a safe and healthy work environment; relevant UK and EC law on safety and health, including the requirements for policy, organisation and arrangements in a work situation. Procedures for risk assessment and risk management. The Disability Discrimination Act (1995), implications for the design of work environments.

Psychosocial and organisational issues

2. Aspects of systems theory and organisational behaviour including: sociotechnical theory and systems performance, systems management and the management of complexity.
3. Key concepts: hazard, harm, injury and health, risk (including subjective risk and risk perception) – their definition, measurement and evaluation.
4. Aspects of stress: theories of appraisal and coping, effects on individual performance and on psychological and physical health, organisational effects of stress.

The problem-solving approach and related procedures

5. The problem-solving framework – control cycle and risk management, including: job safety analysis, work/task analysis, hazard identification and health and safety auditing, risk assessment, design and implementation of control strategies, monitoring and evaluation of outcomes (including cost benefit and cost effectiveness analyses). Team-based problem solving and decision making.

Design of work and work environment

6. Design issues and processes, design of healthy and safe systems of work, role of traditional and cognitive ergonomics, the concept of 'fail safe', the contribution of theories in social and environmental psychology.

7. Job design, work organisation, work structuring and shift work; social-centred design approaches; issues relating to specific social groups, e.g. older workers.

8. Design of physical environment with attention to associated hazards: lighting, temperature and noise, work space.

9. Design of psychosocial and organisational environments with attention to associated hazards; issues of job demands, control and social support; participatory approaches to work design and safe systems of working; alternative forms of work, e.g. homeworking in relation to safe design.

Occupational safety and health

10. Behavioural as distinct from legislative approaches to safety: organisational culture and safety, attitudes and attributions, motivation and safe working behaviour, risk perception and risk-taking behaviours.

11. Systems reliability, the 'human' factor; factors that shape performance and human error.

12. Techniques for promoting safe behaviour; behaviour sampling, modelling and modification; education and training for safe behaviour; communication and safety; organisational development and safety; drugs and safe working.

13. Issues in occupational health psychology: back pain; coronary heart disease, work-related upper limb disorders, sick building syndrome, screen-based work.

14. Employee assistance programmes and workplace counselling, health promotion in the workplace, health beliefs and health-related behaviour.

Author index

Subject index

Note: page numbers in *italics* refer to figures, page numbers in **bold** refer to tables.